HARVEST

HARVEST

BELVA PLAIN

Delacorte
Press

Published by
Delacorte Press
Bantam Doubleday Dell Publishing Group, Inc.
666 Fifth Avenue
New York, New York 10103

Library of Congress Cataloging in Publication Data

Plain, Belva.
        Harvest / by Belva Plain.
            p.   cm.
        ISBN 0-385-29926-5
        I.   Title.
        PS3566.L254H3   1990
        813'.54—dc20   90-34417   CIP

Manufactured in the United States of America

Published simultaneously in Canada

September 1990

10   9   8   7   6   5   4   3   2   1

BVG

HARVEST

1

Carrying the proceeds of the morning's errands, soap from the drugstore, rolls from the bakery, socks and shirts from the boys' store, she was waiting to cross Main Street when she saw his car. There were not that many pearl-gray Cadillac convertibles in town, and it caught her attention seconds before she recognized her husband or saw that a woman was in the front seat beside him. And she stood there, watching, as slowly, through noontime traffic, the car moved past. Sunlight struck the proud MD license plate, and the chrome on the car's fins gleamed discreetly.

Then the familiar, shameful, angry, frightened cry rose in her: Who was she? He likes rich things, my husband does. Rich but not gaudy. His tastes are quiet and refined, even in women.

But no, not always! That girl at my mother's cousin's funeral—the one with three shades of hair and rhinestones all over her skirt—my God, he had to flirt, even at a funeral, even with her.

She began to tremble, dropping the bag of socks. Someone picked it up. A male voice with a smile in it spoke to her.

"Got your arms full, haven't you? Oh, it's you, Mrs. Stern! You don't remember me? Jed Bauer from the hospital?"

One of the interns, she thought, collecting herself. "Yes, of course. Thank you."

The light was still red. It would probably take another minute to change, a segment of time that he, a polite young man, would think it necessary to fill with pleasantries.

"Children all well, I hope?"

"Oh, yes, busy. Back in school."

When the traffic stopped and they crossed the street, he was still talking, feeling an obligation, no doubt, to show respect to the wife of Dr. Theo Stern.

"I've never had a chance to thank you, Mrs. Stern, for being so kind to my wife and me."

"Was I? When?"

"Yes, at the party you had for the new interns last winter. We'd just come east from Idaho, and my wife—she's from a small town—was really nervous that night, but you gave her such a welcome, made her feel right at home. We never forgot it."

Then Iris remembered them, the young bride, still really a girl, in the homemade dress, a girl with a hesitant voice, a gentle face, and scared eyes. She had recognized the girl's bewilderment, had *felt* it.

Iris smiled up now into an equally gentle masculine face, honest and somehow innocent. No guile, no flattery had been intended at all.

"Idaho. Are you pretty well settled here now?"

"We're getting there. Jane's working and I'm learning a lot. Will you give my regards to your husband? I hardly ever see him, but I'll never forget the one time I watched him operate. It was my first experience with plastic surgery. I knew the patient. He almost had to rebuild her face after an accident. I thought he must be some kind of magician, a master magician. Is this your car?"

"The station wagon. Right here. Thanks so much for the help, Doctor. It was nice to see you again." Her voice was still clear and natural. How was it possible?

Huddled over the steering wheel, she sat without energy or will to start the engine. The master. The magician. But where had he been going at noon with a woman? Still, perhaps it was innocent, just giving someone a lift? And yet, and yet . . . His wandering eyes, his courtly compliments, the trace of gray in his dark hair, the trace of a Viennese accent in the fluent English he had learned at Oxford . . .

She thought of their months-long estrangement; it had been five years ago, and she had put it well behind her. The reconciliation had almost been worth the pain of the long quarrel. Were they now to slip back and go through it all again? She thought: I haven't the strength this time.

She took out a mirror. Why? To reassure herself? For she knew what was in the mirror: a slender, sturdy woman, thirty-six years old, with straight dark hair worn in short wings away from the temples; large, dark almond eyes, unblemished skin, a nose too prominent, and good teeth. Pretty enough in a very quiet way, not a woman whom anyone would turn to look after. If I looked like my mother, she thought, it would be different.

And yet, Theo loved her. Knowing that, still she felt cold. The chill trickled down her spine. She talked to herself.

No one really knows anything about anyone else. My husband is one of the best-known plastic reconstruction surgeons in the New York area. My father is one of the most successful builders. I have four children and a house that my father built for us on two acres of greenery. I'm in good health, at least as far as I know. So I have everything, haven't I?

Her daily list, only half checked off, lay on the seat. Market. Shoe repair. Underwear and socks for Jimmy and Steve. See Mrs. Mills about Laura's Brownie scout meeting. Make haircut appointment. Kindergarten parents' day with Philip. Call about Steve's Bar Mitzvah date. Lunch at club with Papa and Mama.

She looked at her watch, ran a comb through her hair, and turned the key in the ignition. Papa was almost a fanatic about tardiness, and since that was one of the very few things that ever made him angry, he deserved to be humored. Thought of her father was sudden comfort; in him lay security. Understanding quite well that there was something juvenile about these feelings, as when a child is consoled by a kiss on his bump or scratch, she felt it nevertheless. So then, she ought to be glad now about this rare event, a meeting in the middle of the busy workweek, and ordinarily she would have been very glad. But at this moment she felt only like running home, like hiding, like being alone.

Now in late September the day was as hot and weary-looking as midsummer, distinguished from it only because the trees were dusty. A smoky haze lay over the street. The center of town was busy with autumn shoppers moving through the Georgian brick stores where, behind quaint bow windows, were displayed in turn the Irish tweeds, Italian shoes, Scottish cashmere sweaters, French tableware, records, books, and gourmet foods that befitted an urbane life within commuting distance of New York.

Before the war the town had still borne the mark of the country village it had once been. In the fifteen years since the war it had tripled in size and prosperity, a fact which seemed to gratify most people, but not Iris. She would have liked it to stay as it had been. In all things she was most at home with smallness and simplicity.

People aren't satisfied anymore, she thought. The country is restless and greedy. Everybody wants better things than his

neighbor has. Theo said it was understandable after what
they'd all been through, the long Depression, followed by the
war. Theo again. Always her thoughts must return to him.

Driving now through the gates of the country club, which
they had only recently joined, she reflected that if it had been
left to her, they would not have done it. This club was far too
expensive, with its large bond and dues. Also, it was too mani-
cured, formal, lavish, snobbish—too everything. But Theo was
expert at tennis, he loved his competitive games, the heated-
all-year pool, the lawns, the grand view—he loved it all.

The lobby was deserted. Those who were not still on the golf
course at this hour were already at lunch on the terrace, from
which came a murmur of voices.

The smart young woman in charge of the dining room came
over. "Mr. and Mrs. Friedman are already here. They're on the
terrace, Mrs. Stern."

This is a talent, too, Iris thought as she followed. Imagine
caring enough to remember all those names! Of course, she
has to; it's part of her job. But still, she must really like to be at
the center of crowds; as for me, I can't imagine it—

Her parents were at a table under an orange umbrella. She
kissed them both, apologizing, "I'm sorry I'm late. I didn't
think of looking out here for you."

"That's all right, darling," Papa said. "Only two minutes.
You're forgiven. Your mother's entertained herself watching
birds."

A variegated congregation of sparrows, blue jays, mourning
doves, cardinals, and pigeons was bustling around a shallow
feeder.

"Look!" Anna cried. "There's a flock of ducks on the way
south. Isn't it a miracle that they know when it's time to leave?"

Her face, raised toward the sky, was young and eager. Her
russet hair, which was barely streaked with a few strands of
gray, was piled high in soft, thick waves. In spite of the sultry
weather she looked cool. Her cotton dress was plaided in lime-

green, black, and white; she wore thinly strapped black sandals
and little jewelry, just a gold choker and the diamond on her
finger. Iris, in her pink sundress and white shoes left over from
last summer, felt suddenly dowdy.

"What are you having?" Anna asked. "The last time we had
lunch together the lobster salad was wonderful."

"That sounds good. I'll join you," Joseph agreed.

His wife touched his hand. "You! At home you're so obser-
vant you won't have it in the house. But outside it's all right, is
it?"

Her touch was affectionate and her tone amused. She has an
aura, Iris thought. A sparkle? No, that's too bright, it's more
like a glow, a light that spreads from her, the light of pleasure,
as if she found the world delicious.

"So what's new?" asked Papa.

"Nothing special. Nothing's changed," Iris replied.

"Then that's good. When nothing's new it means things
must be all right." He reached into his breast pocket, out of
which protruded three black cigars, took one, clipped off the
end, lit it, and drew on it, sending a small, curly puff of aro-
matic smoke into the air. An expression of pure enjoyment
crossed his shrewd, kindly face, an expression that Iris's memory always summoned when she thought of her father.

He settled back in the chair. "Ah, you're a lucky young
woman to have a husband like Theo." He chuckled. "The
answer to a parent's prayer, he is."

Iris made no answer. What had brought that up? Nothing, no
doubt, but Papa's satisfaction and pride in his son-in-law. From
where Papa sat, indeed Theo was an answered prayer, sober
and gentle, an attentive parent, a worker after Papa's own
heart. A good man; a good husband and father had to be a
worker.

What would Papa say if he knew of the ways she suffered?
Although maybe *suffered* was too strong a word? Just say "troubled," then; the ways Theo "troubled" her. And yet it felt like

suffering. It was a matter of degree, after all . . . A small, swift jab above her temples presaged a headache.

But Papa must never know. It would be cruel to tell him, to say nothing of its being pointless and self-defeating. The admiration between the two men was genuine and equal. What was to be gained by destroying it?

Theo admired his self-educated, self-made father-in-law. "Your parents, yes, they gave me the first feeling of home that I had on this continent," he liked to say. Then his poignant memory of the Holocaust, of his lost parents, of his lost first wife and baby boy, would darken his face. "Yes, in their house, for the first time, I began to feel whole again."

"A lucky young woman," Papa repeated now. "Not that you don't deserve it. Our good daughter. You make us very happy, Iris."

It was funny about Papa. He didn't often get sentimental. Something must have inspired his mood, probably their wedding anniversary, which was coming up this week. It was the kind of time when he always said, "I count my blessings." They were no idle words either. In a very literal sense he did count them, for he was truly in his heart a religious man.

"And your children make us so happy. Beautiful, beautiful children! You should have some more."

Anna's laughter rang out. "Joseph! What do you want of her? Aren't four enough?"

"Another child is the last thing I want. What I want is to go back to teaching or to work toward my master's, or even perhaps do both. I want to do something—something with my life," she said, letting the anger speak. Yet at the same time she knew that this anger was only a substitute for that other anger.

Anna was dubious. "With that big household to run?"

"I'm not much of a housekeeper, Mother. You know that."

"Mother," she had said. It crossed her mind that *Mama* was the word for some moods, but *Mother* was the word for this one.

"It's not *my* freezer that's filled with homemade pies, and I certainly don't know how to make strudel dough. *My* vases aren't filled with fresh-cut flowers out of the garden I planted, and I don't do needlepoint," she finished.

Anna smiled. The smile said: I know you're attacking me or else defending yourself in some odd way, and I don't mind. I wish I could know everything about you, but that's impossible. I do try, though, Iris.

"I'm sorry," Iris said. "I didn't mean anything except that I'm not like you, Mama."

She was taking her trouble out on her mother, and it wasn't right.

Joseph intervened. "True, you're not like your mother. But you do well enough. Your family's fed and cared for, as far as I can see."

"Yes. But I want to do something more. Something important."

"Having children isn't important?" Joseph queried. "You know better than that. It's the most important thing you can do."

Anna looked reflective. "That's true, Joseph. And yet, if I had had the education Iris has, I often think—oh, I don't know. I wonder what I would have done in the world—"

Joseph interrupted. "Look what you do now! All your charities, your hospital committee, the League of Women Voters, you do plenty in the world," he said firmly.

It is odd, Iris thought, that Papa, to whom I have always been so much closer, is still the one to whom some things are better left unsaid. He has a picture of me, his happy, grown-up little girl, that mustn't be touched. While my mother—Mama—is ready to listen in spite of the strain that has always been between us, that we never mention because there is no explanation for it. Is it because she knows I am aware of her beauty that I haven't inherited, or because my brother died? No, it was farther back. Farther. I don't know why.

"If Theo wants you to stay home," Papa said, "my advice to you is, put this business out of your mind. Iris dear, be content as you are. Cultivate your talents at home. Remember, a man who works as hard as he does and under so much tension wants a well-run, peaceful household. Especially a European man, brought up before the war in a very different style."

Iris was faintly surprised that her father could have such awareness of a cultural difference. She was also faintly surprised at the unmistakable reprimand in his voice.

Anna hurriedly cut through whatever resentment might be rising to cloud the air.

"Has your dress come yet, Iris? Mine was delivered this morning. It's gorgeous." And without waiting for an answer she said to Joseph, "Oh, you'll be proud of us both at your dinner. But not as proud as we are of you. I've been hearing everywhere that this Home for the Aged is the best thing you've ever built. The man at the bank today called it an architectural gem."

"Well, well, I wasn't the architect. I only built it. Too much fuss," Joseph growled, looking enormously pleased.

"Don't sell yourself short. You had a lot to do with the design. You deserve a testimonial dinner. Did you say that your dress has come, Iris?"

"Yesterday."

"Where did you go for them?" Joseph asked. "To that fancy place in New York?"

"Chez Léa, of course. Where else?" Anna gave a little self-mocking smile. "It's the only place to go. Half the women I know practically live there."

"Her prices are disgraceful," Iris complained. "I haven't been there more than three times since we got my trousseau and my wedding dress."

"But she does have lovely things, you have to admit," Anna said. "And what's more, she doesn't push things on you the way most places do. No high pressure at all. She's such a friendly woman too."

"I never liked the way she looks at us," Iris said. "She's too curious."

"For goodness' sake, what could she be curious about?"

"I don't know. There's just something that bothers me. Anyway, I was ashamed to look at the price tag again when I opened the box."

"Iris," her father remonstrated, "there are certain times when a little extravagance is called for. God knows your mother wastes nothing. But she doesn't mind dressing herself. I like to see my wife dressed up. And I'm sure Theo does too," he finished somewhat sternly.

Iris was conscious again of her dress, which had gone baggy from wear.

And again Anna changed the subject, asking Joseph whether they expected to open the Home in the summer. It was as if she had sensed Iris's discomfiture, almost as if, Iris thought, she could have guessed that money was another very uncomfortable subject.

Yet she could not have guessed, certainly not from the way the Sterns lived, how uncomfortable it actually was. Who would believe that their checkbook balance was so low that Iris was sometimes wary of writing a fifty-dollar check for the household?

She worried about what or whether Theo could be saving. When she asked him, he would smile and answer, "Enough. Let me worry about it. That's the husband's responsibility." He would kiss her cheek or pat her head as if she were a child and she would be left with resentment. And, as if she were a child, she thought, he brought unexpected gifts—adult toys—a blond alligator purse he had seen in a shopwindow, or a pair of gold cuffs studded with lapis lazuli and turquoise that they could not afford. Iris was careful about expenses; she had probably been made that way. When Papa's partner gave her as a

wedding gift a complete flatware service of hand-wrought silver from Italy, she exchanged the heavy, oversized pieces for
something lighter and easier to maintain.

"It would take hours to polish," she had explained. "We
can't afford to pay someone to do it, and I have better things to
do."

"What a pity," Anna had remarked. "I can't understand
you." She had marveled at the magnificence of the chasing and
swirling and would gladly have spent hours caring for it if it had
been hers. But Iris wasn't Anna.

Joseph was leaving. "I'm sorry to run off, but I've got a two
o'clock appointment. This was a real treat, a luxury." And he
bent to kiss his wife and daughter.

When he was out of sight and hearing, Anna asked, "Are you
feeling all right, Iris?"

Could one hide anything from those clear eyes?

"I'm fine."

"You've eaten practically nothing."

"I'm not hungry."

"I don't think you do feel all right."

Anna's thoughtful gaze went to the grass, where pigeons
strutted, picking up fallen seeds. After a moment she spoke
quietly.

"You can postpone your work or study for a few years, you
know. It won't be too late for it then if you still want it."

"I'll want it." Fragmentary phrases, subliminal messages,
flashed before Iris's eyes. *Be somebody. . . . Show him. . . .*

And she said firmly, "Things are changing, Mama. When I
was in college, the dean told us that the first purpose of a
liberal arts education was to make you a better wife and
mother. In fact, I was just reading the same thing before in a
magazine."

Tactful as always, smoothing and soothing, Anna replied,
"Of course there has to be more in a woman's life than that. Yet
there is a little something to be said for—what I mean is, an

educated woman like you should offer herself first to her children. After all, you're not an immigrant like me."

"Don't say that about yourself. You were a good mother, always."

Anna's eyes filled suddenly. For a moment she did not speak. Then she said, "You did so much for your father and me when we lost Maury. I remember—" She stopped.

Remember. . . . Yes, how the storm had rattled the windows that night when the police came to tell them that their son was dead in a car wreck. The rattle of winter wind and rain. . . .

"And all that long sad time you understood how it was for us."

Iris wanted to say, but did not say, Yes, I can always feel for the lost and lonesome. I relate to them.

"Perhaps you don't realize what a comfort you were. We took strength from you."

Iris thought: She sees beneath my skin. She's worried about me. She's reminding me that I can be strong, which I know well enough.

"I'm glad I could help you, Mama."

"I think men take sorrows harder, don't you? Your father especially took strength from you."

"I think it depends on the man. Papa is very, very soft. He only likes to seem tough, isn't that so?"

Anna smiled now. "Yes, yes. Soft as custard inside. You and your children . . . you're his whole life, Iris!"

She's pleading with me to be happy, not to give them any trouble.

"Not his whole life. You're forgetting yourself."

"I'm not forgetting."

Perhaps unconsciously, Anna looked down at the hand on which the diamond flashed. Joseph had brought it home, Joseph made her wear it. The ring was the symbol of his achievement; the young man from the tenements had labored and risen high. Yet sometimes Iris wondered whether, under the serenity, the competence, and the devotion, her mother could be totally satisfied with the man she had married. They were so different! But that wasn't fair, she would think at once, ashamed of her doubt. No man would worship a woman as her father did if the two did not satisfy each other entirely.

How beautiful she is, Iris thought now. Men still linger near her even when younger women are in the room. How must it feel to be adored as Papa adores her?

Anna was very serious. "Iris, I ask you again, is everything all right? I don't want to intrude—"

But you are intruding, Iris said silently.

On the lawn a swooping crow startled the feeding flock, which rose and scattered. Feigning interest in the birds, Iris blinked and, before tears could start, turned in her seat to watch them.

"I'm fine. I'm just feeling quiet. You know how I am."

"You'll work everything out. All in good time. Believe me, you will. Be patient. A woman must make a home for her husband. Life is hard for men, struggling for a place in the world. A woman must be his refuge."

And where does the woman find refuge? Iris asked herself, resenting the trite, simplistic counsel.

"You are of your time," she said only, as they rose to go.

"And you, I think you are ahead of yours," Anna replied.

They walked to the parking lot. A vivid girl in a pleated tennis dress, with red ribbons on her long black ponytail, waved to Iris.

"Who's that?" asked Anna.

"She plays doubles with Theo at the club. He thinks she's stunning."

"Well, she is very striking."

Anna stood for a moment at the window of the station wagon before Iris put it into gear.

"Iris, darling. Just remember Theo loves you." Very carefully, Anna looked away. "You must forget that old business. I do hope you're over that nonsense. You remember what I told you then? Jealousy can eat you up."

Canny woman! She had guessed that more than a teaching career was troubling her daughter today. But whatever could Mama know about jealousy? Papa wasn't a flirt. Papa wasn't out riding around town with another woman at noon.

"Don't worry, Mama. Please, I'm fine. And I have to rush. The kids will be home any minute."

The car sped back through the main streets of town and out through its fringes. It passed the Reform temple to which the family belonged, a handsome modern structure of brown brick set in an evergreen garden. On the highway it passed a desolate string of bowling alleys, pizza parlors, strip malls, and gas stations before turning off on a side road into another world. There, through a tunnel of old trees, it rolled on curving roads flanked by large colonial houses, with here and there a French provincial, or what passed for French provincial in suburbia, and slowed at the blunted tip of a quiet dead-end drive.

The house was framed by an autumn splendor of maples, still partially in emerald leaf but tipping now into gold. Built almost entirely of glass and slender redwood pillars, the house seemed almost to float on a lake of sunlight. Or else it was a crystal box lying lightly on a table of grass.

While it was building, and for a few years afterward, people had come by to look at it, some to marvel and some to scoff at the strange new "modern" structure. Under mild bewildered protest Papa had built it to his daughter's taste. Theo had truly never liked it, either, that she knew. The mullioned Elizabethan windows and nooks that he had lived with in England or the overstuffed central European comfort with which he had grown up were far more to his liking, although he did appreciate the very evident cost of this house. Ironically, its cost was the one thing about the house that bothered Iris. It could have been just as airy and modern, it could have given her just as much pride and joy, if it had been half the size. The enormous rooms, some of which were still being furnished, were almost grandiose, as was the enormous yard with its elaborate ornate shrubbery and garden. Long walls called for paintings, and while it was certainly delightful to make selections at the galleries on Madison Avenue or on Fifty-seventh Street, she always had a sinking sensation while Theo wrote out another check and blithely carried yet another costly treasure to the car. It was he who had failed to object, indeed had encouraged her father when he had increased the scale of the house plan. It was he who had added the terrace and the tennis court, he who had brought in the expensive landscape designer. A simple lawn and the natural woodland would have been pleasing enough, she reflected again.

Steve and Jimmy, with three of their sixth- and seventh-grade friends, were shooting baskets in the side yard. They gave their mother a second's pause for greeting as they whirled.

For a minute she stood watching her boys. Such nice kids, they were. Naked to the waist, sweating in the heat, brown from their summer at camp, they were the products of their parents' —and their grandparents'—care and good fortune. Lucky kids. They couldn't know how lucky they were. God bless them, she thought suddenly. She would have liked to hug them both right there in front of everyone.

There were only ten and a half months between the two. In the first year of marriage Theo and she hadn't been careful at all; he had been a passionate, careless lover, and she on her part hadn't minded. A little smile touched her mouth at the recollection. Indeed, she had not minded at all.

Now here were the brothers, close and in most ways quite alike. Neither was yet, she thought, as strikingly handsome as Theo, but they would become so. The shape of the men to be was already clear, and those men were manly, supple and tall, broad of shoulder and narrow of waist. Their eyes were clear and honest. Steve's, gold-brown and large, were filled with light.

They both did well at sports, at friendships, and in the classroom. Jimmy, the younger, had to work much harder to accomplish what Steve did fast and easily. Perhaps that was why Jimmy could sometimes seem to be the older, the more sober, of the two. Sometimes he could even be protective of Steve; Steve retreated from physical fights—never out of cowardice, but only because of some deep-seated horror of violence that Jimmy, although he did not share it, understood. Jimmy, if need be, used his fists, while Steve's weapon was his tongue. Filled with ideas, he would argue to the death for them. So curious about the world, so alive, Iris thought now, that he almost sparkles!

And, leaving the boys to their game, she went into the house.

In the kitchen Laura, wearing a borrowed apron that fell almost to her ankles, was cutting out ginger cookies. She bent over the dough with a concentrated expression, her underlip tucked in. Her russet hair fell loosely over her cheeks; she was a replica of Anna. Even strangers remarked about it whenever the two were together. The model had simply skipped a generation.

At the far end of the counter Ella Mae was shelling peas.

"All the cooking going on around here this afternoon! I'll make a good cook out of this girl yet," she said fondly.

Laura was domestic already. Anna's genes again! Her room was a pink chintz nest; for her ninth birthday this year she had asked to have her room redecorated, and Theo, to Iris's dismay, had agreed to start from scratch with new furniture, carpet, lamps, and curtains. Theo would give Laura the moon if she were to ask for it. Laura had a dressing table with a perfume tray. When I was nine, Iris thought, what did I know about perfume? And she marveled about the variety of human experience. Thank heaven, Laura also had a mind, though, and shelves of books that she really read.

"Laura was a big help with the apple pie, Mrs. Stern. A big help."

"I peeled half the apples," Laura said, looking important.

"Pie? What's the occasion?"

"Nothing special. Just, Dr. Stern is awful fond of pie."

Even Ella Mae adored the man! And Iris said suddenly, "You're so good to us."

"Why not? You're good to me. You're my family."

Ella Mae had two children who lived with their grandmother in South Carolina. At Christmas she visited them for two weeks, and that was all the contact she had. So she could call these strangers "family." This touched Iris in the heart of her heart.

At the first interview Iris had addressed Ella Mae as "Miss Brown." But Ella Mae had corrected her.

"She calls me Mrs. Stern," Iris had told Theo that night. "It doesn't seem right not to do the same to her."

Theo had been a little amused. "That's the way things are. You can't change the world. And anyway, if she doesn't mind, why should you?"

"Philip's at his friend's house," Ella Mae now reminded Iris. "They phoned to say you needn't go get him. They'll bring him home later. And your mail's on the hall table."

On a narrow marble slab in the hall lay schoolbooks, Jimmy's new sweater, torn already, and a pile of bills at the base of a vase of red anthuriums. Their stiff-angled branches and flat red petals were repeated in the mirror above the table, but her face, mirrored as it was between the angled branches, was fragmented as in some cubist painting, the features nervously separated and disjointed. And abruptly, a memory seized her, a startling recollection of her own familiar childhood's face, and then a recall of fragrance, the same as that which now came from the kitchen, the salty smell of roasting meat that had filled the apartment on that winter evening when she had stood outside a door and heard her mother's soft, pitying voice: "But you must admit, she isn't a pretty child, Joseph."

She turned away from the mirror and, crossing the hall into the living room, stood still there, drawing a deep breath as if to fill her lungs with something pure and calming.

The room was hers, of her, spare as a Japanese graveled garden, gray and cream and still. The blond Danish furniture stood on dove-colored carpet. The draperies were of crisp, self-patterned linen. Tall lamps of Swedish crystal caught the afternoon light and threw it back in rainbow colors onto the floor. A red lacquered screen—how well the Scandinavian and the Oriental went together!—drew the eye as to a point of fire toward the courtyard where, on the other side of the glass wall, a Norfolk pine grew in a large stone tub. In October it would be brought indoors to flourish over the winter.

In a far corner stood the piano, the Steinway baby grand that she had brought from home when she married. On the wall, facing her when she played, hung two rows of etchings, also brought from her room in her parents' house; there were sandpipers running along an empty beach at low tide; there were far, cloudy hills; there was a hemlock under snow.

The contemplation of all these things was comforting.

She ran her hand now over the keys. Their tinkle was loud in the silent room. Philip's lesson book stood open on the rack. Last year, when he was four, he had stood next to her watching her play, and this year she had begun to teach him. As fast as she could teach, he could learn.

"Like mother, like son," Theo had said just last Sunday afternoon when Philip had played for them. She had been happy last Sunday afternoon, and ever since then until this morning, until old fears had come back to plague her.

She walked down the hall toward her bedroom. At the end, where the light could fall upon it, hung a photograph in an ornate frame. Mama had bought the frame and Theo had put the picture in this place of prominence.

"What a wonderful face your brother had!" he had re-marked. "I'd like to have known him. Blond. That must be the strain from your mother's side."

The golden child, she thought now. That's what Mama had always said; the neighbors on the block had given that title to Maury. Iris had seen the street on which they had lived when her parents were poor. The women brought their camp chairs to the sidewalk, rocked their babies, and watched the older ones play.

"He was the most popular boy in school," Iris had told Theo, holding nothing back. Poor dead Maury. Give him all the credit he deserved. "He was on the basketball and the tennis teams."

"Ah! I would have had a tennis partner in the family," Theo had replied.

And she had thought, Yes, I know I'm clumsy at games. I know.

She stood before the picture. The eyes were radiant, eager, as though they were looking out at something new and won-derful. And then it struck her: That's Steve!

Faces and voices merged and overlapped the generations, dissolving and reappearing. All, all a mystery, why we are who we are. What made a person grow to be like Maury, the golden child, or Steve, or Theo? Or me?

There was a heaviness upon her, dragging her down. And the morning had begun so normally, so brightly.

The heat in the house was oppressive. Maybe Theo was right about wanting to air-condition the house. So many people were having it done these days, and the newest houses were having it built in. But it would cost so much. Last year he had added on a small conservatory, although he almost never had time to use it. He did a good deal of free clinic work; he'd even gone to Japan to treat victims of the Hiroshima blast—and incidentally had brought back a necklace of black pearls, whose price he wouldn't tell her; but she had seen the appraisal for insurance and been shocked. He prided himself on his charity work, on keeping his fees reasonable, which was right and honorable and ethical. Still, they never got ahead, in spite of all he earned, and it frightened her. They had four children, and suppose he were to fall ill? Her mind began adding a familiar column of figures: property taxes, insurance—

The telephone rang. "We'll pick you up for dinner at the club." It was a neighbor's voice. "Will seven be okay?"

"Oh, yes," Iris said. "Seven. And thanks."

She had forgotten. A club again, somebody else's country club this time, where few people knew them. When strangers don't know I'm Theo's wife, she thought, they give me a cool stare, but as soon as they see that I belong to him, ah, then, that's different. His reputation goes before him; he does everything so well, whether it's tennis or bridge, and all of them with his European gallantry. I am compelled to be vivacious alongside of him, which is not my nature.

And where was he going with that woman in the car this noon?

"Oh, stop it!" She was furious with herself. "Go take a bath, take a nap, read a book, lay out your clothes, do anything, but stop this and get hold of yourself."

In the closet hung the dress bought for Papa's dinner. The black velvet bodice had a portrait neckline made to display a white neck and shoulders, which she had, as well as an important choker, which she also had. Made of coral, gold, and diamonds, it was original and exquisite; also, she had reason to think it hadn't been fully paid for. The white satin skirt displayed her narrow waist, one of her best features, and had the sweep of grandeur. One had to admit that Léa knew her business. Theo was always urging her to shop there; he took pride in these expensive clothes and, she suspected, even a sensuous pleasure in the very crackle of the tissue paper when the box was opened.

"The dinner's in the fall, and I'd like to see you in velvet," he had suggested.

It was really he who had taught her what little she knew about fashion. Her mother had long ago given up trying, although she had made one suggestion which Iris had no intention of following, that her hair be teased into Jackie Kennedy's new bouffant style.

She hadn't gotten a good look at the woman in the car, only enough to see that she was dark and had long, flowing hair, so she must have been young. . . .

"Oh, stop it!" she cried again.

She must lift herself out of this mood. She must. She went in to run the bath water.

"You were very quiet tonight," Theo remarked while they were driving home.

The convertible top was still down. When she laid her head back on the seat, she could see the stars rushing above the road between the dark trees on either side. It was a relief to have left the evening's chatter and stir behind. Now, after the day's heat, there was a touch of autumn in the air, fresh and clean on the skin. The earth was turning toward winter, away from the sun.

Theo pursued the subject. "Didn't you have a good time?"

"It was very nice."

"You didn't act as if it was. You're so remote sometimes. Without joy, when everybody else was happy."

She sat up. "What do you mean? 'Always'?"

"I didn't say that. I said 'sometimes,' didn't I?"

"I can find more joy in the world around me than any ten of the people there tonight. Or most of them, anyway. Just looking at these stars, I feel—"

"I'm not talking about stars. Tell me what's wrong. Don't pretend you don't know what I'm talking about, Iris. Why won't you let me help you?"

She did not answer. How could she say what was "wrong" with her without appearing to be a victim, unsure of herself and defeated?

"You're not talking?"

"Not now. I don't feel like it."

"Fine. Suit yourself."

"Just remember, Theo loves you," Anna had said.

Now she reconstructed the evening just past. Walking to and fro, and at the table where they sat, how could she not have observed the repeated passage of eyes, his, widened, mischievous, glancing, admiring, and teasing? And the women's eyes answering, as if there were something secret that he and they—each one of them in turn—might know. It was as if something electric were conducted between them, as if Theo were a magnet toward whom they were drawn. He both desired and was desired.

He was a man with great power. Power was even in his fingers; "magical" fingers, that young doctor had said just this morning. Command was his, and strength in the lines that hard experience had drawn upon his comely face.

A hero of the Resistance, a man who had known despair and fought it; how far beyond her reach he had seemed to the inexperienced, romantic, simple girl she had been! Perhaps she ought to have married one of the nice 4-Fs, the fellow teacher or the earnest accountant who had liked her. But there had been no fire in them, and Theo was all fire.

And she wondered now, while the silence lay between them, how far he really ever went with these parlor flirtations that were so painful for her, whether they were no more than that or whether they led to something more, to secret afternoons in bed together. And she was hot with fury, hot with anguish, at the mental image of the bed.

They rode the rest of the way without speaking. At home Theo stayed downstairs to listen to the late news. The children were all asleep, so the house was quiet. The quiet was dismal and foreboding. She undressed, showered, and sat down before the dressing table to brush her hair. All the time her mind worked, churning with bitter questions: Why did he marry me? Because of my mother's cooking; goulash or strudel? The brush swept her dark hair over and over. His first wife, dead under Hitler's blows, had had a cap of blond curls. How carefully Iris had studied that old photograph! She could close her eyes now and see it in every detail: the eyelet cuffs, the short, tilted nose, the dark beads around the neck. Amber? Amethyst?

She was still brushing her hair when Theo came in. The mirror over the dressing table reflected his troubled eyes.

"Iris. I know you're miserable. And I know you're angry. Will you be fair enough to tell me why?"

"I'm perfectly fine," she said, proud in her misery.

"You don't look it. And it's not decent to go around like this without talking to me, is it?"

A lump was forming in her throat. She swallowed, before tears should follow, and still kept silent.

"Don't you feel well? Are you ill?" he persisted.

Her lips tightened. As if you care! she thought.

"Iris, I'm trying to be patient. But I must say you're behaving like a child."

She swung about on the dressing-table stool. Yes, she was carrying this too far; she could see that in his face. Years before, her father's temper, so rarely roused, had been frightening, but Theo's control was far more threatening.

"All right, I'll talk," she said. "What do you want me to say?"

"Well, tell me about your day. What you did all day."

"Nothing unusual. I had lunch at the club with my parents, and before that I did errands. So, what did you do?"

Let's see, let's see what he will say.

He said: "Operated in the morning, as you know, then drove straight to the office, had a sandwich at my desk, and saw patients."

Straight to the office. To let him know? To bury the whole business? Which to do?

He was leaning against the window frame with his arms behind him, drumming his fingers on the sill. He frowned a little, as if he were concentrating.

"What kind of errands were you doing?"

"What difference? I was shopping for the boys, if you must know. Shirts, shorts, and pajamas."

"At the place on Parker Street near the hospital?"

"There and other places. Why?"

"You saw me."

Iris shook her head. "No. No, I didn't."

"Yes, you did. You saw me and that's what's been bothering you all day."

She was hot with shame. This man could strip her mind naked.

"Iris, Iris," he said sadly. "For God's sake, she was a nurse from the OR! She was finished for the day, her child was sick at home, and I offered her a lift a few blocks out of my way. That's all there was to it."

Now tears of humiliation gathered at Iris's eyes. She lowered her head to hide them, but Theo gently raised her chin.

"Look at me. Why? Why do you make yourself miserable over nothing?"

"You lied! You were going to conceal it! You said you went straight to the office."

"Good God, do I have to measure every word? Yes, I guess I do. I have to guard myself against your continual suspicions."

"I think I have reason enough to be suspicious, haven't I?"

"Oh, now we're retracing our steps five years back down the road. . . . Do you have to remember every bad thing that ever happened? Grow up, Iris."

"Why don't you grow up and stop acting like an adolescent, making eyes at everything in skirts? The way you were to-night."

There. She'd said it, after vowing that she would not, she had made herself vulnerable, weak, and foolish.

"You imagine things, Iris, the way you imagined I was on my way to a liaison this morning."

"I know what I see, Theo, just as you would know if it was I making a play for some man at the table tonight."

"Who? Who? The one in the checked sport jacket? He must weigh three hundred pounds."

This enraged her. "Oh, do you think I'm not able to attract another man, is that it? That I can't do better than the fat man in the checked jacket?"

"You'd better not try attracting other men. I'll break your little neck if you do. Ah, come on, Iris, this whole thing is stupid."

"Stupid, is it?"

"No, it's actually more sad than anything. Wasting good energy on nonsense. Do you think so little of yourself that you believe I would change your little finger for another woman? Don't you know I love you, Iris? After all this time, you have to be told? Shall I show you?"

As he moved to put his arms around her, she jumped up and backed against the wall.

"No, you can't get away with that, Theo. I won't let you this time."

"Get away with what? What is this all about?"

He pressed her against the wall; her fists, small and inadequate, hammered his chest.

"Good! I like that. I like it when you fight me." And he pressed her more tightly against the wall. "You like it too. I know you." He kissed her neck. "I know you very, very well. Go on, struggle. Fight. If you can tell me what this is all about, I'll let you go."

She was still crying, yet she was at the point where crying turns full circle into laughter, into a mild hysteria. And she was furious because he was able—he was always able—to defuse her anger. Wasn't that an absurd contradiction? Now his mouth was on hers and his hands were on her breasts; he could do anything he wanted with her; he was doing it and she could not stop him; she did not even want to stop him; damn him, he always won; she would never change him, never make him behave the way she wanted; he knew how she loved him; he was already carrying her to the bed.

2

A hearty country-house fire
blazed beneath a marble mantel five floors above Fifth Avenue.
Tall, formal windows curtained in moss-green damask overlooked cool, naked trees in Central Park, where the wind was
tearing down the last bronze shreds of autumn.

A tall man, wearing a dark suit and highly polished British
shoes, stood staring into the fire, jingling the keys and coins in
his pockets. He might have been of any age between fifty and
sixty, an old fifty or a very young sixty; he had the supple body
of a tennis player. His fine aquiline face, grave now, was bright-
ened by sea-blue eyes, which were surprising in contrast to his
olive skin.

The most beautiful eyes in the world, thought the woman, who had put aside *The New York Times* to pay attention to him.

She was about his age, whatever that might be, thin and seemingly strong. Her skin was very white, her forehead wide and low, her shining pepper-and-salt hair parted in the center in a fashion unchanged since her youth. Her eyes were slanted, alert, and faintly Asian; she was pleasing to look at, although not nearly as handsome a person as was the man. They had been lovers for fourteen years.

Their separate apartments, since he was still a married man living with, or at least occupying the same residence as, his wife, were on opposite sides of the park. She knew that ultimately they would be married, since his wife was now dying in a nursing home. But the long wait had never troubled her; she had endured too much else. Husband and son had died in Europe. Having survived the concentration camps herself, she had come here to America and resumed the practice of medicine. Her life was full.

They made a good pair. Neither of them had ever known what it was to feel time hanging heavily. He was the head of his father's and grandfather's firm of private bankers, a small, prestigious firm in an old building on Wall Street; his grandfather's portrait, wing collar, muttonchop whiskers, and all, hung opposite his desk as a reminder, he would say laughingly, of his responsibilities. And they were many. He was an active member of a dozen boards, with interest in old-age homes, symphony orchestras, museums, hospitals, a foreign policy think-tank, the Sierra Club, problems of Appalachia, American Indian reservations, the inner cities, and surely, too, of Israel.

If his wife had not been childless, he sometimes thought, he would not have had the time or the need, either, to do so much.

His wife. Poor, weak, neurotic Marian, a passive, dependent, frigid woman whom he never should have married, who possibly should not have married anyone. Why had he done it? Because, given the way the world had been in those years of the

First World War and given the "proper" young man from a "proper" family that he had been, it had seemed impossible to break an honorable engagement. He could still remember with shivering distaste that fanfare of congratulations, announcements, dances and teas, the trousseau, and the Tiffany diamond.

And later, through the years? Why, a divorce would have shattered her! Never would he forget her scared eyes or her desperate pleading: "Don't leave me, Paul. Promise me you'll never leave me." He could no more have hurt her than strike an infant in its bassinet.

Now, of course, she was bedridden and unconscious. He could quite simply divorce her behind her back and marry. But whether she lived for another year or died tomorrow, he would not. He would let her die with the dignity that had meant everything to her in life. Let her die as a married woman: Mrs. Paul Werner. How she had cherished the title engraved with a dark blue swirl on Crane's best cream-colored notepaper!

Nothing had she ever known of his other life; call that hypocrisy if one wished to, but at least it had preserved their peace, her peace. Nothing had she known of the woman who sat in this room with him now, and certainly nothing of that other, so much longer ago, that other beloved girl, she of the russet hair and golden eyes, whom he had forsaken when he kept his promise to marry Marian. Nothing had she known of that single, accidental encounter long after he was married and the girl with the russet hair was married to someone else, which resulted in the birth of a child, a girl who did not know, would never know, the truth about herself.

The woman in the wing chair let the paper fall from her lap. She sensed exactly what was passing through his mind, and she was soft with pity. Worldly and experienced in human foibles as a skilled physician can be, she knew how thoughtlessly a man is able to scatter his seed and move on without a thought to the harvest. But not this man.

At that moment he turned away from the fire.

"Ilse," he said, "do you know that never a day goes by when I do not think of Iris?"

And the mother of Iris too? she might have asked, but did not. There was no jealousy in Ilse. What was past was past. She, too, had had a life and other lovers. The present alone was precious and to be savored. The future was nothing to count on. That she had learned well.

"I still think," she told him, "you shouldn't have gone to that dinner. It's upset you too much. And you must have made *her*— Anna's—heart stop with terror for a second or two when you walked in."

"I'm a trustee of the Home for the Aged. It was entirely natural for me to be there."

"I'm not questioning that. I'm thinking of the poor woman."

"We only exchanged a few words. Very formal, in the circumstances. She knew I just wanted to see Iris."

He had not seen either mother or daughter in years. He had given his promise to stay away, to cause no harm, and he had kept it. Except, he thought now, for the day when I hid with Ilse on the sidewalk in front of the temple where Iris was married and saw her walk out in her white dress, and saw Anna, too, on her husband's arm as they watched their child go away. Anna. And the man who had no reason to think that Iris did not belong to him.

"They danced so well together," he said. "A handsome young pair. A couple in love." His voice trailed away, leaving a wistful note in the air. And he resumed, "The husband must have quite a practice. Plastic surgery, you know. Iris wore some grand jewels, I noticed. Her dress came from Leah's place, black velvet. Leah told me what she would be wearing." His smile flared for a second and as quickly died. "A fine thing, a fine situation, to have to pick up crumbs from my cousin about my own daughter! And if Leah didn't happen to own Léa, the most popular dress salon in the city, I wouldn't even have those crumbs."

Ilse gave gentle reproof. "Ah, Paul, will you ever get over this?"

"Will you ever get over your son?"

"My son is dead. Your daughter is alive, dancing in a velvet dress."

Despising self-pity, he was instantly ashamed. "I'm sorry. I have no right to compare them." And he repeated, "I'm sorry."

"Darling, I don't mind. It's just that I hate to see you unhappy."

"At least I know that Iris is happy. Oh, she reminded me so much of my mother! It was uncanny. When you see the bones, the height, the eyes—very bright and dark, almost too large for her face—when you see all that copied in another generation, it's startling, to put it mildly. Startling."

It would be better, Ilse thought, if Leah would keep her crumbs of information to herself, few and far between as they were. Maybe sometime, should the right moment arise, she would suggest it to Leah. Different as they were—Ilse the professional, bookish, reserved, and analytical, and Leah the ambitious, talkative and clever, maneuvering in the fast track—they were yet good friends. Leah had been Ilse's first real friend in this new country. Never would she forget the generous wardrobe that Leah had insisted on providing for her, more beautiful than any Ilse had ever owned before. But Leah was more than merely generous, she was trustworthy and loyal. And it was their common loyalty to Paul, most of all, that united them.

Leah had known about Paul's child since long before Ilse's time. Why Paul had confided in his cousin, Ilse did not know and had not asked; she supposed it was understandable that he had needed to confide at least in one other human being. So now there were just two people who knew.

Now and then, Leah liked to bring up the subject.

"She's a beautiful woman. The mother, not the daughter, I

mean. I have a hard time to keep from staring at her when she comes in to shop. It's an odd feeling to know something like that about a person who could have no idea you know it."

And Ilse, listening, would feel a certain distaste, as if there were something prurient in her own curiosity. In one way she wanted to listen to Leah and in another way she did not.

"When Paul knew about the child—it wasn't till five or six years after she was born—he begged Anna to leave her husband. But Anna wouldn't. She had some sort of conscience about it; he loved her, they had a little boy, she couldn't destroy a good man, he must never know—that sort of thing."

Leah loved the drama, the poignancy, of the situation.

"I know. He has told me," Ilse would say.

"Of course, it was all so long ago. Now it's the daughter who haunts him. He wanted children so badly. It's a pity. He's just one of those men who should have had children."

Paul had gone back to stand before the fire. The flames turned orange and snapped, sending a piny fragrance into the room. Ilse spoke silently to the tall, straight back in the dark suit: I came too late, my darling; how gladly I would have given you a child! Or more, as many as you wanted.

Aloud she said, "Paul, it's half-past two. Your guests should be here pretty soon."

"Yes, yes, of course." He stooped to kiss her cheek. "I'll go take a look at the preparations."

Thanksgiving was his favorite holiday. He had insisted on being the host this year, although both Leah and his cousin Meg argued for it. Only a few blocks from this apartment, near the Metropolitan Museum, Leah lived in a sumptuous town house in the Federal style, complete with fanlight over a green door, a brass knocker, and tubbed evergreens. Meg and her husband, Larry Bates, were veterinarians in New Jersey, living in a restored clapboard farmhouse surrounded by fallow fields and untouched woods. But Paul had gotten his way this time and he was the host.

His apartment, in an old prewar building, spread sheltering arms around him. He had been living alone in it for the past year, and yet in spite of its enormous rooms, high ceilings, and long halls, it did not seem either empty or too large. His possessions, like friends, spoke to him. Over the mantel here in the dining room hung his glowing Monet landscape, the first important acquisition in a lifetime of learning and collecting. Underfoot lay a rosy Persian carpet from his grandparents' house. In the corner on its pedestal stood the wonderful crystal horse that a German cousin, long since murdered during the Holocaust, had given to him. A long antique table, English mahogany and bought in London, was now set for twelve; he saw with satisfaction that Katie, the housekeeper, had arranged it exactly as Marian would have wished, with Royal Crown Derby service plates and the Baccarat glasses, three at each place. At the center of the table she had copied Marian's traditional cornucopia of oak leaves, squash, and wheat.

Then he remembered he must go to the kitchen to thank Katie. Actually, he had no need for a full-time housekeeper. A weekly cleaning of the rooms would have sufficed, since he took most of his meals with Ilse or out, either at a restaurant or the Yale Club. Often enough, he stayed the night at Ilse's place. What Katie's thoughts about his absences might be, he couldn't imagine, faithful churchgoer that she was. But they were fond of each other, and she had no wish to retire. This apartment, after all these years, seemed as much her home as his.

When he had gone into the kitchen to admire the glistening brown turkey, the cranberry molds and pies that were cooling on the counter, when he had praised Katie and greeted the woman who was her helper for the day, he went through the apartment on inspection.

There should be flowers in the bowl on the piano, he remembered. Yes, Katie had remembered, too, what belonged there: a bowl of yellow roses in full bloom. A broad shaft of cold sunlight fell through the corner window, silvering all the pastel silks and the pale Aubusson rug. It was a lovely room, comfortable and welcoming, so well put together that one was aware only of the whole, never of the fact that every object in it was a treasure of its kind, from the tall clock inlaid with satinwood, to the Waterford chandelier and the Winslow Homer watercolors, Caribbean palms blown askance in the tropical breeze. Slowly, through the years, the room had assumed its present shape and, having attained near perfection in Paul's eyes, had undergone no recent change except, yes, except for the painting he had hung only last month between the windows.

He examined it now again, a portrait of a woman, nude and pregnant. She had red hair, and she lay in a pose of complete languor against a pile of violet cushions. He had bought this picture in Munich between the wars, on that horrible day when he had witnessed his first Nazi march. He could still see too vividly those ranks and files of brutal thugs goose-stepping to the cheers of a crowd that had gone demented.

In contrast he could still remember the tired, famished-looking gentleman in the gallery.

"An imitation Klimt, Herr Werner, not the sort of painting that a man with your knowledge should add to his collection," he had remonstrated gently.

But Paul had understood the painting's worth, or lack of worth, and had known, too, why he wanted it. That woman, that soft, white, red-haired woman! Marian had found it vulgar and certainly inappropriate for the living room, and so, rather than argue, he had hung it in his little study. But now it hung in full light, bringing a leap of the heart that he had never expected to feel again and had not felt in just that way for years. It was absurd at his age.

Ilse was right. Whether to see Iris—for whatever reason—he should never have gone to that dinner. No, definitely, he should not.

"There's the doorbell," said Ilse from the hallway. "They've arrived."

The convivial hubbub of the holiday filled the house. It had been a long time since these rooms had seen such a pleasant mingling, for Marian for the last few years had been disinclined to have guests. And Paul, surveying his lavish table, felt a special joy in Ilse's presence in the hostess's seat. Today had brought the hidden, obstructive times to an end. Today she could at last be displayed before everyone; when a man's wife lay in a coma that might last for years, it was understood that a man was entitled to have a lover.

Katie's dinner was superb. The turkey was stuffed with oysters, the biscuits were hot, the yam pudding had the tart taste of oranges, the corn soufflé was airy, the beets were carved into roses; asparagus, thick and creamy, had been flown in from some warm part of the world, and the wines were very old. Champagne came with the desserts: pumpkin pie, of course, along with Katie's special almond-chocolate roll.

Now, overfed but nevertheless quite comfortable, the party dispersed into the living room, the library, and the wide foyer, which was a room in itself. When Katie came with a tray of after-dinner drinks, liqueurs and brandy, Paul took the tray over her objections.

"No, no, you've worked hard enough today, and you've still got all the cleaning up. I'll do it."

He was enjoying the role of host. Lamps had been lighted against the darkening, short November afternoon. A harsh wind had risen, shaking the windowpanes with a sudden gust, and this awareness of the looming winter out of doors enhanced his sense of enfolding shelter. From room to room he went with the silver tray, stopping to say a few words, to listen, and watch what was going on.

Most of the people there had been connected to each other and to Paul for the greater part of his life or of theirs.

Leah and her husband, Bill, were playing Scrabble with
Meg's daughter Lucy and Meg's husband, Larry. For a while
Paul stood there as if to observe the game, but actually his mind
began to wander, as it usually did, to the players. He was, he
knew, an inveterate people-watcher, apt to indulge in the
hobby even at long-winded business conferences that were
getting nowhere. The contrast now between the three worldly
New Yorkers and the simple, rather innocent manner of Bates,
the country veterinarian, was interesting to him. Leah, of
course, was always interesting. She had wit and energy. Like
Ilse, but unlike Meg, who looked older than she was, Leah had
been gently treated by time. Her lively pug-nosed face—
"Monkey-face," the family had lovingly called her when she
was a child—was so carefully made up that it seemed she wore
no makeup at all. She knew how to create an image, fashionable
yet not conspicuously so. Her smooth black woolen suit was
perfectly cut, her white lace blouse was obviously handmade,
and her antique gold bracelets were discreet.

It struck him that Meg's daughter Lucy, in her gray woolen
suit and massive silver bracelets, might also be a clone of Leah.
Divorced now, she had used some of the inheritance from her
father to buy a partnership with Leah, who wanted to take life a
little easier. Certainly there was nothing of Meg in this daughter. Her clever, keen expression was her father's, as were her
seductive eyes, heavy lashed and round lidded. No, there was
nothing of gentle Meg in her.

And reflecting thus about the diversity of people, and of his
cousin's offspring in particular, Paul left to see what Agnes,
Meg's youngest daughter, might be doing.

He found her in the living room examining the painting of
the pregnant nude. Herself an artist, she would know what she
was looking at, but understanding as he did the family dynam-
ics, Paul knew that she was not so much interested in the
painting as she was in avoiding her sister. Agnes had removed
herself geographically from the family almost as far as one

could, having bought a small house in the mountains between Taos and Santa Fe. She still wore the air she had had in childhood, that of the outsider looking in without wanting to be in. Her hair hung straight to her shoulders; she wore sandals, granny glasses, and a long patterned skirt joined to the blouse with a turquoise-and-silver Navajo belt.

He offered her a drink.

"No, thanks. When did you get this? I don't remember seeing it in this room the last time I was here."

He smiled. "That must be four years now. Do you actually remember what was in this room then?"

"I remember what wasn't in it."

"Ah, well, I had this hidden away. Do you like it?"

"It's not bad, though not up to your usual standard. Of course, it's an imitation of Gustav Klimt."

"I'm afraid it is. The man might not even have been aware of that when he painted it, though."

"What's the difference whether he was or not? Everything—poetry, architecture, everything—comes out of something that went before. An imitation with some new twist to make it original. Who's Ilse?" she asked abruptly.

Paul raised his eyebrows. "Who? Well, she came from Germany after Hitler—"

Agnes interrupted. "I know that. I sat next to her at table. What I meant was, are you going to marry her?"

"Good Lord, Agnes, I have a wife, remember?"

"Certainly I remember. But they tell me she's dying. And when she does, you ought to marry Ilse before she gets away from you."

"Thanks for the advice," he said somewhat dryly. And yet it was amusing how relatives felt it was their privilege to give unasked-for advice.

"I hope you take it. She's a real person. Real."

"That I know. But speaking of marriage, what about you? You're somewhat younger than I am, by twenty years or so."

"Twenty-two. And not interested. Maybe I'll have that drink after all, please. A brandy."

Paul gave her the drink and then went to the library, where Meg and her son Timothy were having a conversation with Ilse.

He sensed that a connection had been made between these two women. An outsider might wonder why this should please him so much, but no matter; it just did. And he drew up a chair to join the group.

Timothy Powers was Paul's favorite, and had been all the time he was growing up. He had been an appealing boy, large, fair, healthy, and a vigorous athlete; he had also possessed an eager mind. Now a man in his thirties, he still had all those qualities, and was as different from either parent, as well as from either of his twin sisters, as human beings can be different from one another. For some years he had been teaching modern literature at various universities, chiefly in the Middle West, so that Paul saw him too seldom.

"But let's get back to the subject," Timothy said, explaining to Paul, "We were talking about the displaced persons camps after the war."

"If it hadn't been for the British blockade, I would have been in Israel—Palestine, then," Ilse replied. "That's where I really wanted to go."

She clasped her hands with an unconscious gesture that Paul recognized; it was the result of tension whenever this particular aspect of her past was mentioned. And she continued softly, "The French were supposed to be our friends, yet Franco— isn't that crazy?—Franco of all people let in twenty-five thousand Jews during the war and refused to send them back to the Nazis. But the French sent them readily to their deaths."

"To our shame, we didn't do much for them either," Paul said.

"I thought Roosevelt was always sympathetic to the Jews," Timothy remarked.

"He made sympathetic statements," Paul replied, "but neither he nor Churchill, for that matter, would consent to bomb the tracks that carried the trains to the extermination camps. Weizmann pleaded with Eden, but he refused. It's well known that he had a particular fondness for Arabs, perhaps because they looked picturesque in their kaffiyehs."

"Fascinating," said Timothy. "I had no idea. This is all new to me."

Paul knew though, but did not and could not have said, It is a never-ending surprise to me how few people know what really happened during those years.

"But I'm curious about it all, Paul. And I've been thinking I ought to see Israel myself. You've been there, I know."

"Twice. I was there in forty-eight, when the state was established."

"If you ever go again, I'd like to join you."

"Well, I intend to go again, maybe even next year."

"Ever since the Suez Canal fight three years ago, I've wondered what it was actually all about."

"What it was about? In essence it was to prevent Nasser from mastering the Arab world and driving Israel into the sea."

"I suppose," Timothy continued, "I'm especially curious because Grandpa was Jewish. I grew up knowing it in the back of my mind, but I never thought much about it. There was no awareness of it in the family, so one could easily forget it."

Very true. Uncle Alfie hadn't let himself be aware of it if he could help it. And yet he gave generously enough to Jewish charities. Meg was shifting in her chair; was that a coincidence, or did the subject really make her so uncomfortable? It seemed strange to Paul, whenever he thought about it, that Meg, like himself, should be the grandchild of the old lady with the blue-white hair and the black silk dress, proud Angelique of New Orleans, of the DeRiveras from the Savannah and the Charleston congregations, the elite of the Jewish establishment that was in existence a hundred years before there was a United States. And all of this past, like a stream diverted, had trickled away and disappeared in Meg. Of course, there was also her mother's heritage, equally honorable. It must have been confusing to the child Meg. He had no way of telling how confusing. He knew only that Iris alone was the last of the line, and she was hidden. . . .

"I wish you'd let me know definitely when you plan to go," Timothy urged.

"When the trouble dies down," his mother said anxiously. "It seems much too dangerous right now."

Ilse interjected quietly, "The trouble will not die down for a long time. I get letters that tell me things that never reach the newspapers, attacks by the Egyptian fedayeen, people shot on the roads coming from work on a quiet evening, bombs planted in the marketplaces on a quiet morning—"

"Do you have family there?" asked Meg.

"I have no family anywhere anymore."

There was a silence. And Paul saw that Meg was moved. Then, to his relief, there came a burst of laughter and talk from the other room. Ilse rose.

"I'll go see what Leah's up to," she said.

Timothy followed, leaving Meg and Paul alone.

"She's lovely," Meg said. "We've talked for the past hour, and I feel as if I'd known her a long time. You ought to marry her someday, Paul."

He felt slight irritation at the second admonition of the day. "Am I to marry every lovely woman who comes along?"

"Don't be silly. You've been—going about with her—for ages." Meg laughed. "Yes. Did you think West Eightieth Street was a secret?"

Paul felt himself blushing like a boy. "What on earth—"

"Oh, all right, I'll tell you. We've got some friends who met you once at our house and who happen to live across the hall from Ilse. They've seen you coming and going for years. You're a person people remember, you know. And that's the story," she concluded, still half laughing.

Paul had to laugh too. "And I thought we were so well hidden. Such a tight secret."

"You thought I wouldn't approve? That's why you never told me?" Meg was slightly reproachful.

That was just what he had thought, but he merely shrugged. "Well, there's Marian, and—"

"Everybody in the family knows that Marian's been sick for ages. And now—goodness knows, I don't wish for her death, yet maybe it would be kinder in the circumstances to wish for it —but when it happens, I think you deserve someone wonderful for the first time in your life, someone just right for you."

Not for the first time, he thought, but was touched nevertheless and replied simply, "Thank you, dear Meg."

From the hall came sounds of impending departure. Meg looked at her watch.

"Goodness, we ought to be starting home! It's been a beautiful holiday, Paul." She kissed him. "And remember, when the time comes, you and Ilse must be married, and I want to be at the wedding."

"No doubt we will be," he said.

"You made an impression," Paul told Ilse when everyone had left. "Everybody wants to make sure that we'll eventually get married."

"Who is 'everybody'?"

"Well, to be exact, Meg and Agnes."

"Darling, that's wonderful, but it's not what they think, it's what we think."

"There's no question about what we think."

"Marriage won't make any difference in the way we feel."

"No, but I'll be glad when we can make it official. It does make a difference once you go out into the world beyond your own walls. I'd like everybody to know—ah, well, you understand what I mean."

"I understand."

Paul poured two brandies and they sat down on the sofa to

talk about the party. He reflected that this was what well-married couples did after a social evening.

"They were all very nice people," Ilse said. "You were right about Meg. She's wholesome and kind. I can see why you love her."

"She's been like a sister to me."

"You never let me meet her before."

"Maybe it was foolish of me. I just didn't think it right while Marian and I were living together, or I should say, occupying the same house. But you know, Meg guessed. She'd known it all the time, anyway."

Ilse laughed, and Paul added, "I'll take you there for Christmas. Meg and Larry make a real country Christmas. It's like something out of Dickens."

"Tell me about who was Jewish in her family."

"Meg's father, my Uncle Alfie. He took off his Jewish coat when he married Emily and tried to wear an Episcopalian one, but it didn't quite fit. However, that was his business, not mine. He was a kind man, and I was fond of him. I miss him. I miss that whole generation." He stared at the glass, tipping the amber liquid as if in its depths faces long gone might be reflected. "Meg's had a hard life—not like yours, but hard in its way. Her first husband, Donal Powers, was a millionaire many times over, a real estate tycoon who got his seed money running rum during Prohibition. On the surface he was a polished gentleman, but underneath he was a killer. He made a second fortune with investments in Nazi Germany, then knew enough to get out in time. In short, he was a bastard. I don't like to speak ill of the dead, but the truth is the truth." He paused. Ugly memories fled through his mind. "Everything blew up one night at Leah's house. It was Uncle Dan's seventieth birthday, 1938, a few days after Kristallnacht. And Donal Powers sat there among us, all of us terrified and grieving, and he said, he actually said, that we'd all better make our peace with Hitler because he was going to win. Oh, and that anyway, Hitler had restored order to his country and must be given credit for that. He said it was unfortunate that some innocents had suffered, but that was inevitable whenever great changes took place. 'Unfortunate'! God, he made a shambles of that evening, I can tell you. I never came so close to striking a man as I did then. It was Meg's last straw too. She left him the next day. Took the five children and left. She should have done it long before. Am I boring you?"

"No. Tell me the rest."

"After the divorce she went to veterinary school, met Larry, and married him. And they've been perfect for each other. Incidentally, she never took a penny from Donal, even when she needed it for her tuition. She didn't have a cent of her own."

"I'll bet I know who gave her the money for the tuition."

"Well, so I did. What's money for, but to use it where and when it's needed?"

"Oh, I like you, Paul! Have I ever told you I like you very much?"

"I don't remember. Tell me again, please."

"I like you, Paul. You are the best—so good, so smart and wise, and it's extra nice that you're handsome besides, a real bonus. Also, you buy me diamonds."

This was a private joke, because Ilse had been awkward about accepting the diamond earrings, so that he'd had to argue her into taking them. She was wearing them now, and they made two very becoming sparks against her pepper-and-salt hair, which was also becoming.

"Tell me about the pale one, the artist. She's tender under the prickly manner, I think. Very tender. I had a sense that she's a lesbian. Is she?"

"Quite possibly." Paul reflected, "Donal never cared about her. She was too arty for him. So naturally she had no love for him either. And for another thing, she knew where his money came from."

"I don't think that bothered Lucy too much. She's a man-eater, isn't she?"

This was a game Paul enjoyed, gauging the accuracy of Ilse's perceptions, which were usually correct. He laughed.

"You have to admit she's stunning. A lot of men wouldn't mind being devoured by her."

"No question about that. And Timothy," Ilse went on, "he's different again. Doesn't he look like a prophet with that beard? A prophet in a biblical desert."

"Yes, I've always found him the most interesting of the lot. He's got a brother who works in the State Department, the Foreign Service, a real brain, too, and nice enough, but a little stiff and set on himself. Tim's much more likable. He must be a splendid teacher, very open-minded, uncluttered, unfettered." And, pursuing his subject, Paul added, "You know, he made over his share of their father's estate to Agnes. He wanted no part of it. She didn't want it, either, but he felt that an unmarried woman, an artist with an unreliable income, should have security, and he made her accept. It bothered Meg a good deal, and I daresay it was foolish of Tim, but still I have to admire him for standing by his principles. He saw it as dirty money. Besides, he doesn't believe people should inherit things, anyway. So you see," he finished, "Meg has complicated children."

Ilse stood up and went to the window, looking out into the darkness. After a moment she said, "Just having children is complicated." Her tone made a small, plangent echo in the room, and Paul knew she was remembering her own son, whose death had been somewhat "complicated."

A moment later she forced brightness. "If I shot an arrow straight across the park from here, I'd just about hit my apartment." She turned around to face him. "I can't believe how long I've been there. Fourteen years!"

"You should have moved long ago. I've always told you it's much too small and cramped for you."

"But this place of yours! I had no idea an apartment could be as gigantic as this. It's intimidating."

"One gets used to it." And he thought, When the time comes, she will.

She moved to the mantel and examined a pair of birds. They were of Chinese enamel, the color of a blue jay's wing.

"These are pretty, Paul."

"They're very old. Yuan dynasty."

"I didn't know. And these? They're jade, aren't they?"

In a small hanging cabinet stood a collection of jade figurines, moss-green and cream and pink.

"Do you like them?"

"Oh, yes! They're beautiful. Dust collectors too."

He was amused. For some reason this aspect of an otherwise appreciative woman pleased him. Probably it was because she was so unlike himself in this respect. She had no collector's instinct at all.

"If it were up to me, Paul, I would have a wonderful soft feather bed, chairs, a desk, a table, bookshelves, and nothing more. Except paper plates," she added.

"Sounds like a kibbutz in Israel."

"Oh, I know a lot of people say they could live like that when they really couldn't."

"I believe you could," Paul told her.

"But you couldn't."

"You're absolutely right. I don't want to live in Israel on a kibbutz or anywhere else. I know how to raise funds for them, though," he finished somewhat defiantly.

"Darling, I know that. And I know you've done far more than you'll admit to doing."

That was true. After all this time there were still some things he never talked about to anyone. He thought of those black days in 1948 right after the state was founded, when within hours, the Arabs had attacked it from all sides; the need for arms had been so desperate and immediate that the means for getting them overseas were at that moment unimportant, even if it had meant seeking connections with the mob on the New York waterfront. It was not a means or a neighborhood with which Paul had ever had anything to do, either before or since, but—had not Roosevelt himself pardoned a gangster and sent him to Italy to help save American lives during the invasion?

Ilse picked up the coffee cup and gazed at him over its rim. "Yes, this was a lovely day. Tell me, why is it you never told Meg about your daughter? Surely you trusted her."

"I don't know. I suppose—my parents were living when it happened. . . ." He faltered. "And then there was Marian. I sort of closed it away. It was a thing one puts in a locked drawer."

The tall clock clicked and struck the half hour with a brazen bong. A minute or more passed before either of them spoke again.

"What are you hiding from me now, Paul?"

He looked up, startled. "Hiding? Nothing. Nothing."

"Yes. You haven't been yourself all day."

"What are you talking about? It's been a happy day."

"Outside, but not inside. You were quivering inside."

He tried to make a joke of her remark. "You can see inside me, then, Doctor? Without a fluoroscope?"

"As a matter of fact, I can. Right into your head. Come, I can always tell. It has something to do with Iris, of course."

The clock went hurrying, hurrying, along with his heartbeat.

"You needn't be ashamed to tell me."

It wasn't shame, it was just a reluctance to spill out, even to Ilse, his deepest, oldest, most intimate longings. Perhaps it was even a fear of being a bore to her. Yes, yes. . . . Oh, years ago when all his friends were becoming fathers, he had used to imagine himself with several sons, two or three sturdy boys in blazers and school caps. And his vision had ended with one daughter, unacknowledged. A stranger. He could count on the fingers of one hand the times he had had a glimpse of her. All he had was an impression of intelligent eyes and a rather lovely voice.

"Iris looked at me so strangely when I was talking to her mother," he blurted now. "And I've been wondering whether my face or my manner could have revealed something. Yet I'm sure I was perfectly correct. But she looked at me with dislike. I'm sure of it. I saw it. Dislike."

Ilse didn't try to comfort him with a contradiction. Most people would have said "I'm sure you're mistaken, you imagine it, there's nothing about you to dislike." As always, she was a realist, and he was grateful to be believed.

"Sometimes people just don't like other people," she said. "Isn't that so?"

Yes, it was so. Painfully so. And he shook his head as a swimmer, emerging from the water, shakes off the clinging drops.

"At the dinner," he resumed evenly, "I had an interesting conversation with Iris's husband. You'd have enjoyed him. He's from Vienna. You'd have a lot in common."

"Vienna is a long distance from Munich for us to have much in common, if that's what you mean."

"I meant that you're both from Europe, Hitler's Europe." He was fumbling, and he knew it. "We passed a few remarks about the economy. I'd been introduced as a banker, you see, and he said something about needing advice, about opening an investment advisory account. He said he didn't know the first thing about finances. Most doctors don't, not if they're any good as doctors. They don't have the time, as you should know better than I do."

Ilse looked unmistakably severe, so that Paul had to ask what the matter was.

"All right, I'll tell you. You shouldn't have gone to that dinner. I know I said, when we discussed it beforehand, that I could understand your excitement over getting a look at your daughter. But I was wrong. You're going in far too deep for your own good or anybody else's good. Now you want to make contact with her husband! I can't believe my ears."

"For God's sake, it's only business, Ilse."

"It's not only business, and you know it isn't. Since when does a man in your position go drumming up customers as if he were a bond salesman? It's ridiculous, Paul." Her voice was low and urgent. "Don't phone him. Make believe you forgot."

He felt chastened. "I guess you're right," he said at last.

"I know I'm right."

He stared out across the room. At the far end the copper hair and the milky skin shone out of the shadows. He shook himself and stood up.

"Katie's gone to stay at her nephew's house. I gave her the rest of the weekend off. Will you sleep here tonight? You never have."

"Sure you don't want to go over to my place?"

"No. You're not the only mind-reader. I can read yours too. This apartment makes you uncomfortable. And it mustn't, because someday you'll be living here. You might as well get used to it now."

"It's too grand. It's formidable."

"It's not grand at all. It's my home. Come on."

Two rooms faced each other at the end of the hall. The doors were open, allowing the hall light to shine through to a pink-and-white room, in which twin beds were piled with lace-covered pillows. A flower-skirted dressing table under a gilt rococo mirror stood between a pair of windows on which the taffeta draperies were looped and flounced.

Paul caught Ilse's expression. "Marian had her own room for years, you know that. Here's mine."

And he led the way into another room, equally large, but totally different. Bookcases stretched along one wall. There were paintings, a grouping of American primitives. There was a great chair for reading, an ottoman for resting the legs, and there was a simple, dark blue bed.

"It's a three-quarter bed. Plenty of room, as you can see," he said.

"Oh, this is nice!" Ilse's quick glance took in the photographs on top of the bookcase. "Who are all these people?"

"My parents. My Aunt Hennie. She was a second mother to me. These are friends from Yale, taken on commencement day. I still see some of them. And this is my cousin who was killed in France during the First World War."

"Family. It seems to be more important to you than to many people. I almost said 'most' people."

"Yes," he said shortly.

He had no idea why he should possess such a trait. He knew only that, whether or not it was excessive in him, he had always had this sense of family identity.

Even as an adolescent he had wondered about who he was and why he was where he was. Centuries before us our ancestors made decisions that put us where we are. Iris exists because her mother, a poor immigrant from Poland, was beautiful in my eyes. And her children exist because Hitler had made their father flee from Vienna.

Oh, well! Wasn't everybody looking for his roots these days?

"It's so strange," he said suddenly. "Imagine, I have a grandson who is going to be Bar Mitzvah. Imagine!"

Ilse laid her hand over his. "I know how that must hurt you, but you mustn't do this to yourself. Paul, listen to me. I fear for you. You're playing with fire. Or one could say you're practicing brinksmanship. Tell me you'll stop all this and stop thinking so much about it. Tell me."

"I haven't been this way often, Ilse. I haven't in years, you know that." He forced a smile. "And I promise I'll stop."

"You said Katie made some sandwiches. Why don't I bring them in here, and we can pretend it's room service in a hotel? Remember the first night we slept together in the Black Forest?"

He met her mood. "Do I remember? Yes, feather bed and all. I wish we had one like it tonight."

"We can have the wine, though."

"Good, I'll get it. I know where it is."

"Wine has a certain effect on me. Darling, do you mind?"

Did he mind? Wine acted fast upon her. It made her very, very warm. It made her young, and her resilient, healthy body made him young too. How wonderful that sex and love could last so long!

Oh, he did love her, loved her humor, her honesty, and the way she loved him. He even liked the way she said "darling," a word that could be so affected, but when she said it in her faint accent with a little purr, he only wanted to hear it again.

"I'll get the food," he said quickly. "And you get undressed so we won't waste time. I'll be back in a minute."

3

A mild wind crumbled the yel-
low blossoms of the locust tree and spilled them onto the
terrace. Even if you were to close your eyes, Iris thought, you
would know by the softness of the air that this is spring and not
some equally warm afternoon of fall. You would know by the
smell of the damp earth and the freshly watered geranium pots
on the brick wall. For an instant, proving the point, she closed
her eyes, then opened them to the scarlet blaze of the geraniums, to the young birches clustered between the pool and the
tennis court, and to the garden umbrella spread like a para-
chute under the blue silk sky. She breathed long and sighed the
air out. She was having a rare, delightful sensation of well-
being and expectancy. This was one of life's high moments.

Pearl spoke through the kitchen window. "Weatherman says another fine day tomorrow."

"Thank goodness for that. We'll be able to serve drinks and hors d'oeuvres outdoors. This crowd has grown bigger than I ever expected. Everything does look lovely, though, doesn't it?"

Pearl shook her black curls. "I sure do love a party, the whole family happy."

Ella Mae would have rejoiced too, but she had gone back for good to South Carolina. Iris missed Ella Mae, her warmth and strength and sound advice.

"Feels almost like a wedding," Pearl said.

The caterers had crowded the kitchen with their oversized utensils, ready for the next morning's work. They had already set some of the tables with royal-blue cloths. The dishes were palest yellow, and tomorrow's flowers were to be yellow tulips and blue iris. A pair of flowering white azaleas stood in tubs at the front door.

This is the reason people crave ceremonies, Iris reflected, because ordinary life comes to a stop for a little while and everything is happy, smooth as cream. Happy. Theo was enjoying it too. He had invited a long list of colleagues, both from the New York hospital and the local one. Papa had added another long list. After all, this was the Bar Mitzvah of his first grandchild, and there were so many relatives who must not be omitted; he could always manage to dredge up distant cousins whom one never saw except on occasions like this one—or at funerals, she thought now, laughing a little. Papa had such a generous sense of *family*. Almost any idiot, as long as he could prove descent from some remote ancestor of his or of Mama's, was welcome.

The front door banged open and shut, unmistakable signs that Steve had come home. He stopped short in the doorway, regarding with startled eyes the long views on either side of the hall, from the blue-skirted tables in the living room and dining room to the imposing silver candelabra which Anna had insisted on lending.

"Dad home?"

"Not yet."

"Soon?"

"Yes, why? Anything I can do?"

"I have to talk to him and you together."

There was unusual urgency in the boy's tone. The worrying mother, always worried—and she knew it—pressed him.

"Can't you tell me now?" And as she saw his hesitation, pressed again. "Is it important?"

His eyes were cast down. When he raised them, she saw their wet gleam.

"Yes, it's important. Very."

"Come in here," Iris said. She closed the library door. "If it's that important, though I can't imagine what it can be, I'll phone Dad."

"I suppose I could tell you now."

She became aware of terror. What was it? A pain? A growth he had discovered? Some mysterious lump on his body?

"Maybe it'll be better if I do tell you without Dad."

Suddenly all Iris's well-being, her pink-and-gold *happiness,* drained away.

"Don't keep me in suspense, Steve. I have enough on my mind today, a hundred things to be looked after between now and tomorrow."

"That's what I hate. I've been thinking all day"—now the words rushed out—"all day! And I decided, I decided I'm not going through with this. I'm not. I can't."

Iris went cold. The chill went up her arms and traveled down her back.

"I'm not sure that I'm hearing you right. Not going through with what?"

He didn't look at her. His eyes were focused on the air above her head.

"The Bar Mitzvah. I hate this fuss. All the strange people staring. I don't even know most of them."

Calm, calm. The boy is scared, that's all. It's not so unusual, this last-minute panic. Poor child. He had the beginning trace of an Adam's apple, which bobbled now above the edge of his T-shirt.

"Oh," she said, "I can imagine how you feel. But you do know lots of the people, and the ones you don't know are all here because they want to be. They want to celebrate with you, Steve."

"No, they don't. I've heard you and Dad say you've gone to Bar Mitzvahs only because you were invited and couldn't say no."

"Yes, that's been true sometimes. A few times."

"Not a few times. And you said you were bored—"

"All right. I guess we were now and then. But this argument isn't making much sense, is it? You're making a rather trivial objection, wouldn't you say so?"

"Stupid fuss. Look at this house. Everything so fancy."

"It isn't fancy at all. Actually, it's rather simple. It's just a luncheon with some good food and some nice flowers around the place. And friends. That's all it is. Friends to wish you well on your important day."

"It's not an important day, to me."

She was harried, hurried, and losing patience.

"Steve, you're hot and tired and nervous. Why don't you go upstairs, take a shower, and relax. Or maybe, better yet, go out first and have a catch with Jimmy and Philip. The exercise will clear your head. Then take a shower."

Steve looked straight into her eyes.

"You haven't been hearing me. You haven't paid attention at all. I can't go through with this, I said. Don't you understand?"

"Steve, stop this. Talk sense."

"For one thing, I don't believe in God."

"Steve, this is no time for a theological discussion." Now she was angry. "There've been a thousand times when we could have talked about God or anything else, but today of all days—really, it's outrageous to do this to me."

"I think this *is* just the day to talk about it."

He stood up and walked the length of the room, paused at the glass door to stare out at the locust tree, which was still showering yellow crumbs onto the grass, turned to the piano, and ran his fingers over the keys, making a shrill decrescendo. Then again he faced his mother.

"How can any intelligent person believe in these superstitions? 'The loving God.'" His high voice, still childish, mocked. "Look at the world and see how loving! I should think, after the Holocaust, after what happened to Dad's family—do you think *he* believes? He doesn't, only he won't let his children know it. The word from Mount Sinai, the Law laid down for all time, this is right and that's wrong, why should I accept it? What's right for me may be wrong for the next guy. You want me to listen to childish fairy tales in a scientific age when we're on our way to Mars."

There he stood with his hands in his pockets, suddenly audacious, with no longer a sign of tears. His nice, even features were contorted into a frown. At this moment, thought Iris, he actually looks old. Old and worried. How to cope with such a crazy, unexpected rebellion? What if he really should refuse to appear at the temple tomorrow morning? Oh, my God! The rabbi, the whole community, the busy telephones, the gossips meeting at the club and the supermarket, destroying his reputation! To say nothing—and her scared glance fled toward the closed door beyond which they would now be putting out the place cards on the table—to say nothing of all the people who had been invited, friends from Chicago and Boston and—oh, my God!

She swallowed hard and tried to speak very, very reasonably.

"As to science, Steve, maybe you don't know what Einstein said. He said that the more he learned about the universe, the

more he marveled at its grand design. It's true he didn't practice religion in the sense of going to services, but he did believe
in an orderly world controlled by something that many of us
call divine. And he wouldn't have found anything foolish about
a Bar Mitzvah, nothing incompatible with science. No, not at
all," she finished, almost pleadingly. "Listen to me. He would
say to you, go ahead and carry out your obligation."

"You knew him?" Steve queried, raising his eyebrows. "So
that's how you know what he would say?"

She strove for patience. Hold on. The only way to win is by
keeping your anger down.

"I know," she said carefully, "that he deplored the way society is drifting. He saw that the old religious ways—oh, I don't
mean fanaticism, but what we call morals, keeping your word
and having respect, keeping the commandments—were good
ways. They made life decent. You promised many people,
Steve, that you would be at temple at ten o'clock tomorrow
morning, and it would be terribly, terribly wrong for you to
break this promise."

"What's this, a private discussion?" Theo, coming in from
the hall, stood looking from one to the other, from Steve to Iris
and back again to Steve. "What are you arguing about? I heard
you out in the hall."

"We're not arguing. Just discussing," Iris began, and
stopped. Oh, please don't let this day be ruined, she implored
silently, wringing her hands. And then, feeling the gesture to
be theatrical, she laid them on her lap. Helpless hands. She felt
suddenly helpless. "Steve says, he says he doesn't want to go
through with the Bar Mitzvah."

"What? What the hell are you talking about?"

"He says," Iris continued, "he asks how there can be a God
who permitted the Holocaust. Perhaps you can talk to him,
Theo." Her voice broke.

"Now, the night before, you come with such a question? All

these years in religious school you could have discussed it. I'm
sure they did discuss it many times in religious school."

"I told him," Iris said, "I told him it is perhaps an unanswer-
able question, anyway."

"Yes," Theo said, "like how many angels can sit on the head
of a pin. Listen, Steve, we'll talk about this some other time.
Right now you have a commitment, one of the most important
in your life."

"You see it that way," Steve muttered, "but I don't."

"Maybe you don't, but you're going to meet that commitment anyway, my boy."

"They all say the right things," Steve said, ignoring Theo's
statement. "But have they done anything to change the world?
Look at the slums, look at the wars, look at the Negroes in the
South or our soldiers in Vietnam. Clean up the world. That
would be religion."

"I suggest," Theo said, "that you go clean up your own room
for starters. It's the next thing to a pigsty."

"That's all you can think of? Not what's in my head, not my
self-respect, but some dirty socks on the floor of my room?"

"Maybe you should have enough self-respect not to live like
a pig in its sty."

The two males glared at each other. And again Iris wrung her
hands, then pulled them apart. It's a cliché; one wrings one's
hands. But it's true, she thought. One does so, in despair.

She spoke softly. "Don't, don't, both of you. The world and
his room are both irrelevant."

"Agreed," Theo said. "Steve, you have services tonight at
half-past eight, and tomorrow morning, and after that you'll
come back here and you'll smile and be courteous to your
guests like a civilized human being. I don't want to hear another word about it."

"Look! We made a ton each of chocolate chip and lemon!"
The front door opened and Laura, the cookie baker, came
carrying a platter high and proudly. "Look!"

Behind her in the doorway appeared the cheerful faces of Anna and Joseph. A second later Anna set her platter down on the table.

"Tears, Iris? What's wrong?"

Theo answered. "We're having a problem, Papa. I just walked in on it myself. Our son here has decided he doesn't want to be Bar Mitzvah tomorrow."

Joseph stared. "What? Is he sick?"

The boy, standing at the center of the adults' circle, seemed to have grown even smaller in his defiance, and this frailty in contrast to his elderly expression, in which Iris saw the anxiety beneath the challenge, filled her, in spite of her outrage, with foreboding. Perhaps her father would reach him, grandparents being a step removed from daily discipline. All this went through her mind in seconds.

"Tell me," Joseph repeated, laying a hand on Steve's forehead, "are you sick? No, you've got no fever. Scared, that's what you are. It's nerves, that's all. Listen, come on outside with me. We'll sit under a tree and we'll talk. You'll feel better." And he took Steve's arm as if to propel him toward the door.

But Steve pulled his arm free. "I won't feel better. I'll feel better tomorrow when I don't have to be in temple doing something I don't believe in."

"You don't believe?" echoed Joseph, who had with great effort made a still-uncertain transition out of Orthodoxy. And this, his grandson, was telling him he "didn't believe"?

The room was very still, waiting. The grandfather, too, seemed to have grown suddenly smaller, as if he had shrunk. He looked the boy up and down from his beautiful head to the dangling laces on his sneakers and back to his head.

"So then tell me," he said slowly, "when you reached this brilliant conclusion, and why you waited till the last minute to torture everyone with it?"

"I've been thinking about it for a long time. It just hit me today coming back from school, and I knew I couldn't do it. That's all."

Joseph nodded. He sought a chair. "Suppose you tell me just what it was that 'hit you.' "

"I told you that I don't believe. Not in any of it. Because there is no God."

"I see. No God. You, Steve Stern, you can prove there isn't."

"But you can't prove there is! You only want to believe there is because you're old and you're afraid of dying."

At once Iris's pity was transferred to her father. On his behalf she was incensed. "That's a horrible, horrible thing to say to your grandfather!"

"Let him be, Iris," Joseph said. "But I do think Laura shouldn't hear this. Laura darling, take the cookies to the kitchen, will you?"

Of course Papa wouldn't want Laura to be corrupted.

Now Theo took over, trying another tack. "You're a scholar, way ahead of your age. I've always admired you for it and given you full credit, haven't I? So listen, surely you've heard of Nietzsche—"

"Yeah, he's the one who said God is dead."

"Yes, but what he really was saying was that because so many people no longer believed in anything, there was an emptiness in the world, a vacuum. And he predicted that evil men would fill it, men who believed in nothing but power. Fascists. He was saying that we need God."

Theo was struggling. He was defending order and peace and this family. He was defending Joseph too, Iris knew, and was grateful.

Steve had plucked a leaf from the plant on the piano and was now twisting it into a thread. He could only repeat himself.

"But this fancy stuff has nothing to do with all that." He waved his arm toward the dining room. "It's just social, that's all."

Anna objected. "This isn't fancy at all. Your mother is a very simple person."

"That she is," Theo assured him. "I would have had an orchestra. Your mother settled on a string quartet."

For a moment it seemed that the atmosphere was lightening, and Steve relenting. Again the room was still, waiting.

"I can't do it," Steve said.

Iris felt desperation. It was almost six o'clock. She resorted to pleading.

"Steve, please, we love you. For my sake, for all our sakes, no matter what you think of it all, don't do this to us or to yourself. I beg you—"

Theo laid a hand on her arm. She felt the quivering of his hand.

"No, Iris, a mother does not beg her thirteen-year-old son for anything." He looked about, as if he were addressing an audience. "Discipline! I have said it again and again in this house. Parents are all afraid of their children in this country. Well, I'm not afraid of mine, not afraid to give an order. I love and respect my children, and I expect them to do the same to me." He looked straight at Steve. "No, I expect a little extra from my children, because I am the head of this family. So. You will carry out your job tomorrow. Jewish boys are Bar Mitzvah and you will be too."

"I'm not interested in being a Jewish boy. I'd as soon be an Arab, if you must know."

"Good God," Anna whispered.

"Ah," said Theo. "Perhaps if you'd been alive then you'd have favored Hitler too? You'd have been a storm trooper?"

Joseph just shook his head. "Maybe, I'm thinking, maybe my grandson needs a little clout on the behind?"

"Maybe so," Theo answered.

The light had gone out of everything. The sky that dazzled beyond the sliding doors, the new grass, the rhododendrons in full crimson flower, all had no reason to be so beautiful. Iris gave a deep, sobbing sigh.

Anna spoke quickly. "Iris, don't make yourself sick. I'll tell you, Steve will come home with us, back to our house for the night. It will clear the air here. He can skip temple tonight. We'll say he seems to be getting a cold, and we want him to be right for the morning. Steve," she commanded, "run upstairs and get some clothes. Pajamas, I mean. We'll bring you back early tomorrow to dress."

"I'm not coming back here in the morning," Steve said.

Again the boy was close to tears. If Ella Mae were here, Iris thought, she would be able to do something with him, for he had loved her. But also, he loves Mama, she thought.

"Go, Steve," Anna said sternly.

"I'm not coming back here to get dressed for anything in the morning," Steve told her again.

"All right, all right. Tomorrow's another day. Let's talk about right now."

Surprisingly, or not surprisingly, since obviously he was being offered an escape from the crisis, Steve went to fetch his things. The rest of them, dispirited, stood looking at each other. Theo spoke first.

"Yes, best to get him out of our sight. I don't know what's come over him. It's one thing to have opinions, and he's always had strong ones, but this—this scornful expression on his face—"

"He's just scared, Theo. It doesn't seem like him, I know, but he's just scared," Iris repeated.

"Bullshit." Then to Anna, "Excuse me, Mama, that's not my usual language."

"It's all right, I've heard the word once or twice before." Anna took charge. "I'm going to get him back here in proper shape tomorrow morning if I have to talk to him all night. Now you both go get something to eat and try to think positively."

· · ·

Anna was true to her word. At seven o'clock on Saturday morning she telephoned.

"Joseph is driving him over now and will stay to see that he's properly dressed. No offense meant, but I think it best that neither of you talk to him. Don't upset the applecart. It's very tippy."

"Thank God, and thank you," Iris cried. "However did you do it?"

"Don't ask questions. I haven't time now. Just one thing more. He'll do his part at the temple, but he won't go to the party. We're to say he's not feeling well and he'll stay in his room."

"Well," Iris told Theo when she hung up, "it's half a loaf, and that's a lot better than no loaf."

"It feels more like crumbs. Stale crumbs. At this point I don't even feel like going, if you want to know."

And so, all in their best new clothes, the family set forth. Laura's bright hair was brushed out roundly in a childish imitation of the President's fashionable wife. Laura will be a clothes-horse, Iris thought fondly as she tied the blue silk sash, and marveled that her children could be all that different from one another. She ought to have four different personalities herself to deal with them.

At the temple Steve performed well. His flawless memory made the ritual prayers go without a second's hesitation, and his little speech about charity flowed with his customary eloquence. In her front-row seat with her children beside her, Iris was aware of the picture they made. She wore a pale green, flowered silk suit that Anna had argued her into buying at Léa's: "You owe it to the occasion to look perfect, and one can't fail at Léa's," Anna had said. Jimmy looked like a man, and Philip was round-eyed with awe as his grandfather handed the scroll of the Law to his father, and his father handed it to Steve. Indeed, this was an awesome moment, this giving from generation to generation, and Iris should have been thrilled, moved, proud—anything but what she was, tense as she caught the anxious glance above Steve's head between Joseph and Theo. Her palms were wet, her back was rigid, and she was terrified of some disaster. When none happened, she went weak with relief, thinking: Who would guess? Here we are, such a good-looking family—yes, we are; prosperous, successful and happy, we seem—

It was over. They stood in the lobby to receive congratulations. People came up to praise Steve, to commiserate with him for being sick on his big day, and to marvel that he had done so wonderfully in spite of it. The party at home was a beautiful success, thanks to fine weather, expert caterers, and the efforts of Joseph and Anna, who went about greeting everybody and being enthusiastic, so that any lack of liveliness in Theo or Iris would not be noticed.

When the guests had departed, the tables been removed, and the house settled down for the night, Iris and Theo took off their shoes and stared at the library wall. This long-anticipated day, this miserable day, was past, and nothing remained but a house full of flowers, a freezer full of leftovers, and a deep bewilderment.

Theo stretched, and with pounding temples laid his head back on his chair. Goodness only knows what my mother-in-law did last night, he thought, what magic she and the old man wrought, but whatever it was, the victory was temporary, and fundamentally it changed nothing.

Steve. Who was he? Theo frowned so hard that his eyeballs ached from the pressure. I've always thought of him, of Jimmy too, he said to himself, as my all-American boys. Bigger, with heavier bones than the boys I remember from when I was growing up, and with an air, something easy and sure of themselves, something just verging on what my mother would have called impertinence. These boys were so different that their European ancestors would be astonished to see them. He had to smile at the thought. Was there some mysterious change, a sea change, when you crossed the ocean?

The little smile died back again toward the frown. Lately, even before this current crisis, Steve had begun not to fit so exactly into the picture that Theo had drawn. Things he said were sometimes astonishingly adult, and often very wise. There might be more than a little truth in the saying that at thirteen the boy becomes the man. . . . And that's good; one wants to see one's children prepare to step out into the world. Of course. Still, if one could only see ahead a little, see where they plan to step?

And, as if he were ticking them off on his fingers, he counted his children. Laura, the darling beauty, was probably being spoiled, but she was sweet, and a little spoiling wouldn't hurt her. Philip, the baby, was still hardly out of his mother's lap. Jimmy was fairly predictable; Theo could see clearly enough the straight conventional path that he would walk. But Steve, with the volatile, quicksilver mind, what of him? It was plain to see, judging by yesterday's words alone, that his would be no conventional way. God only knew what heights and peaks it might reach! So earnest, he was! The earnestness was his mother's. . . .

Opening his eyes a crack, Theo saw from beneath his lashes that Iris, reclining with her feet on the ottoman, was also pretending to be asleep. Her face was pure, innocent, gentle, and refined. A lovely woman! But so painfully insecure! Often he wondered what it was about her childhood that could have made her so.

He loved her. He would go, as they said, "to the ends of the earth for her." He couldn't say he had adored her when he married her, but perhaps that was just as well. Such madness didn't last. In his case it never had. This steady trust was better. Except that Iris—he winced at the thought—Iris obviously adored *him*, and that troubled him. It was such a heavy responsibility to measure up to, when he saw what was in her eyes and in her heart.

Iris spoke. "He has no use for tradition, he says."

This reminder of their situation angered Theo all over again, driving out all the compassion of the previous moments, and he burst forth.

"They want to throw us on the dust heap. Rebellion, that's all it means. These kids . . . their dissonant music, everything . . . it's all protest these days. Against what, I ask? Don't know how lucky they are. What people go through! His own half-brother murdered in Austria—"

He saw Iris flinch. It was quite visible, that faint tightening of the cheek muscles. She was still not used, probably never would be used, to the fact that he had had and lost another family. Now he was sorry he had reminded her of it again. He hadn't meant to.

"Was he calling for attention, do you think? What can he lack?" Iris asked.

"Don't be so psychological. You heard what your father said. A clout on the behind is what he lacked. The whole thing was disgraceful."

"You can't mean that, Theo. Papa didn't mean it either. He's too kind and too intelligent for that. He was just upset. Oh, God, it was awful! I'm worn out."

"So am I. I think I could sleep for a week. On the other hand, I'm afraid I'll be awake all night."

"Poor Theo. But you wouldn't really have cared," she said wistfully, "if he'd had no Bar Mitzvah at all. You always say that organized religion doesn't mean much to you. You only go to services to please me, which I appreciate. You said that the first night I met you, I remember."

"You're missing the whole point. It was a question of responsibility today, of not humiliating the family, of honoring the family, especially your parents. It was a question of character."

"I wonder what Mama could have said to persuade him. She

did have a chance to whisper to me for a second. She said we should leave him alone. Don't nag him, she said. He has strong principles. He'll grow up fine."

"Principles! We'll see."

And Theo, looking again through that long tunnel into the future, was suddenly overwhelmed with tiredness.

"We'll see," he repeated. "We've got a job, Iris. We've got our work cut out for us, and it's not going to be easy, I'm thinking." What he was thinking was: The boy will need wise guidance, and a lot of patience. What crazy influence can have overcome him just now? Does he just want to show his independence? And he took Iris's hand as if to mitigate the sternness of his caution. "Come. It's been a long, long day. Come to bed."

It took some time for the atmosphere to lighten. By tacit agreement little more was said about the Bar Mitzvah in that house. No photographs of it were displayed. It was almost as though it had never happened.

Steve knew that everyone must have talked about what had happened between him and his grandmother that night. He guessed that she would have told them that something she had read to him had influenced him. In the upstairs den, long after his grandfather had given up and gone to bed, she had pulled a book from a shelf and brought it to Steve.

"See? Your grandfather showed me this a long time ago. I think it's quite beautiful. But see what you think. It's an essay that Tolstoy wrote in 1891, called 'What Is a Jew?' " And in her soft voice, still with its minute trace of an accent from somewhere in middle Europe, she had read, " 'He is the source and the well from which all other nations have drawn their religions and beliefs. The Jew is the discoverer of freedom. The Jew is the symbol of civic and religious tolerance.' "

Her pink, perfect nail had drawn a line between the words as if to emphasize them. He could imagine what she would have said to his parents: "You have to understand the boy. He has a social conscience. I do believe that those words are what finally touched him."

Yes, they had been splendid words out of a great mind, but these words were not really what had moved him. His grandmother and he had talked until very late, past one o'clock in the morning, and he had seen how weary she was growing. In the daytime, with her bright hair, her bright dresses, and her quick steps, she did not look like some of the grandmothers he met in other boys' houses; but in the lamplight deep shadows had hollowed her eyes, so that for the first time he had been shocked into an awareness of old age.

All of a sudden her alert replies and arguments had subsided, as if the strength for them had gone out of her, and she had turned to him, saying, "All right, I've said what I can say, Steve. Now you must do what you think best."

And as she had turned to leave the room, her face had shown more than all the words that she and the others had spoken to him during the last hours how much the morning's ceremony really meant to her. His heart had filled with a sudden amazing compassion, and he had known what he must do.

So grateful, she had been! She had kissed him and blessed him, and he had felt large with generosity.

In the spring night, under the white sky, the house was dark and still. Steve got out of bed to raise the window higher. The locust tree, at eye level, swam in a silvery fog. Beyond it, toward the rear of the yard, he could sense the dark, wet gleam of tree trunks. Water dripped from the eaves. And he stood quite still, inhaling the cool night air. As it filled his chest, a new feeling of elation ran through him, and he spoke aloud.

"I will do great things in the world. I'm not sure what, but I know I will."

4

When he had hung up the telephone, Paul turned to Ilse.

"Meg says Tim's planning to be in Israel when we are. He's going with a university group over Christmas. We'll be at the end of our month when he arrives, but we'll overlap by two days. I told her to have him meet us at the King David."

"Ah, yes, the young man who's curious about the part of him that's Jewish? I remember."

"A small part. Just enough to be—picturesque, should I say? Not enough to feel any of the ancient fears."

Almost three years had gone by since he had last seen Timothy, and he looked forward to seeing him again. It had been interesting to watch him, for that matter to watch all of Meg's children, grow up, to observe what a superb education was able to make of the extraordinary intelligence they had inherited, chiefly from their amoral father. Happily, they had been blessed, given that particular father, in having Meg for a mother, she with her plain, innate, old-fashioned *goodness.*

"Yes," he said now, "it'll be nice to show him a bit of the old-new country."

"I can't believe," Ilse cried, "that we're finally, actually, really going. If you knew how much I've wanted to go!"

He smiled at her. "I think I do know. I think I've heard you talk about it once or twice."

"Come eat. I've chilled a bottle of champagne to celebrate."

In the ell of her small living room she had set the table with bright blue pottery and a wicker basket of daisies. From the record player came the clear, pure notes of the overture to Mozart's *Magic Flute,* and from the kitchenette came smells of coffee, of something sugary rich in the oven, and then of something else, compounded of rosemary and perhaps thyme. Roast lamb, he guessed, sniffing the fragrant air. Anyway, it would be something savory, for Ilse could cook.

"Can I help?" he called, knowing what the answer would be.

"Of course not. There's barely room for me to turn around in here. Just sit and relax a minute. Goodness knows, you need to, anyway."

And he had thought he had concealed his mood so well! Actually, it was more than a mood; it was, rather, a deep gloom, most unusual for him. But this, after all, had been a dreadful year, starting last November, when one had sat in disbelief before the television set, watching the horse with the reverse stirrups as it followed the flag-covered body of the murdered president across the bridge to Arlington. And that had been only the beginning. He stared down at the pattern in Ilse's carpet. His antennae were sensing trouble for his beloved country, hard, hard times for the United States. Ominous rumblings rose out of an ancient kingdom in what had once been called French Indochina, to which we had been sending first money, then a trickle of young American men, and now a stream of them.

It was in connection with these events that he had had occasion to read Tim's name in the newspapers when Tim had spoken at various rallies, on and off campus, against any involvement in Vietnam. Paul could agree with much of what he said, although some of it did tend to sound overly dramatic. But one understood that; it was youth's fervor and youth's impatience. For Paul anyone in his thirties was still a youth.

Now Paul's antennae, reaching into Washington, were quivering again, for strange reports were being rumored there: that Kennedy, after the Bay of Pigs disaster in Cuba, had confided that America must have a victory and Vietnam was the place to have it. This, in spite of warnings from the military that the victory might require three hundred thousand troops! This, in spite of the warning that Eisenhower had left behind against becoming involved in a war in Asia. There could be no greater tragedy, he had said. But no one was listening. Hard times ahead for the United States.

And then there were other, personal reasons for Paul's mood. For so long after the stroke had Marian hovered at the brink that her death three months before could only have brought relief, and yet her final days had been so pitiable that they would have torn any heart with feeling in it. They had torn his heart, which had never been lifted to any joy at the thought or the sight or the touch of her. Yet after all their years together there were poignant memories. There had to be. Her punctilious consideration, her anxiety to do everything expected of a wife according to the code that had been handed down through generations of well-bred, dutiful women—he remembered them all. In a death that was not yet quite death she had lain through those last days with her knees drawn up in fetal position, her flesh shriveled and gray; her hands were birds' claws, and her eyes deep sunken in their blue-gray sockets. And as he had stood looking down at her in the bed, he had thought of her pride. She whose hair had been "done" three times a week! She who had come to the breakfast table at eight o'clock fully dressed for the day, whose immaculate, unwrinkled housecoats at home in the evening had always matched her slippers, whose modesty about her body—well, the less about her modesty, the better—had had to lie like that! He remembered so much. And he thought now, What baggage we carry about with us!

Yes, he needed to get away.

In Israel there was plenty for him to do. He'd been sending money to help resettlement of the latest refugees, an ingathering from exotic places like Persia. People thought Persians were all rich merchants from Teheran, bankers, or dealers in rare carpets, but the truth was that most were miserably poor, ignorant, and frightened. He wanted to see for himself what was happening to people like them, how the funds that he had raised were being spent and what else might be accomplished.

"Give me your plate," Ilse said. In the center of the table she set a platter of lamb, asparagus, and roast potatoes. "You can open the bottle, while I serve." She looked at him sharply. "You were very grave just now. May I know why? Or not?"

At the moment he didn't want to reveal himself. "Not grave. Thoughtful. I was looking around the room. You really have some nice things here."

"Thanks to you. Yes, I've grown quite fond of them all."

From time to time he had bought things for the apartment. "I spend so much time here," he had insisted over her protests. "Honestly, I'm only doing this for my own benefit."

The plants, all flourishing, for she had a way with them, were hers. A basket of ivy geraniums hung at the window where they sat. In the bathroom ferns were lavish, for, as she had explained, they throve in the moist, warm air of the shower. Books, which were everywhere on shelves, tables, and floor, were also hers. But the handsome cloisonné lamps were his gift, along with some rather fine watercolors, an old English silver fruit bowl, an antique, yellowed map of the Americas, and a collection, handsomely framed, of nineteenth-century photographs of New York: brownstone stoops on Washington Square, the brand-new Flatiron Building, and Fifth Avenue with cobblestones and scrubbed front yards.

Paul's thoughts now ran: Now that Marian's gone, we shall have to make room for some of these things in my place. We'll wait a decent interval, and when the year's up, we'll be married. Or maybe even by spring, before we get back from Israel.

"How soon are we leaving?" Ilse asked.

"How soon can you get ready?"

"As fast as you can get plane tickets. You know me. I have someone to take over for me at the clinic."

Indeed, he knew her, and he needn't have asked. Unlike Marian, so fussy and cautious, and unlike Leah, so conscious of fashion, both of whom would need days for deliberation—and for that matter unlike most women—Ilse would be ready in a moment. A good raincoat, some extra shoes, a few skirts and fresh blouses would suffice, all in one sturdy suitcase. She would look as well as, perhaps even better than, any other woman anywhere.

"I'll take care of it tomorrow," he said. And with those words, already, he began to feel gloom fading.

From the window of their room in Jerusalem's King David Hotel, Paul, with a sweep of his arm, pointed around the compass. Ilse, not the least tired after the long, tedious flight, was too exhilarated to unpack.

"The city's divided now from north to south. Over there's Mt. Scopus with the Hadassah Hospital and the Hebrew University, both idle." He shook his head, aware of the indignation in his voice. "No one except an isolated Israeli police garrison can go there. Every two weeks a convoy sends supplies under the United Nations flag. And over there, that's the Old City, in Arab hands now. They've destroyed almost all the Jewish quarter that had been there since Solomon's time. Sixty synagogues they wrecked." Now in his own voice Paul could hear the strains of wrath and sadness. "They tore out the tombstones in the ancient cemetery on the Mount of Olives and paved the streets with them." His words died away into silence.

It was almost evening; hazy clouds were closing over the lavender sky. Then, thrilling the air, there came the nostalgic chime of church bells, almost under their window. From some far corner of the city the chimes were answered and answered again. Peaceful bells. I suppose, Paul thought, when you come down to it, that's all there is to history, a cycle of violence and peace, over and over.

"I want to see everything," Ilse said. "You must show me everything." And he understood that she was reminding him again how long she had waited to be here in this place.

So began their days in Jerusalem. In the mornings they walked. No eager youngsters in from the countryside to see the sights could have covered more ground or done it with more excitement than they did. The huge stone blocks of the mausoleum, just a few blocks from the modern hotel, were the remains of King Herod's family tomb, Paul explained. The great stone wall around the Old City had been built by the Turkish sultan Suleiman the Magnificent in the sixteenth century, but its foundations, layer upon layer, had been laid by the Roman emperor Hadrian, and before him, and before . . .

He took Ilse to Mt. Herzl, where the dreamer, and so one might say the original founder, of the state lay buried. Almost half a century after his death they had brought the body of Theodor Herzl from Vienna, where he had first had his dream of a Jewish state. He took her to the Hill of Remembrance, the memorial that contains the name of all the Jews who perished in the Holocaust.

"Shall we . . ." Paul hesitated. "Do you want to look—"

"For Mario? No," said Ilse. "I don't want to see my son's name."

They turned away. He took her hand, and they walked down the hill.

On some days they separated. Paul had consultations with the experts, bankers and politicians and civil servants, on the dispersal of funds from overseas. Ilse went to visit hospitals, well-baby clinics, and homes for the aged, sickly poor.

"Such need!" she would cry to Paul when she rejoined him late in the day. "These are newcomers here from Arab countries, who don't even know the simplest hygiene, not even how to use a toothbrush. And no matter how many doctors there are, and there are plenty, there seems to be need for more."

In the evenings after dinner they often heard a concert, for the city had superb music; the world's artists flocked here to perform. Sometimes, though, they just liked to wander through the streets, watching the people: Arabs, Christian pilgrims, French nuns in white sailboat hats, Greek patriarchs with their heavy, swinging crosses, old bearded men in the broad velvet hats and black coats of the ultra-Orthodox, and always, tourists from everywhere, wielding their cameras.

It was the first time they had ever been away together in a new environment. Before now they had had only brief excursions whenever Marian was in Florida, escaping the cold. So these days were totally new, exhilarating, adventuresome, and totally free. When he looked at her as she strolled along in her rubber-soled shoes, with her hair tied up against the wintry drizzle in a red bandanna, or smiling on the other side of a table with a glass of wine in her hand, he seemed to feel renewal, as if he had only just met her, and he felt—he felt young! What an extraordinary companion, so filled with curiosity, with knowledge, sympathy, and humor! He couldn't believe his own age or hers; he couldn't believe how eagerly he awaited the night and the bed together.

In the middle of the second week they began to travel out of the city.

"Only three days more," Paul said. "Tomorrow we're going

south through the desert to Eilat. It's four hours each way, too long a trip in a bus, I think. So I'll rent a car, and we'll start while it's still dark.''

Their route ran southward to Beersheba and through the Negev toward the Gulf of Aqaba. At dawn Beersheba was a dusty, ramshackle, pioneer town out of the American Old West.

"If the young men were on horseback instead of pickup trucks, it would look like a Wild West movie,'' remarked Ilse.

And he reminded her that there had been a town here as long ago as Abraham's time.

The land was a thorny brown waste without shade. Here and there a line of tamarisks and acacias marked a settlement, an Arab village clustered about a sandy, rubble-strewn market-place where camels, sheep, and goats were traded for coffee, sugar, and cloth. Of the men in their kaffiyehs and the black-veiled women, Ilse said that they were figures in a surreal landscape. In empty stretches between villages, there could now and then be seen an Arab family living in a black, goat's-hair tent pitched on a stony field. Once they passed a little boy standing at the side of the road with a tethered camel; the child stared and waved. Ilse was entranced.

The sky, even now in December, began to burn like a blue flame. In the distance the rimming mountains were purple.

"Solomon's mines are only a few miles from here,'' Paul said. "See those rocks ahead? Guess what? Those are the Pillars of Solomon.''

"This is what Mario always wanted to see,'' Ilse replied.

It was the first time she had spoken of him since they had gone away. Paul thought, Perhaps after all we shouldn't have come to Israel, regardless of what she wanted. I should have taken her on a trip through Spain or the Greek islands, or anywhere. But he only remarked cheerfully that they would be in Eilat in time for lunch.

"If I remember correctly, they get the best fish in the world out of the Gulf. I'm starved too.''

The wind in Eilat had died down to an agreeable breeze, just enough to sway the palms along the shore. Paul hired a glass-bottomed boat and they went out over the coral reefs, where Ilse recognized queer specimens of marine life that Paul had never even heard of.

"Don't forget how many years I had to study biology," she reminded him.

"Now I'll have to boast about the years I studied history. Do you know that Solomon probably shipped copper from this very harbor? And probably brought back gold from Africa."

"This place," Ilse murmured, "it's strange—it's all new to me so that every time I turn a corner I'm amazed all over again —yet it also seems that I've known it all before, that everything I see and hear, I recognize. As if I had been here long ago. I don't know how to explain it," she said and, stopping, looked far off to where the sun drew a glittering stripe across the water. And in her eyes, Paul saw, tears glittered too.

At midafternoon, leaving the Gulf behind, they started back along the barren way. There was very little traffic on the road, just some dusty trucks, some tired-looking buses, and a few neat new rented cars like theirs. The motor hummed nicely.

Ilse stretched and yawned. "It's all that sunshine making me sleepy."

"Take a nap," Paul said.

It had been a long day, a fine day to remember as the trip wound down toward its end. All in all, he reflected, this had been a wonderful time in spite of his moment of misgiving earlier that afternoon. Of all the gifts he had ever given to Ilse, this trip was probably the best, because it was something she had really wanted. She really wanted so little, he thought. The smallest things delighted her. The angora kitten he had seen in a pet-shop window had become her close companion. The dependable watch on an inexpensive leather strap had been her own choice. To give such pleasure to most of the women he had known, the gift would have had to be something small and dazzling in a velvet box.

Yes, this had been a wonderful time together.

But he was quite ready now, he was even feeling an eagerness to leave. There was a rhythm about traveling, first the anticipation, then a peak of excitement on arrival, a plateau of enjoyment, and finally an abrupt dropping off from the plateau, with thoughts of home.

Remembering something, he started to say "I suppose we'll have a message from Tim at the hotel desk," and had just gotten the first words out when he rounded a curve in the road and brought the car to such a screeching, jolting halt that Ilse sat up with a little scream; and seeing then what Paul was seeing, screamed again.

"Oh, God! Oh, my God!"

In a narrow, shallow ravine alongside the road a large bus lay smashed, turned over with its complicated, grimy undercarriage exposed and its great wheels slowly spinning. Around it glittered an enormous spread of broken glass. A car and a small truck had also apparently just come upon the scene, for the occupants of both were still in their seats staring in shock at the bus, which loomed like a cliff above them all.

Then at the same moment, everyone leapt out of his car and stood in eerie silence staring at the horror.

"What? What?" someone whispered.

Terrible cries, wailing, shrieking, and groaning came from the bus, and Paul's memory flashed in a second to sounds of the battlefield, where the wounded lay beyond the trenches in the no-man's-land of that old, old war of his youth. Another flash: What to do? What to do? In those first seconds the little group of passersby stood paralyzed.

Then came pandemonium.

Where the windshield had been there was only an open hole framed by jagged glass, wicked as carving knives. A man was now trying to crawl out through it.

"Go back, go back!" the truck driver shouted. "Let me cut the glass away first. Sam," he called to the boy with him, "get the stuff out of the toolbox. Hurry!"

Paul was jarred into motion. Open the safety door at the rear of the bus. . . . Makes sense. . . . Open it. Then he saw in an instant that it was crushed. He tugged at the handle, but it wouldn't move. No use, no use, only an acetylene torch would do it. He ran back to the front of the bus.

In the meantime the truck driver, burly and panting, had managed to mount the slippery hood, from which, in precarious balance, he was attempting to reach the handle of the side door.

"You can't reach it," someone shouted. "And anyway, for God's sake, it's locked from the inside."

"Isn't there anyone in there who can open it?"

The truck driver called the question through the windshield and shouted back the answer. "It's jammed. The front seat's blocking it. Sam, where the hell are you?"

"Here, here," called the boy.

He carried thick gloves and, Paul saw, some sort of cutting tool. Agile and young, he took the driver's place on the slippery hood and began carefully to cut away the lethal shards, which he handed down with equal care to his partner and to Paul on the ground.

This positive action suddenly galvanized everyone else into motion. Ilse got out the traveler's first-aid kit and ran to the bus. A man ran to flag down approaching cars, while Paul ran then in the other direction, from which any speeder coming around the curve could quickly pile disaster on disaster.

"Go on, go on!" he cried to the first car that approached. "Drive ahead, get help. Ambulance and police. Hurry! Hurry!"

Now came the first passenger from the bus, crawling through the space where the windshield had been. He was a workman in overalls, gasping and sobbing, but apparently unhurt.

"I was an extra, sitting on the floor beside the driver. He was shot, and I grabbed the emergency brake. It saved me from smashing into the side when we keeled over. Oh, my God! But there are people in there, on the other side where the window's broken! Oh, my God, what's in there!"

"If only I had something better than this first-aid kit," Ilse cried.

Must get them out now. Help is miles, minutes away. And again Paul saw that flash: only yesterday in 1917, somewhere south of Armentières, only yesterday. . . . He began to climb up on the hood.

"Give me a leg up on the wheel," he commanded Ilse. "Then I can grab the side mirror."

"Paul, you can't! You're not a boy, come down!"

"Damn it, Ilse, hold my foot up, I said."

He hoisted himself, thinking, Not easy, but not too hard either. Shows what keeping in shape will do.

The boy Sam had already crawled inside the bus. Now his face appeared at the window in front of Paul.

"It's hell. They're lying in heaps on the bottom. I think some of them are dead. It's hell."

"Can you get anybody out? Some children? If you can, I'll take them and hand them down to the ground."

"Josh, hey, Josh! Stand there. We're going to try to hand some down."

"Wait, Sam. I'll come up too. Wait," Josh called back.

"You're too fat, and there's no room. This guy here can do it."

"I'm Paul. Shall I crawl in there too?"

"No, stay. There's no space in here. You'd be standing on top of somebody."

Now, abruptly, the first terrible cries had stopped and given way to a prolonged, low moaning, more ominous, more fearful even than the first hysteria had been. In the open space appeared a young girl from whose forehead blood streamed over one eye and cheek.

"My mother's in there. I think something's broken. I think she's fainted, I don't know," she whimpered.

Paul helped her climb through and held her while he fumbled in his pocket for a clean handkerchief to cleanse her eye. Her body shook in his arms.

"We were being followed. There was this car full of men, fedayeen from Egypt, they were. I've seen them before. They kept playing with us, speeding up to pass us, then falling back and going so slowly that we had to pass them. Oh, we were all so scared, we knew something was going to happen, we knew it. And then—then—they shot the driver, and we—then my mother—"

"Yes, yes. We'll get help. They'll be here," Paul murmured. *Damn them to hell and back. Damn the bastards.*

Sam's face appeared again. "Can you put that one down? I've a few more here, a mother and a kid."

"You'll have to slide," Paul told the girl. "I'll hold your hands, I won't let you fall. Josh, here she comes, grab her feet."

So, one by one, they began a slow removal of those few who were still conscious and able to move. It must have taken half an hour, Paul estimated later as he relived events, before help arrived. Given the distances, it was a miracle that anyone got there so fast. But arrive they did, police and ambulances and wreckers with torches. Traffic was blocked where a small crowd was collecting; some were mere curiosity seekers, but most pitched in to help. They lifted and comforted, offered blankets and handkerchiefs, water or whiskey. Several were doctors, unmistakably tourists, some of whom spoke neither English nor Hebrew; but comfort, Paul thought, can be given without speech. And outrage, too, needed no common vocabulary. It was on every grim face, in every shouted command, every sob and every curse.

Once the rear of the bus had been cut away, Paul climbed inside. Chaos was there, the unhurt climbing over the ruined seats, over the injured, and perhaps the dead, in their haste to escape. They were treading on the side, on the broken windows. From the opposite row of windows above their heads, an occasional shard of glass was jarred loose.

Somebody handed a child to Paul just at the moment when a jagged piece of glass fell and caught him on the shoulder. When he emerged with the child, he was bleeding.

"You've cut yourself!" cried Ilse, who took the child and set it on the ground. "Take off your shirt. Oh, it's deep, straight across your old wound!"

"Over my scar," he corrected. "Don't get excited, it's nothing."

And it really was nothing compared with the pain of the original wound, which a Nazi sniper's bullet had given him on the day the Americans marched into Paris back in 1945. He felt a small, foolish laugh rising. He seemed to attract wars.

Ilse had gotten an antibiotic from the ambulance and was now carefully and competently tending the cut.

"This probably should have a few stitches." She worried. "It can't heal evenly over a puckered scar. It was never treated right in the first place. It should have been fixed up years ago. I've nagged you and nagged you."

He was impatient. "Stop fussing with me. I'll take care of it when I get home, okay? Will you look at these people instead?"

For a young boy was staggering across the road, grasping his left shoulder from which his arm dangled. Ilse ran at once.

"A tourniquet! Give me something." She ran to the ambulance, rummaged, and came back. "I can't find anything. Paul, give me your belt."

She tightened a tourniquet around the boy's arm, led him to one of the ambulances, and spoke to the driver.

"This one can't wait, or he'll lose his arm. He's in shock. Take him quickly."

At the side of the road a woman sat holding her wounded baby, its pink face cut diagonally from eye to chin. She rocked back and forth, back and forth, whispering, "I want to die. I want to die." It was like a song, a crooning, a macabre lullaby. "My baby. My pretty baby."

Paul walked around to the other side of the bus. As it keeled over, the luggage racks had spilled their contents through the windows, and these innocent contents lay scattered in the ditch: carrots in a string bag, new shoes in a box that had split open, a book of piano exercises.

"Bastards, bastards," he said aloud, clenching his fists.

Someone standing near to him inquired in English, "You're from the States?"

Paul nodded. His throat was too full for speech.

"Then you're not used to seeing things like this. We see them all the time. Yes," the man said, his voice rising, "all we want is to live, you know? They don't want to let us live. That baby there—what has it done to deserve this? What have any of us done? God damn," he said, and walked away.

And Paul just stood there, staring at the carrots in the string bag. A redheaded lizard, queer creature, scurried along the ditch. A small wind seized a page of piano exercises and blew it down the road.

Ilse came up in tears. "This is carnage. In all my years, in all the emergency rooms where I've worked, I've never seen anything like this."

"You were never in a war."

"This *is* a war," she said quietly.

For a moment there seemed nothing to add except to ask him how his shoulder felt.

"Stings a little, but it's all right." He turned to her and smiled. "I had a good doctor."

She said glumly, "It will take more than any good doctor can do to patch up some of these people. I've seen two with broken backs. They'll be paralyzed. One of them had three kids. The kids were screaming. They thought their mother was dead. She might just as well be, anyway."

Now the police were clearing the road, and the ambulances were moving off.

"We're blocking the way," Paul said. "There's nothing left for us to do, so we'd better get going."

He was starting the car when a policeman approached. "We're asking for lifts for some of these people. Can you take anybody?"

"Of course, as far as Jerusalem. There's room for two."

Two men climbed into the backseat. They were stained and disheveled, but unhurt except for a bruise that was already turning livid on the younger man's jaw. Ilse asked him whether he was having pain.

"A little," he was able to mumble.

"The best I have here is some aspirin. Take two for now. We'll stop at a roadside place for water."

"I think we could all use a hot drink," Paul said. "It's getting raw out."

For a while no one spoke. It was as if they were all still absorbing the full impact of what two of them had endured and the other two had witnessed.

Finally, at a roadside shack, they sat down at a battered table, ordered coffees, and began to talk.

"Cold?" Paul asked Ilse. "Are you still so cold?" For she was warming both hands around the cup.

"Nerves. I always freeze."

The old man spoke. "Can you let me off the other side of Beersheba if you're going that way?"

"You're not together?" Paul nodded toward the older man; the younger one was pressing his scarf to his jaw.

"No, we don't know each other. I have a grocery store in a village. We're almost there." The man sighed, stirred his coffee, and sighed again as if he were about to say something. At last he said, "My grandfather came here in 1906 with Ben Gurion. It took two weeks on a tramp steamer from Russia." He spoke in a monotone, as if he were talking to himself. "He worked as a laborer on a farm. The Arabs used to raid the farms, so they had to defend themselves. That's how the Haganah began. The first defenders, they were. A good thing, too, because it was the Haganah that was ready when the Arabs attacked the state. We were only a few hours old, and sponsored by the United States, when they attacked. A couple of hours!"

Paul responded quietly, "I know. I was there."

"Did you know that when we captured Egyptian officers, they had swastikas on their jackets and copies of *Mein Kampf* in Arabic?"

"That I didn't know."

Ilse was shivering. Paul put his hand on the tabletop to cover hers.

"This is your wife?" the old man said.

"Yes," Paul told him. "My wife."

The other man now removed the cloth and in halting English added his remarks.

"They are preparing for war again. This thing today, this terror, is to soften us up. Farmers have to carry guns when they work in the fields. My cousin had a boy, fourteen. They shot him. He was walking down the road going home. That boy wrote a poem once about Israelis and Arabs, they should be friends. A poem."

For a moment the young man looked as if he were about to weep. And Ilse said quickly, "We'd better start. You must see a doctor for your jaw the minute you get home."

So they set forth again, and again no one spoke. The young man appeared to be sleeping, and the old man, whom Paul could see in the rearview mirror, was just gazing out at the dusty air, thinking perhaps about the grandfather who had come here with Ben Gurion. And one by one the two passengers arrived at their stops. The old man was the last.

"I wish you luck and better times," Paul told him. "I wish for no more days like this one."

The other raised his hand in farewell. "Thank you. But it will be worse before it gets better. In the meantime, courage. No choice, as we say in this country."

The afternoon was dying. The low light fell on red roofs, terraced hills, and on the final peak where Jerusalem stood. Paul glanced over at Ilse, who was looking straight ahead toward the peak. And he saw that she, like himself, was mentally exhausted.

She asked abruptly, "Did you look at the young one? Did you see his eyes?"

"Not really."

"You didn't see? They were full of tears when he told about the boy and the poem. Such fine eyes, intelligent gray eyes. Mario would have looked like that if he had lived to be that old."

Paul had nothing to say. They entered the suburbs, passed through the gardens and villas of Rehavia, and neared the hotel. He remembered then that this was the night they might hear from Tim, and he certainly hoped they would. Already he could see before him the lively face, the football shoulders, and the hearty smile. Charisma, Tim had. It was a word much overused and Paul disliked it, but for the moment he could think of no better one. Tim would give a happy turn to the conversation at the dinner table tonight, which, along with a glass or two of a good wine, was just what Ilse and he himself needed.

At the desk there was indeed a telephone message. Tim would meet them at the hotel for dinner at seven unless he heard to the contrary.

"Oh, great!" Paul said.

The desk clerk was staring at Paul's torn sleeve and the stains on Ilse's rumpled jacket, so Paul answered the unspoken question.

"We got mixed up in a terrible accident on the road. Terrorists. They shot a bus—"

The clerk, unsurprised, gave a sigh of profound resignation.

"Ah, yes, we heard it on the radio. It's already the third time this winter. They sometimes mine the roads, blow up the whole bus."

"When is this going to stop?" cried Ilse as if she were demanding an answer from this pale young man, who merely turned up the palms of his hands.

"God knows."

They went upstairs to shower and dress.

"I'll change your bandages in the morning," Ilse said. "If it doesn't hurt you, I'll leave it alone for now."

"It doesn't hurt too much."

She brushed his lips with her own. "Your wounds. Your poor wounds."

"At least I was on the right side again. Anti-Nazi and anti-terrorist, each time." He smiled. "Wear your red blouse, something bright. There's no sense looking mournful. These people who live here all the time with this kind of thing aren't mournful. Haven't you noticed? They can't be. They have to work and hear music and laugh and make love. Otherwise they'd go crazy, wouldn't they?"

"You're right, of course you are. The red blouse, then."

Tim was waiting when they came downstairs. With his height and blond beard he was conspicuous, a bright figure among neutrals. When he came toward them with both hands out, Paul grasped them.

"Good to see you. I was beginning to feel we might miss each other. We leave the day after tomorrow."

"No, no, I've been looking forward to this too much. How are you both? You're looking splendid."

Paul doubted that. Fatigue was visible in spite of Ilse's attempt to hide it with powder and lipstick, and he had no reason to believe he looked any better.

He had been about to say "We've had a horrendous day,

we're not at our best," but deciding abruptly not to darken the evening with the subject, made welcome instead.

"Let's go to the dining room. The food's not bad here, and I hope you're hungry."

They chose a quiet corner. Paul ordered drinks and they sat back to survey each other.

"It's so good to see you," Paul repeated. "A face from home is a fine sight, especially since I haven't seen you in a couple of years. You know, after a month away, I'm ready to go home." As he spoke, he was aware that his flow of speech was inconsequential. Ah, well, it was nerves. "How's your mother? I called up to say good-bye before we left, and she seemed fine then. Been putting on a new back porch, she said."

"Oh, Mother is always busy and fine," Tim said. "She's really found her place in life with her house, her animals, her trees, and the right man to share them with."

"Nothing wrong with that. Sounds good to me."

"Oh, I don't know. With so much going on in the world, I sometimes wonder how anyone can hole himself up like that. However, as long as she's happy. . . ."

The comment surprised Paul, and he replied, "She deserves some happiness, if anybody does." After all those years with your miserable father, a man as far removed from herself as Sweden is from Tibet, he thought, and went on. "So what have you been seeing since you got here?"

"Walking my feet off. Covered a lot of ground in a week, Haifa, Tel Aviv, Galilee. Everything. Saved Jerusalem for the last. Plan to spend all next week here before going home."

"You'll find plenty to fill the week, I promise you. Tell us what you think of this country."

"Fascinating. I've been meeting and talking to all sorts of people. Interesting types, especially among the Arabs."

"Oh, Arabs," Ilse said. "We met, or almost met, some very interesting types this afternoon too."

Paul, annoyed that she had introduced the subject, frowned

slightly and corrected her. "We're not sure. They might have been Egyptians."

"Egyptians, then," Ilse retorted. Her eyes flashed angrily. "Same result. What's the difference?"

Tim looked from one to the other. "What happened? May I know?"

"Excuse us if we seem a little shaken up," Paul said. "I wasn't going to talk about it, so I'll make a long story short."

Reluctantly and as succinctly as possible, he related what they had seen on the road from Eilat. In the telling his heart began to hammer just as it had while the experience was being lived.

"I should have ordered whiskey, two or three stiff drinks, instead of wine. Well, too late," he finished as the waiter refilled his glass. "At least this will make me sleep if I drink enough of it."

Timothy shook his head in sympathy. "Needless suffering. . . . Terrible! But what do the politicians care? The lot of them, on either side."

"On either side?" Paul asked. "But on the Israeli side all they're asking for is peace. It's not the Israelis who are shooting at buses and killing farmers at work in their fields."

"Well, I suppose. . . . Of course, it's too bad, the bloodshed you saw. But I mean, when people are desperate, one has to try to understand," Tim concluded somewhat vaguely.

Desperate? Who? Survivors of the concentration camps? What did he mean? Paul wondered.

"After all," Tim said, "they have been kicked out of their homes and—"

"Oh, but, Tim, that's totally untrue! I know, I was here. It was the Arab leaders who told them to flee. The Israeli authorities were distributing leaflets, were actually going through the streets with loudspeakers assuring them that no harm would come and urging them not to leave, but to stay and live in peace."

"I don't know. People all say—"

"Who says? What people? With my own ears I heard the Arab leaders telling them to flee. In Haifa I saw them fleeing in boats."

Ilse touched Paul's arm. It came to his mind that it was she who was usually the emotional one and he who gave the signal for calm. And he subsided, saying quietly, "I stood among the crowds outside of the museum on Rothschild Boulevard in Tel Aviv on May 14, 1948, when the state of Israel was proclaimed. The United Nations had voted for the partition of Palestine, Jordan to the Arabs and this land to the Jews. And I was so proud, proud of America my country, which had brought this about."

Timothy shrugged, implying that he found the subject at best uninteresting and at worst unpleasant.

Something forced Paul to explain, to convert. "So you see, it was all entirely legal," he said. "Legal before all the world."

"What's legal isn't always just," Timothy answered.

It was as if the two men were challenging each other, each with a plate of almost untouched food before him. What was to have been a happy meeting was turning into a forum. And Paul looked down at the white cloth, on which a red stain had drawn a circle. It looked like blood.

"Justice," he said bitterly. "Was it justice or law when the British sent back from here to the displaced persons' camps— in Germany, of all places—the pitiful survivors of the death camps? A pretty sight it was when they were herded onto the ships, I can tell you."

"I understand your emotions," Timothy said.

The tone was cool and condescending. Or in the whirl of a sudden exhaustion, was Paul imagining all this?

But he wasn't imagining the woman who had held her wounded infant today, nor the woman's cry: "Oh, my baby, my pretty baby, I want to die!" No, nor the bag of schoolbooks, and the carrots, the harmless carrots in the string bag.

"Of course you're upset over what you saw today," Tim added. "It's unfortunate in these situations that the innocent sometimes have to suffer with the guilty, the good with the bad. But that's nothing new. It's always been so."

There was a throbbing in Paul's head. Years before, he had confronted this young man's father across another dinner table, in New York. He could still see it all, the crystal, the massed flowers, Leah's diamonds, and the horrified faces.

"The good," Tim's father had said, dismissing them with a shrug of well-tailored shoulders, "the good have to suffer with the bad."

Thus he dismissed the slaughter in the concentration camps with the same words that his son, so different from him, was using now. It was uncanny. This son had despised his father and his father's wealth; this son was an intellectual, charming and sunny. It wasn't making any sense.

And Paul said aloud, "This isn't making sense."

"Most talk doesn't, when you think about it. You don't change people's minds when emotions are involved, especially when you're dealing with explosive subjects like racism."

Tim buttered a roll. The calm movement of his fingers and the ordinary act of biting the crisp crust affected Paul as if, in their very ordinariness, they were mocking his feelings. And Paul paused to refill his wineglass. This was more than he ever drank, and it was beginning to muddle his head, but he didn't care.

"Racism?" he repeated. "How does that enter here?"

"Well, Zionism. Surely it's a form of racism, isn't it? Don't you have to admit that it is?"

Ilse gasped. In fury she reached across the table as if she would meet Timothy hand to hand.

"We admit nothing of the sort! It's preposterous! Are you hearing this, Paul? Are you?"

"Timothy, I don't understand," Paul said, controlling himself. "Ilse herself, and all these people"—he waved toward the windows as if to include the whole city—"know better than anyone else what racism does. And you yourself—perhaps you don't know it—but there were cousins on your mother's side, people I knew, who perished because of it. So how is it possible for you to say such a thing?"

Ilse had risen. "Stop, Paul! There's no point in this! You're talking to the wrong person. We went through enough today." She was trembling and weeping. "I'm going upstairs. Excuse me."

Paul also rose from the table. "It's all right. But she's not feeling well. You have to excuse us. I can't let her go up alone like this. The dinner will go on my bill." And repeating in some confusion, "I'm sorry, excuse us," he followed Ilse out of the dining room.

In their room she drew the curtains back. He stood with his arms around her, and they stared out into the nighttime sky where clouds were roiling, and out across the Kidron Valley, where lights made gold polka dots in the blackness.

"Is there no end to the hatred? Will there ever be?" she asked. "Even that young man, your oh-so-nice young cousin, even he."

"Hatred? Do you think it was hatred on his part?"

"It was ignorance and indifference to violence. It's the same thing in the end."

"Yes," Paul said. "Crazy, isn't it," he reflected, "that under all the rhetoric the world sees the whole tangled mess in this poor little country mainly as an oil problem. That's the worry at the bottom of it all. Tim's father made a fortune in oil. It was natural for him to take up the Arab cause. But Tim? Crazy again, the father and the son, the opposites, meeting for opposite reasons at the same point. Oh," he cried aloud, "I am so sorry to be at odds with Tim! Heartsick, Ilse. I knew him before he was born, and I watched him grow. How can he have grown so cold? Cold and—and mean. His mother's one of the last people in the world I'd want to hurt. Don't ever mention this at all when we go home, will you?"

"Of course not. But I doubt you'll be seeing much of Tim. He'll go back to his university, and you haven't been seeing much of him recently anyway."

"I feel—all of a sudden I feel as if I've lost him," Paul said. "The boy. The young man I knew." A deep sadness flooded in his chest. And he added, after a pause, "I can't wait to be home. After today and now after tonight, I've had enough."

He put his arms around Ilse, turning her away from the window.

"Come. Let's rest together. We need it."

"I don't feel sleepy at all," she said. "I don't think I'll be able to sleep a wink."

"Perhaps some more wine will help you. I'll ring for some."

"No, no. I shan't drug myself."

"All right. I'll just hold you in my arms until you fall asleep. We'll count sheep together."

She twisted out of his arms to face him. "You're so good to me, Paul. Sometimes I wonder whether I tell you often enough how much I love you."

"You do. But I can always hear it once more."

She touched his cheeks, holding his face between light fingers. "I love you, Paul. I want you to remember that I said this tonight, no matter what happens."

"What's going to happen? As long as we have each other—"

"I don't know. How does one ever know? But do you promise to remember?" Her brilliant eyes were glossed with tears.

"I promise to remember," he said gently. "Now come to bed."

In the morning Paul had a new thought. They would never be able to wipe yesterday's horror away, but life had to go on, and a little pleasure would do no harm right now. So what about a few days in Spain, a stop on the way home? They'd stay at the Ritz in Madrid, and linger at the Prado across the street. They'd walk in Retiro Park, where nursemaids in dark blue capes wheel the babies, sit in the wintry sunlight and watch the strolling lovers, have tapas in the Plaza Mayor—

On the pretext of a last-minute appointment with a man at the refugee housing office, he left the hotel to make arrangements for tickets to Spain and a room at the Ritz. After that, pleased with the thought of Ilse's surprise when they should reach the airport the next day, he turned back toward the hotel.

He walked slowly down King George Street, marveling again at the fine shops and restaurants and at the growth of this beleaguered city. As he passed a small jewelry store, his eye was attracted by a flash of silver bracelets and rings under the sign A. HEMMENDINGER AND BROTHERS. They had purchased almost nothing in their time here and really, he told himself, one ought to have some memento of the trip. This was Yemenite stuff, handwrought and attractive if one liked that sort of thing, which he didn't. But he knew that Ilse did. He could see her wearing one of these broad, simple bracelets, even when in her white doctor's coat. And he went into the shop.

The proprietor, undoubtedly one of the Hemmendinger brothers, was an old man with a pince-nez on a cord, a pronounced European-accented English, and a courtly manner. He brought out a tray of bracelets, Paul selected one and was on his way out when his eye fell upon something else in a small display case and he stopped.

On a heavy rope of woven gold, a collar that would fit snugly around the base of a woman's neck, there was fastened a large pendant containing on its face a portrait in miniature of a beautiful young woman. It was painted on ivory and framed in a wide band of brilliant round diamonds. Paul's eyes widened involuntarily.

"Ah, you admire that? It's a treasure, my finest treasure. Here, I'll show you. Pick it up. Go on."

The necklace lay heavily on Paul's palm. It had the sensuous feel of silk or fine wood, and his eyes recognized the hand of a master, a Cellini or a Fabergé.

"To judge by the style of décolletage, I would guess about 1870. Am I right?" he asked.

"Maybe thirty or forty years later. They wore such ball gowns in certain circles in Vienna right up to the First World War. This is a court piece. Look at the box alone. Someone in Franz Joseph's court had it made for his young wife or sweetheart. Who knows?"

The gold grew warm in Paul's hand. "Yes, it's a work of art."

"I see in your eyes that you're a lover of beautiful things. Am I not right?"

"I do know a little about painting and antiques, but I'm an amateur," Paul said.

"Well, let me tell you about this piece. The diamonds are blue-white, the purest. And the rope—it takes one man one month to weave such a rope out of gold thread. And the miniature is the work of a first-rate portrait artist." Herr Hemmendinger was almost in raptures.

Paul laid the necklace back in the box. "A wonderful piece," he murmured. "But my lady and I don't go to balls."

"Ah, but this is basically gold, and can be worn with a quiet dress at dinner. You don't need to wait for a ball. However, it's up to you, of course. I never urge anyone. It has been here since I came from Vienna twenty-five years ago, so it can wait some more."

Paul felt his curiosity mounting. He felt drawn to the old man. "Why have you held it for twenty-five years?"

"Let's say I'm sentimental, and I wanted to hold it for the right person."

Paul was amused. "What on earth makes you think I'm the right person?"

"How can I answer such a question? Don't we all have impulses, impressions, that we can't explain? Just because one can't explain them doesn't mean they aren't true."

"I suppose you will want a good deal of money for it."

"I want what it's worth, no more. There's the price on the little ticket under the velvet flap."

Paul looked. "Expensive, Herr Hemmendinger."

"Yes, of course. There are several trustworthy appraisers here in the city. If you are interested, you may take it with you and verify its worth."

Paul was not yet ready to declare himself, and Herr Hemmendinger continued.

"There's a story behind almost all of these old pieces. Sit a minute while I tell you. I was a jeweler. I had one of the most beautiful shops, near the Ringstrasse. Third-generation jewelers, we were. That's not uncommon, or wasn't, in Europe. When things went bad—I suppose I needn't describe how it happened. You know enough about it."

Paul nodded. "I do."

"Well, then, when things went bad and I knew I had to emigrate, I began to collect diamonds. I was lucky. I mean, I was lucky to have a way to get things out of the country. I had connections, it doesn't matter how. So I went about among my old customers, buying things. Most of them wanted cash."

Paul knew about cash for bribes. If you happened to know the right money-hungry Nazi, it was sometimes possible to arrange things. But not often, God knew. Not often.

"I had access to the best houses in Vienna. They were my customers and my father's and my grandfather's before me. That's how I got this piece." Herr Hemmendinger sighed. "It belonged to an aristocratic family. Jewish aristocrats. I don't know how they got it, probably from some impoverished noble family that had gambled itself into beggary. Anyway, I remember going to that grand house. Frau Stern was a proud, elegant lady, and they had beautiful things, a marble staircase, silver, paintings, everything. They were in a big hurry to leave, especially to get the young people out, the grandchild and the young daughter-in-law. The son was already in France on his way to America, and she was to join him with their baby. I don't think—well, I heard they didn't make it. They were caught."

"Stern," Paul said.

"Yes. It's a common name."

"In America too."

"But I remember them especially because of that grand house. The son had just finished medical school. Theodor. He was going to be a plastic surgeon. They were very proud of him." The old man, reminiscing, rocked on the stool. "Yes, yes. I sold the young man the engagement and the wedding ring, I remember. Dr. Theodor Stern."

Paul felt the blood tingling up his neck. "Whatever became of him? Do you know?"

"I seem to recall that somebody said he had gone to New York. Why, do you know him?"

"It's strange, but I think perhaps I might."

"It would be odd if you knew him. Sometimes the world turns out to be small, doesn't it?"

Paul's flush was spreading, burning his neck. "Yes, very small."

"If you want to think about the necklace, please do. And if you don't want it, I'll put it back. No harm done."

"Don't put it back. I'm going to take it," Paul said.

He hurried back to the hotel with two wrapped boxes.

Ilse was reading the *Jerusalem Post* in their room when he gave her the silver bracelet. But the real treasure was burning a hole in his pocket. He was like a child with a new toy who has to show it off to his friends. Why wait until dinner? And he gave her the second box.

"Oh, Paul, two presents? This bracelet's enough, it's lovely."

"Oh, that! That's a little nothing I knew you'd like well enough even to buy for yourself. But this is for me, something I want you to have. Open it."

It was entirely natural that she should be startled by the lovely piece that shone on the velvet bed. But he, who was

watching her face so eagerly for the delight he expected to see
there, was himself startled. Could it be pain that, for the frac-
tion of a moment, drew her brows together and quivered over
her mouth?

"How beautiful!" she cried. "Oh, you shouldn't—"

"—have done it," he finished, laughing. And, with this repetition of her usual objection, was reassured. "Here, let me
fasten it. First take off your sweater."

In her slip, bare shouldered and bare necked, she stood
facing the mirror. The gold rope made a perfect circle around
her throat, and from the center point at the hollow the pendant
shimmered.

"It's one of the most beautiful things I've ever seen, Paul.
You shouldn't have done it," she repeated.

"Give me one reason why I shouldn't buy what I want for my
wife. My almost and forever wife."

"I don't know. . . . I mean, it must have been so expensive."

"That's stupid, Ilse. You know I don't like to hear it."

She looked contrite. "Okay, I'm sorry. It's just a habit of
mine to say it, I guess."

Yet he was vaguely disturbed. He was sure that there was
something different about her. She was subdued. That was the
word: subdued. But it was probably that she had not yet recovered from yesterday. One didn't get over such things so
quickly; perhaps one never really did, and would be haunted
from time to time all one's life by the sight of the crippled bus
with its spinning upturned wheels and the sound of screams.

But the day passed pleasantly enough. As if by tacit agreement neither spoke of yesterday. They went to dinner. A
woman at a nearby table flicked a glance across the new necklace, and that pleased Paul. They talked of inconsequential
things, a popular new artist, a Yemenite restaurant, the
weather. But Ilse was still quiet and ate little. He tried to lift her
out of her mood by telling about Herr Hemmendinger, making

an amusing little pastiche of his pince-nez and his antique manners, only omitting the part about Dr. Theodor Stern. There must be some subtle reason why he omitted it, he said to himself, although he didn't really know why.

"We should go to bed early," he proposed. "We have to be at the airport at the crack of dawn."

A little smile, which he suppressed, touched his lips, for he had held on to the secret about Spain all day and was not about to spoil the surprise now.

Upstairs in their room, after they had repacked quickly, Paul read the newspaper and Ilse sat down to do her nails. The room was still except for the rattle of the paper. When he finished reading, he looked at her and was suddenly moved to go to her. When he bent to kiss the nape of her neck, on which the gold chain still gleamed, she neither moved nor looked up, just switched the buffer to the other hand, working it across her nails.

Then he unclasped the necklace, saying lightly, "This will be your opera jewel. I shall get seats in the parterre for next season. We'll dress and be gala."

At that, casting the buffer aside, she turned to him with a little moan. "Oh, Paul, oh, my dearest, I can't! I can't!"

"Can't what?"

She began to weep and, laying her wet cheek against his, repeated, "I can't, I can't."

"What is it, Ilse? For God's sake, what is it?" he cried.

"I'm not going back to America with you."

He was aghast. "You're *what*?"

"All evening during that dreadful dinner with your cousin, and then afterward, I didn't sleep all night. I got up and sat at the window here for hours and thought and tried to think, first one way and then the other, and I was tortured. Because I don't want to leave here. And because I love you. Oh, Paul, you know I do! God, you know I do!" And putting her hands over her face, Ilse wept.

He loosened her hands and stared at her anguished face. For a moment he was unable to speak.

Then, wonderingly, he asked, "I think I heard you correctly but I'm not sure—did you really say you're not going back home with me? Did you really?"

She looked away and spoke very low. "It isn't home."

He had been pierced with a knife someplace between throat and heart.

"America isn't—hasn't been home for you?"

"America is wonderful, but it isn't mine. Out there"—and she gestured toward the window—"out there is where I knew I always wanted to be. That can't be a surprise to you, can it? And now that I have seen it, please will you try to understand?" she implored.

There was a hot, cruel pulse in the knife wound. He could only manage to say rather stiffly, fighting the pain, "I thought— I should think home was wherever the man you loved might be."

"That's true, and that's what's torturing me and always will, unless," she said, trying to firm her voice, "unless you can make your home wherever the woman you love may be."

He stared at the tears that were pouring down her face, and could not answer.

"At dawn I was watching the sun come up. I watched you sleeping . . . and I thought, This is a little bit like dying. To part from you! Unless—unless you will stay here with me."

"I don't believe this," he said, while the pain mounted in his chest.

"Would it be so hard for you to stay here too? Oh, my darling, will you?"

He was aware of strange feelings, a confusion of shock and grief, of pity and even of a thin strain of resentment toward fate, or whatever you wanted to call it, for twisting everything up this way.

He found speech. "You forget that I was born in the United

States and fought for it in two wars." The words rang in his ears, giving rise to a soft, queer nostalgia; he saw a sudden picture of a graveyard in New Orleans where lay the bones of ancestors who had lived there before there even was a United States. He shook his head and, almost in a whisper, said, "I can't leave it, Ilse. No, it's impossible."

She threw up her hands. "I suppose I had a hope. . . . But I should know better. We have our separate histories." She could not finish.

Her sobs tore his heart. A few hours ago he had bought the necklace, bought tickets for Spain. How was this possible?

"Home. You don't know," she wept. "I've never had one except here in this place, in my soul. First we fled Russia and Communism, then we fled from Hitler and he followed to Italy. I went to America only because the British wouldn't let me go here, where my heart is."

There was a long, long silence in the room. In the corridor outside it there sounded a bustle of tourists, coming and going, calling instructions to each other about luggage and flight time. And in Paul's pocket his own air tickets lay like stones.

But it was his way, his characteristic reaction, which he recognized in himself, always to stifle weakness wherever he could, to pierce with caution through confusion and let reason prevail. So, pulling himself together, he made an appeal.

"Listen, Ilse, I think I understand what's happened. Yesterday's horror has just gotten to you, that's what it is. You feel you can't simply run away from this little country that's so beleaguered. You feel it would be abandonment. Am I right?"

When she nodded, he went on, "And you think that because of your history and especially because of your profession, there's room for you here, and need for you here, and that it's your duty to stay and help."

She interrupted now. "Not duty. It's wanting to. It's love."

"Good! Good! That's marvelous. I, too, want to help. I have helped, and I always will. But you don't have to live here to help them. You, Ilse Hirschfeld, can't change things that much just by being here."

Ilse's gaze went to the window, below which Jerusalem lay sleeping. "America is your country, I know. But this has been mine, since Mario was only ten years old and we talked about coming here. I've told you that. And if things had been different, we would have been here together." She turned to Paul. "Oh, I am drawn here, Paul! I have no other words to tell you, except that now that I am here, I am incapable, yes, incapable, of getting on a plane and flying away. You have to believe me." And seizing his hand, "Don't you think . . . can't you possibly live here too?" she pleaded again.

Now where the pain had been lying, a chill crept over him, because there was only one answer he could give. "No," he said. "First and always, I am American and I must live in America."

"Dear God," she whispered.

"Then are we up against a stone wall? Shall I beg you? I do beg you. With all my heart—" His voice broke. Catching her hands, he pressed them to that heavy heart. "Don't do this to us, Ilse."

"It's nothing I want to do," she replied, in a voice equally broken. "Oh, don't you understand that I don't *want* to?"

Once more, then, he summoned reason. "Come, let's talk very, very sensibly. How do you expect to manage here? One doesn't live on ideals alone."

"I can manage. I'll get a job at a clinic. I don't need much money, anyway. I never have."

"That's true," he said somewhat ruefully, and gave a short, bitter laugh. "You won't have much use for this necklace, will you?" he asked, picking it up from the bed where he had laid it.

"I guess not. Perhaps you'd better take it back to the shop."

The pain bit sharply again in his chest. He stroked the gold rope and smooth diamonds, as though they were animate and could feel rejection. "I'm not going to take it back, Ilse. You'll keep it, and one day you'll come to your senses and return to me."

"Darling, I have all my senses right now. If I didn't have them, I wouldn't be bleeding like this."

He took her in his arms then, and they stood, clinging to one another. They sat down again and they spoke again, going over and over the same terrible, hopeless argument.

"Let's not quarrel," she implored at last. "Oh, please, Paul, don't let's make it harder for each other. Please."

The evening melted into a late night. After a while there were no words left for any more explanation, persuasion, or appeal. In hopeless silence they lay close on the bed, counting hours as the alarm clock ticked their time away.

A chilly dawn came at last, and a white sun climbed up a white, cold sky. The suitcases, packed and fastened, were ready at the door. His flight was to leave at noon from the airport north of Tel Aviv.

"Don't see me off," he said. "I couldn't bear it."

"Nor could I."

He sat at the window craning down to see what he might never see again. The plane rose and circled. Small houses, square as a child's blocks, clustered along the highway and scattered across the flat land among the orange groves. In the distance, behind the path of the plane, stood the rising towers of Tel Aviv with a fringe of hotels on the Mediterranean coast. To the left the surf made a thin scribble along the shore, and far to the right, dimly seen through his tears, lay the long, dusky line of the Judean hills.

5

All through that first long year,
gradually and then a little more rapidly, Paul fell back into his
routine. He had been hurt most grievously, so deeply that,
when waking in the middle of the night or even when walking
on his way to an appointment, he could be suddenly arrested
by this incredible truth: Ilse has left me. A physical place had
meant more than a person, a lover and trusted friend. It
seemed to him at such moments that she was beyond any
possible forgiveness. Yet there began to be other moments,
random times when snow was melting in the park and the
damp, cold air, regardless of gasoline fumes, began to smell of
April coming, or perhaps when in his office the telephones
were ringing and three different people at once were calling

respectfully for his opinion, that he was able to understand the power of *place;* just as she had said she was "drawn" to Jerusalem, so was he "drawn" to this city and to this life. Why, he could no more leave here than go to colonize the moon!

So in the end he was able to say to himself, not without pain, that to live was to win, to lose, and, perhaps, to win again. This was not the first time he had lost. . . . There had been life before Ilse, and there would have to be life after her. And he resolved not to let bitterness fill his soul; bitterness was wasteful and corrosive.

This resolution was not easy to keep, especially on the day when he went to her apartment to arrange for the sale of her possessions, and found himself standing in the center of the room waiting for the bustling lady who was to manage the sale, the breaking of two lives. On that day he struggled hard against anger, regret, and disbelief, demanding again how she could have done this thing. And yet, knowing her strong will and strong beliefs and her rage against injustice, he could begin to understand it.

As for himself, he wanted nothing now out of these pleasant rooms in which they had been happy, nothing except her photograph.

So life continued with the resumption of long-lived friendships as well as his few family ties. Occasionally he drove down to Meg's place, occasionally met Leah and Bill in the evening or, whenever he happened to be in the neighborhood of Leah's shop, would meet her for lunch.

They had always been perfectly frank with each other, and so it was to Leah that he spoke of Tim. But she turned out to be more interested in Ilse, and bluntly asked him whether the parting could have been in any way his fault, whether he might have discouraged Ilse with "any lingering old obsession."

"I swear not," he replied with indignation. "My God, I begged her to come back with me! We were up all night in the hotel arguing the case. . . . You're looking at me as if you don't believe me."

"No, no, I know you're truthful. I'm only wondering whether there could have been something in the back of her mind, something that she perhaps didn't know was there."

"What the deuce are you talking about, Leah?"

"Don't be angry. I'm only saying—you went to that dinner and she may have some idea that you—"

"Good Lord, Leah, I went to get a look at my daughter. And that was a couple of years ago, anyway."

Leah did not reply but, looking rather doubtful, merely stirred the milk into her coffee. Was Ilse really troubled about Paul's situation? Was that the reason? No. No, it was Israel and all her past that had cried out to Ilse. That and nothing more.

"After all, I couldn't force her to stay, could I?" he said, and fell silent, thinking that the only two women in all his life who had rejected him were the only two he had really loved. The irony of this brought a faint smile to his lips.

"What are you smiling at?" Leah asked.

"Just thinking. Ilse was—is—a remarkable woman. A wonderful woman. I shall keep on missing her for the rest of my life."

"She writes to you?"

"Of course. She even writes descriptions of her cases."

And again he had to smile, recalling their dinners here in New York over which Ilse had so often related the encounters of her day, the tragic or comical or extraordinary people she had met. She'd had a way of telling things that was never boring, but always succinct, like a dart to the very core.

Her letters now reminded him of those conversations, so that he looked forward to finding the thick envelope on the hall table when he came home. Sometimes she sent snapshots of the apartment that she had somehow managed to wangle in a city so woefully short of space. It looked familiar, crowded as it was with books and plants. She sent a snapshot of herself in her white coat holding a pair of twin babies. "Rescued from disaster," she wrote, "their father shot in Lebanon and their mother too sick to care for them." She related funny stories about learning to cope with landlords and marketing in a new language. And sometimes, too, she wrote of her longing for him, of inner conflict and some regret, of love and memories and her persistent hope that he would change his mind and come to her.

This last would fill him with a few minutes' worth of resentment. "Never a thought about changing *her* mind!" he would grumble to himself.

"Apparently," he said now to Leah, who was waiting for him to say something, "she's as busy as ever. She seems to have made a good many friends already."

"Naturally. Ilse would make friends anywhere."

"I know. The janitor's wife or a cabinet member are the same to her, just people."

"She does seem to have made some important connections, though. In my last letter she mentioned intelligence people and army people, big shots. I wonder whether—oh, well, never mind."

"Go on, say it. What do you wonder?"

Leah raised her eyebrows. "I was thinking about men. A man."

"She would tell me if there were," Paul said quietly.

Leah looked straight at him. "Yes, of course. Stupid of me. You were always honest with each other."

"She wants me to visit," he said.

"Will you?"

"Maybe. . . . I don't think so."

What? Get used to each other again, only to go through another parting? No, he and perhaps she, too, was too old for any more of such painful ups and downs.

"No," he repeated, "I don't think so."

"Well, there's time to decide," Leah said. "Plenty of time."

She regarded him affectionately until they both laughed. Plenty of time? They both knew better than that. Time was speeding away.

One weekend late in the second September after his return home, Paul was invited to a beach house on Long Island Sound. It was there, while on water skis one morning, that he injured his shoulder again, striking it on a ski as he twisted the line and fell.

"It looks nasty," said his host, stanching the blood with gauze. "I'm taking you in to town to the doctor," he insisted over Paul's objections.

"It's just a cut," Paul said, feeling embarrassed by the fuss. "The same damn old shoulder every time, can you believe it? A bullet wound in France, a cut in Israel, and now this. It's ridiculous."

Nevertheless, he was taken to the doctor, a general practitioner who gave first aid, sprinkled the wound with antibiotic powder, and advised him to see a plastic surgeon.

"I don't like to criticize, but that ugly welt shouldn't have been left like that."

"There were far worse wounds in Paris that day. They needed more attention than I did."

"I'm sure. Still, it must have bothered you all these years."

"Now and then. Just if I happened to knock against something."

"All the same, it needs attending to. Do you want the name of a plastic surgeon in the city? A top-notch reconstruction man?"

"Well, if you say so."

"I do say so. Here, I'll give you a list of three or four good people. Take your choice."

Back home he put the matter off for a month or more. But after a while his clothes began to rub the wound again, and one night when he turned over, he felt the sticky ooze of blood.

Then he knew he was being stubborn and stupid and must take care of it.

"A top-notch reconstruction man," the doctor had said. This shoulder was certainly no great reconstruction job. He might even be making a fool of himself, walking in with a little problem like this one. Still, the doctor had said he needed a competent plastic surgeon, hadn't he?

The word *reconstruction* rang in his head, and it was then while lying awake that the idea struck him. It's an absurd idea, he told himself at once. Absurd and dangerous. Brinkmanship, playing with fire. That's what Ilse would say.

Still, a man could sometimes use a little fire, risk or danger in his life. Properly handled, though, what danger would there really be? He was tempted and tantalized. His daughter's husband! If he were to pick up just two crumbs about her life, it would be worth it. A few casual words that a man might let drop, even in a professional relationship, would be worth it.

The alarm clock ticked in the darkness. Yes, it said. Yes. No, said Ilse's voice, chiding. Forget and stay away. But she isn't here now to chide me, Paul thought ruefully. Wide awake now, he got up, turned on the light, and felt for the telephone book on the bedside table. Here it was: Dr. Theodor Stern. The New York office wasn't far away, only a pleasant walk's distance. As if that mattered! And he went back to bed to resume the argument with himself.

By morning, however, he had resolved the argument and made an appointment to see Dr. Stern.

"It was a Nazi sniper in Paris," Paul explained, "almost twenty years ago."

Back in the consulting room after the examination he now faced Dr. Stern across the desk. And it was he upon whom Paul concentrated; the shoulder was secondary. Dignified, he was thinking. Really impressive. You can tell first-rate people at a glance, no matter what their field. Friendly without being effusive. Thoughtful but also positive.

"And you've lived with this since then? I have to tell you, it was a very untidy job."

"You're the second doctor who's said so. Well, they were in a hurry, on their way to Germany."

The doctor seemed interested. "Excuse me, but were you young enough to be in the army?"

"No, but I had been appointed to a presidential fact-finding commission. We followed right behind the first Channel crossing, the invasion, and the fighting all the way to Paris. I was supposed to follow to Germany too."

Paul spoke almost by rote. He was concentrating now on the surroundings, on the well-furnished office with its burled walnut, oxblood leather, and pale linen curtains. It had an atmosphere of quiet prosperity. Discreetly, his eyes absorbed all of these things and came to rest on the large photograph behind Stern's head: Iris, in an informal pose, was standing with three sons and a little girl in front of a bank of flowering shrubs. Azaleas, he thought. There was an aura of light around the little girl's head. She must have inherited Anna's hair, for Stern, like Iris, was dark. Paul's eyes wanted to linger, to focus on the young mother's bright expression. She wore a sweater with a white collar; she had one arm around the smallest boy.

"I suppose, then, you never got to Germany," Stern was saying.

"I was ready to go, I wanted to go, but they sent me home on account of the shoulder. Damn shoulder!" he cried, suddenly afraid that his roving, curious glances had perhaps made him seem queer.

"I went across with the British army," Stern said. "I, too, wanted to get to Germany to kill Nazis, and I did."

There was a silence. A common horror had entered the room.

"Well, it was a terrible time," Paul said, and wanting to expel the ghost of that horror, he added, "It's amazing how Europe has recovered. The Marshall Plan, and the simple, human will to rebuild, to endure. Amazing."

"I have never gone back," Stern said. "Especially not to Germany or Austria. I don't ever want to be reminded of them. I don't speak German anymore, although it was my mother tongue. I've tried to make myself forget it. I can't bear the sound of it."

The wife, Paul thought. Hadn't that old man in Jerusalem said something about the wife, "a pretty blonde," and a baby? And he thought, too, of Ilse, who had once made the same declaration about speaking German. "If my son hadn't died in a concentration camp," she had said, "maybe I would be able to remember that German is also the language of Goethe and Schiller."

"I understand," Paul said now.

Stern recalled himself to the present. "Well, this will not be too difficult, Mr. Werner. We'll have you in and out of the hospital in a couple of days. I assume you want a New York hospital. I do operate in Westchester, too, where I live."

"New York, please."

"Fine. My nurse will schedule you for about two weeks from now." Stern looked as if he had just noticed something about Paul. "By the way, haven't I met you somewhere before? I can't remember, but I feel as if I must have."

Paul smiled. "You have. It was a few years back, at a banquet for the Home for the Aged, of which I am a trustee, or was at the time. My term's over."

"Of course. Now I remember. You're the banker and we spoke of investments, about which I've still never done anything. And didn't my wife know you too? Or had she met you someplace when she was a child or something?"

"Years ago. I was acquainted with her mother."

"Really? But surely you haven't come to me because you saw me once at a banquet."

"No, no. Your reputation, Doctor!" And Paul, keeping the encounter as normal, as natural, as possible, made the usual inquiry. "Will you give me an idea of your fee?" He was surprised when Stern named it. "That's very modest. Not that I'm complaining," he added, since a touch of jocularity seemed also natural and normal.

Stern's response was entirely serious. "I didn't go into medicine to become rich."

"That's a refreshing thing to hear these days."

But this office cost plenty. There was an excellent Ispahan rug under Paul's feet that he had not noticed until now. If the man hadn't gone into practice to become rich, then, unless he had inherited a fortune, which seemed doubtful in the circumstances, he must be living up to the last penny.

Nevertheless, Paul liked the sound of the remark. For some reason it had not sounded sanctimonious, as it might have done. It sounded believable.

He rose to go. "Tell me, will I be playing tennis again soon? It's my love, you know."

"Really? Mine too. Oh, give yourself a few weeks before you go back to it."

"That's good news," Paul said.

Walking away down the street, he felt a blend of strange feelings, a rapid palpitation, and burning curiosity, as if he had read only one chapter of a book that had then been taken away or had come in for the last act of an absorbing play. That photo of Iris and her children! His grandchildren! This was simply the excitement of touching the forbidden; he knew it as well as if Ilse or Leah had been there telling him that he should not have done what he had done. He knew it, but it was too late. He was in for it, and that was that.

And in his exhilaration he walked faster. Imagine being actually overjoyed at the prospect of an operation! Oh, I like the man, he thought. He's cultured and manly, just what I would have wanted had I been her proper father and responsible for her. And he went on under the mellow blue sky of a warm fall day, with the last chrysanthemums, still bronze and gold, and the warm wind in his face. He had to stop himself from whistling all the way to Park Avenue.

He felt so pampered that he was almost ashamed of himself. Leah and Lucy had come on every one of the three days he had been in the hospital. Meg had telephoned every morning. People from the office had sent so many flowers that there was no place to put any more. He was surrounded by piles of books and fruit and chocolate, most of which he had given away.

Now Leah came, bringing an enormous sandwich, corned beef on rye and pickles.

"How did you know that's just what I was thinking about?" he demanded.

"I ought to know. I've known you umpteen years, haven't I?"

Meg, who had brought the last roses from the garden, had to leave. "We have a new kennel man, and Larry's laid up with a cold." She kissed Paul. "Don't forget, we expect you at Christmas. Tim's coming, we'll all be there."

"She's a darling," Leah said when she had gone out.

"Yes. Always was." It made him glad that these two were close friends. They made an odd pair, just as Leah and Ilse had been an odd pair in their way, but all of them had heart and honesty, which were what counted in the end.

Paul was sitting in a chair by the window, through which he could see the East River and the bulk of buildings and chimneys on the other side, now blurring under a fall of snow. He opened his mouth to say something that had been on the tip of his tongue each time he had been alone with Leah in this room, then closed his mouth for a second, and said instead, "It looks like a winter storm. Strange, so early in the year."

"That's not what you were first going to say."

"Wasn't I?"

"No. You want to tell me something that's on your mind."

He really couldn't keep it in any longer. "Well . . . have you any idea who my surgeon is?"

"You didn't tell me."

"Theodor Stern." And when Leah looked blank, "Iris's husband."

She leaned back and blew out her cheeks. "Whew! For God's sake, whatever made you do that?"

"I woke up one night and the idea came to me. I couldn't resist it, that's all."

Leah looked severe. "That's not all, you damned idiot. Oh, are you looking for trouble! Do you actually want something to slip out? Is that it? Suppose he mentions this to . . . her, to Anna? What then?"

"It's highly unlikely that he'll go home and discuss who is or is not his patient. And if it were to happen, well . . . she . . . Anna would trust me, that's all."

"Frankly, I think you're a masochist." Leah shook her finger, jangling a wristful of bracelets. "Do you know, in all this time, and I don't keep secrets from my husband, your secret is something that even he doesn't know? And why? Because it's your secret, not mine. And it's you who are deliberately putting it at risk." She put on her fur coat and stood over Paul scolding. "I believe you like to torture yourself, I really do. Damn it, Paul."

"I'm not torturing myself. As a matter of fact, I've felt fine since I spoke to him. Some of the nagging curiosity, even some of the hurt of separation seems to have lifted. That's a fact, Leah."

Her snapping bright eyes were kind. "But are you going to be satisfied with this? Once you're discharged as a patient, you won't be seeing the man again. I should think it would be better for you, then, never to have seen him at all."

"You may be right. But it's done, and I can't undo it."

"It needn't go any farther. My advice is, don't get personal."

"We haven't," he put in quickly.

"Well, don't. Get out of this hospital and forget the whole business. There's nothing you can do to change anything."

"At least," he said, "I know now that Iris has a good man."

"Well, fine. Listen, I have to go. I have to meet Bill. But remember what I said. The less talking you do with this doctor, the better."

When she had gone, Paul sat for a long time with an unread book on his lap, staring out at the storm, which was growing rapidly more ominous. It was about this time during these past few afternoons that Dr. Stern had come to his room, staying only five minutes or so to examine him and exchange a few remarks. On the previous day Paul had been reading *The Wall Street Journal,* so they had had an extra minute or two of comment about finances. This had been the whole of their conversation since that day at the office. Of course, such tantalizing contact made no sense at all; once it was past, he would have to be reconciled to the occasional, inconsequential tidbit received from Leah whenever Anna or Iris might happen to come to the shop for a dress.

Thick wet snowflakes clung to the glass, dimming whatever weak light remained outside. He got up and looked out of the window to see snow streaming onto the sullen black river. Restless now, he turned on the television and heard the weather reporter telling him what he could see, that a ferocious autumn storm was upon them. Service on the New Haven and Long Island railroads was interrupted, and travelers were rushing to get onto trains before it was too late. Many had already been stranded and would either have to find a room somewhere or spend the night on the benches in the railroad stations. He turned off the television, went back to the chair, and fell into a doze.

It was dusk when he awoke. Outside a grim night had closed in, making a grateful haven of the warm, lighted room. And he remembered his delightful shivers during childhood summers in the Adirondacks, being safe indoors when trees swayed and broke and thunder crashed outside. He was thinking of that, and at the same time remarking how amazing it was that one could summon up such feelings so precisely after so many years, when the door opened.

"I looked in before, but you were sleeping," said Dr. Stern, "so I went on to teach a class of residents."

A tremendous gust shook the windowpane as if to blow it in.

"Looks like a real blizzard," Paul said. "One of those that they'll still write about fifty years from now."

"I'm afraid so. They tell me there isn't a taxi to be had." Stern made a face. "They say the trains are stalled. But it's a tough walk to Grand Central, anyway. Too slippery underfoot."

"Oh, yes," Paul agreed. "And you can't afford to break a leg, can you? Now I, as a banker, can sit at my work."

"Well, don't you go breaking anything either." Stern lifted the dressing on Paul's shoulder. His touch was feathery. An expert's hands, Paul thought, having winced when less expert hands had touched him.

Stern replaced the dressing. "Looks neat, if I may say so. You'll have no more trouble with it."

"Do you still say tennis by spring?"

"Unless you do something crazy, like tearing it open again or getting into any more wars."

"I won't," Paul promised.

Stern sighed and sat down. "Mind if I catch my breath for a second? It's been a specially rough day. But that happens once in a while."

"Sit down, stay. You know, I've been wishing for a chance to talk to you about something other than my shoulder."

"Really? What about?"

"Oh, nothing that important. Just a coincidence. When I was in Jerusalem two years ago, I think I met someone who knew you in Vienna. A man named Hemmendinger."

The other shook his head. "The name doesn't register."

"Probably a mistake, then. A jeweler, a funny, old-fashioned fellow, very courtly. He asked me whether I knew a Dr. Theodor Stern, a plastic surgeon in New York. I said I didn't, but yesterday, for some reason, he came to mind, and I wondered."

"It does seem odd, the name and the profession." Stern's interest was aroused. "I'm trying to think."

"He said he had a shop near the Ringstrasse. The business had come down from his grandfather. He knew your mother well—"

"Oh, oh! Of course. Yes, I do remember. I just didn't think of the name. My mother was very fond of jewelry. She bought a great many things in that shop. Later she tried to sell them to save our lives. Terrible times, Mr. Werner. You can't imagine how terrible."

"I'm afraid I can. I've had a lot of contacts with Europeans and European affairs in my time through my business and my work with refugees. I always feel an urge to talk to Europeans about how they've come through this awful century. And then, I'm curious about people anyway. I like to ask questions," Paul said casually, as if he were amused at his own little weakness. Then he added quickly, "That is, if people don't mind talking to me."

"I don't mind," Stern said. His smile was grim. "If you want to hear my story, I'll tell you. It's brief enough. Nothing unusual about it, unfortunately." The smile fled. "I lost my entire family, down to the last cousin, in the extermination camps. I happened to be abroad arranging to bring them out of Austria when Hitler struck the country, so I made my way to England and fought through the whole war with the British army." He extended his palms in a gesture of negation. "It's as I told you, nothing unusual."

"Yes, I'm all too familiar with it, working in the Joint Distribution Committee. We did a great deal to help people get settled here after the war. I always thought it was especially hard for the doctors, taking the licensing examinations over again in another language and struggling through, with no money except the little we could lend them."

"I was somewhat better off than most in that respect. My father had sent some funds to the States before the war, so I had a cushion—not much, but enough to get started on. Then I married into a wonderful family, and they helped heal me— emotionally, I mean. They gave me a home and people to belong to again. What that meant . . ." Stern shook his head. "You can't know." He stopped.

For an instant Paul had a feeling of remorse for having opened up a subject that must be agonizing.

Stern resumed. "They took me in and made me their own. My mother-in-law—it's not often that a man can speak so lovingly of a mother-in-law." He tried to laugh. "But it happens to be true. She's a warm and charming woman, so much—I mean no offense—so much like the European women I knew when I was growing up. And my father-in-law is the salt of the earth. That's the right expression, isn't it? Salt of the earth. His kind is going out of fashion, I'm afraid."

"Yes, it's a good thing when one has family behind him to give some support," Paul said, ashamed to be actually extorting information from this innocent stranger, information that was none of his business.

"Right now he's helping raise funds from big givers to enlarge my department in the suburban hospital. We need a lot more space." Stern looked at his watch. "I'll never get back tonight. I'd better get to a phone."

"Use mine, please do." And as Stern hesitated, "Why not? Use mine, I insist."

Again guilt flooded, and Paul picked up the newspaper, willing himself to pay no attention to the conversation on the telephone. "You're cheating, you're nothing but a voyeur," said one internal voice, while the other replied, "You're doing no harm, Paul. Your desire is natural and harmless. What human being in your position would do otherwise?"

He imagined the voice on the line, Iris's voice, and supplied the other end of the conversation.

"It's miserable," Stern was saying. "No, I can't possibly make it. The trains aren't getting through. Don't worry, I'll get a bite of something in the cafeteria and find a bed in the residents' quarters."

By now Paul had summoned a picture of the face on the other end of the line, and it troubled him, because all that he seemed to remember of that brief encounter was a pair of dark eyes with a look of disapproval in them. But that was absurd! What reason could she possibly have had? Absurd.

"What?" Stern said. "If the walks haven't been cleared, they can miss a day of school. Of course. The hill's too icy. Yes. All right, dear. I'll call you in the morning. Yes, my coat's warm enough."

He hung up, smiling almost sheepishly. "I have a good wife. She worries about me."

Paul wanted to hear more and more. "You're lucky," he said. "After all you've been through, you've come to a happy ending."

"Yes," Stern said after a moment, "this is my second family. My first wife and my little boy were among those I lost." And he said, almost dreamily, "But you never forget. It's odd," he continued, "they say a man falls in love with the same type of woman each time, but in my case it wasn't so at all. Liesel was a blonde, very vivacious and athletic. Iris is dark, serious and sedentary." Stern gave a slight shrug. "Who knows? Who can ever understand why we do what we do?"

It shot through Paul: He is remembering the other woman with regret, just as I used to remember Iris's mother.

"Who knows why?" he answered, being purposely vague to make the talk last before Stern, who was already halfway out of the room, should be gone forever. The next time they met would undoubtedly be the last time.

"The whole business of love between men and women—I've

lived a lot longer than you and I haven't solved it yet," Paul added with a little laugh.

To his surprise the other responded as if Paul had made a meaningful statement instead of a banality, a mere time-filler.

"I often think it's really less complicated than it's made to be. A man has a little flirtation, a little affair, and the wife falls apart, breaks up the marriage. . . . Do you have children, Mr. Werner?

"No."

"Ah. Maybe that's sad for you, and maybe not. Sometimes one wonders. I shouldn't say that, I know, because of course I don't really mean it, and I have four, but one of them is more trouble than the other three put together. I'm so terribly worried about him. He's the oldest, a gifted boy, our pride. Such a brilliant mind, a photographic memory! He glances at a page once and gets the whole meaning of it. Now he's all mixed up in this damned Vietnam war." Stern shook his head. "And I can't seem to reach or reason with him at all anymore. I just don't know what to think about our Steve."

Paul studied Stern's face, on which grave distress was written. Although before now he had always been strict and professional with Paul, it was clear that at this particular moment he had reached the point at which almost any human being will, even against his better judgment, spill out to whomever he happens to be with the thing that most presses on his heart. In a different mood, without the storm or his fatigue or Paul's connivance, he would not have loosened his tongue.

"This damned war," Stern repeated. "I don't know what to think anymore."

"That makes two of us," Paul agreed.

"Flower children! Peace. Love. Twenty thousand of them gathering to hear a lot of befuddled professors tell them to drop out of the system. My son just started college this fall but, you know, even while he was still in high school he was receiving literature from some of these people. Urging these kids to go on marches, to get beaten up and arrested and ruin their lives. There's one fellow—I can't think of his name, but he's always in the newspapers—and, damn it, I think he teaches where Steve is. Lord, if that's so I hope Steve won't get mixed up with him! But he's just the type, a young idealist."

Befuddled professors, Paul was thinking. *Always in the newspapers.* And he remembered Jerusalem, remembered Tim's excusing the terrorists, seemed to see again the bus overturned at the side of the road, and seemed to hear the cries.

"My wife says I worry too much. How can I not, the way things are these days?"

Then, as a nurse came in with Paul's supper tray, Stern finished apologetically, "They say storms bring out people's anxieties the way they frighten animals. I hope you'll excuse me."

Paul was about to say "There's nothing to excuse," but the nurse, a new one whom he had not seen before, spoke first.

"You're not saying you're frightened, are you, Doctor?" Her eyelashes fluttered. "I cannot imagine *you* being afraid of anything," she added sweetly.

Stern laughed. "Only afraid of girls like you." And to Paul, "I'll see you tomorrow and discharge you. Have a good night."

"He's a wonder, isn't he?" the nurse cooed, when Stern was gone. "You're lucky to have him."

"A fine doctor," Paul replied.

"But human, I mean. Not stuck on himself the way some are. Don't you think so?"

"Oh, very human, yes."

"What I mean, he looks at you, not through you. You feel the warmth, I mean. His wife's got to be a lucky woman. We're all crazy about him. Who wouldn't give her eyeteeth for a man like him?"

Paul looked at the plump curls under the white cap, at the full lips, so richly red, and the inviting shape under the uniform. Crazy about him. I'll bet you are, he thought.

And picking at the supper, for he had been overfilled with the food that Leah and Meg had brought, he began to think about Stern. The thoughts were disquieting. That remark about "a little affair," for instance. And the little exchange between him and the nurse just now. So he played around, did he? Yet who am I to talk? Paul asked himself. Is my life an open book? But Iris is my *daughter,* damn it! That's where the difference lies. She's my daughter, and now I don't know and never will know whether she's miserable . . . although probably not, if she worries about him, as he said. Yet I don't *know,* do I? But I liked Stern! I still do like him! Oh, hell, Ilse was right. I would be happier not knowing anything about Iris or about their boy either. He must be a real worry, that boy. There must be more to it than Stern said in those few words, or he wouldn't have it so much on his mind. Oh, hell, there's nothing I can do about anything. And I was a lot better off with my fantasies of Iris, with those few mental pictures of her in her wedding dress that time I stood on the sidewalk watching for her, or at the dinner a few years back, dancing in Leah's velvet gown. Yes, I was better off.

6

On Christmas morning Paul drove down with Leah and Bill to Meg's house. This was not their holiday, but it was most people's, and it was very welcome, a beautiful time for what was left of the family to be together, along with a pleasant assemblage of friends and neighbors who came every year.

Three of Meg's children were there, Agnes in from New Mexico, Lucy with her current man, and also, to Paul's slight discomfiture, Timothy. The two exchanged the briefest of greetings and turned toward other people.

The scene was a Rockwell illustration or a Currier and Ives print, Paul thought. Outdoors, the lawn was white, and on the old stone wall, snow lay frozen into crested billows, like waves caught in midsurge. A splendid tree, covered with a lifetime's collection of glass ornaments, glittered in the living room. On the mantel stood an array of Christmas cards and at either end hung red cotton stockings.

"Stockings for the dogs, too," Meg said. "We never forget Penny and Dave at Christmas."

Penny and Dave were a pair of Irish water spaniels who shared the master bedroom with Larry and Meg. Their mild gold-brown eyes, flanked by drooping chocolate-brown ears, observed the party from the dining-room corner where they had gone to lie down when dinner began.

Things changed. Meg's proper mother would never have allowed dogs in the dining room during dinner. There were no more maids in gray silk uniforms to serve the meal, which had been prepared by Meg and was served by an elderly helper. But other things did not change. The old house was there, only slightly modified by the transformation of the solarium into an office wing, with boarding kennels across the courtyard. And the dinner table was the same. Pine branches trimmed with smaller glittering balls and narrow red velvet bows made the centerpiece. There were turkey, roast beef and Yorkshire pudding, turnips, mashed potatoes and creamed onions, hot rolls and homemade cranberry sauce with orange peel, just as Paul remembered it; cider and wine and a bowl of eggnog on the sideboard, marzipan and stuffed dates in Grandmother Angelique's silver bowls between the candelabra on the table.

He would not have wanted to miss this day. It's the continuity that charms, he reflected, the fact that some things in a world that is so frantically whirling can remain; it gives you an anchor. One didn't find many places like this anymore; young Meg—"young Meg" was almost sixty now—was still living in her parents' house. And he, her cousin, still kept in touch. He looked down the length of the table. Lucy and Leah were chatting; you'd think they'd see enough of each other in the shop every day. Paul stole a quick look at Tim, who, in his open-collared, wrinkled, plaid woolen shirt was obviously "making a statement" to all who were dressed in conventional holiday clothes. Childish, when you came down to it, Paul thought. A childish defiance. At one time he would not even have noticed Tim's shirt or cared if he had noticed it. It was the event in Jerusalem that made the difference. So now his thoughts went to Thomas, the brother whom he had never favored, and he found himself wishing that Thomas were here today or that he would be safe in Vietnam. And once again he felt the familiar awareness of blood-tie.

A man's voice interrupted his mental wanderings.

"I don't believe we've been introduced."

Paul looked across at an urbane gentleman in his mid-forties.

"I'm Paul Werner," he said cordially, "a cousin of Meg's."

"Oh, I'm sorry," said Meg, who, at the foot of the table, sat between Paul and the stranger. "I thought I had introduced you. This is Mr. Jordaine, Victor Jordaine, a good friend of Tim's."

Jordaine picked up the conversation. "Of course I know who you are."

"How so?"

The man looked surprised. "The Werner banking house? How could I not know?"

Paul didn't like the remark, which it seemed to him smacked too much of flattery. And he replied, "It depends what business you're in, I suppose, or where you're from, whether you know it or not."

"I'm in a number of businesses. And generally speaking, I say I'm from Europe. That covers a good deal of space." Jordaine smiled pleasantly.

Mindful of his duty as a guest to continue the conversation, Paul remarked, "You must enjoy traveling."

"Not really. I do what I must do for business. And I hate hotels. I keep my own apartment in a few cities, Paris, London, et cetera."

As Jordaine spoke, Paul tried to "place" him. He had a very faint foreign accent. And he certainly did not resemble any of Meg's other friends here. Those were hearty country types, or rather they were city people who, through taste and habit, had evolved into country types; the kind of people who showed dogs, kept sheep, talked about fescue grass, and, like responsible citizens, manned the polls at election time. This man in his dark, expensive suit with his dark, sardonic face was different.

Meg, the proper hostess, explained, "Mr. Jordaine is our neighbor. He has a lovely house down the road."

"Thanks to your son, my good friend, who let me know it was available."

"Oh, you're a friend of Thomas's?" Paul asked.

"No, of Tim's. I've never met Thomas."

Despite the fact that it was none of his business, Paul was curious. Surely Jordaine and Tim made a strange pair? But making no comment, he waited for someone to say more.

"The house down the road is only rented. I needed a place to stay while my New York condominium is being built. In the meantime I stay at the Waldorf during the week when I'm in the States. But as I said, I hate hotels."

Suddenly Paul lost interest. At the far end of the long table a vigorous discussion, in which Tim's voice dominated, was taking place. His emphatic tone had brought a pause in the general conversation.

"When you make a political statement and nobody listens to it, then violent action is the only remedy."

"I don't agree," Bill replied. "Of course, there's much to be said against this war in Vietnam. I myself am one of those who think it's a bad mistake for us to be there, but I still don't see what bombing the telephone company is going to accomplish. Except to destroy valuable property, and maybe lives too."

"You're a lawyer, so quite naturally you take a legalistic point of view," Timothy retorted. "You represent the propertied classes. That's what most lawyers do, isn't it? Unless they happen to be pro bono people, and I doubt you're one of those, are you?"

"Bill does plenty of pro bono work!" Leah cried indignantly.

Bill waved her aside, as if to say that he was able to defend himself, and proceeded calmly. "This is, thank God, a government of laws. If you don't agree with the laws, make it known by your vote, that's all. That's our system."

"Again, spoken like a lawyer," Timothy argued. "One gets fast nowhere that way. Young people, and I still count myself one of them, don't want to wait an eternity. They want to get things done."

"Your brother wouldn't agree with you," Lucy said angrily. "He's in Vietnam now. Remember?"

"Our brother. It's been a long time since he and I agreed on anything, if *you* remember."

Larry, good Larry, intervened. Although he must surely be used to the hostility among his wife's children by now, Paul sympathized with him.

"Well, these are hard times. One hears so many theories, the domino effect and appeasement and what-all. Only time will tell. Meanwhile, it's Christmas, and—"

One of the neighbors, whom Paul remembered as an elderly type of dignified curmudgeon, interrupted.

"That's the trouble with the young today. Still wet behind the ears and think they ought to run the country. What's happening on the college campuses is a disgrace. I don't understand it. They all live on the fat of the land. What more do they want?"

"Oh," said Timothy, quietly now, "I can easily tell you what they want. You say they live on the fat of the land. Yes, many of them do, but the interesting thing is they don't want to live on it. They're sick of fat. This isn't the fifties any longer. This generation's different. This generation questions the society in which it lives."

"Marxism," Lucy said scornfully. "That's what it is. You

don't just want to get out of Vietnam. You also want to tear up the country."

"Possibly. Tear it up to rebuild it. It's the old cliché: You don't make an omelet without breaking eggs."

Agnes admonished Tim mildly, "You shouldn't let people think you're a Communist, Tim, because you're not. You're a freethinker."

Tim smiled at his sister. "That's right. Agnes understands. Russian Communism is the last thing I'd want. I'm of the New Left, not the old. I suppose I'm more an anarchist, actually, than anything else. I don't want government to order me around, to tell me to go to war or what to wear, or to be anything except my freeborn self. That's what the young people want today, to be spontaneous, to seek their natural pleasures. A cultural revolution, that's what it's all about," he finished.

"In my book," Lucy told him, "your cultural revolution has nothing to do with bombing the telephone building."

"Well, I assure you all that I personally am not making bombs," Tim said. "But I have to tell you that the young people who do make them are very often the most idealistic, the most committed, the most talented. They're willing to risk everything, even their lives, to stop this war. I take my hat off to them."

"Bullshit," Lucy said.

"Oh, my," said her mother.

Paul's glance met Victor Jordaine's, which was amused. To Paul that seemed like a cold reaction, since there had been nothing funny in seeing so much hostility between brother and sister. It troubled him that this should have happened at Meg's beautiful table. And he was angry at the cause, at Tim, who sat untroubled in his blond glory, as sure of himself as he had been at the table in Jerusalem. And suddenly Paul remembered Dr. Stern and the boy Steve.

"Victor," called Tim, "you haven't said a word!"

Jordaine, still with the amused expression, answered quietly, "I listen, I'm a European. Vietnam is not my business. I let you Americans worry about it."

"If you've all had enough of everything else," Larry called out, "I'd say it's time to bring on the plum pudding."

So it was carried in, flaming, with a sprig of holly on top. Then pies were brought, and the tension gradually subsided into the relief of trivial conversation about someone's departure for the Caribbean, and someone else's entry at the Westminster Kennel Club Show in the coming February.

After dessert the company dispersed. The house was large enough for people to separate; some went across the hall to the piano, where somebody began to play; some went to look at a Christmas program on television; others went out for a tramp in the snow to walk off the food. Paul, Meg, and Leah were left alone in Meg's little study for a while.

"I'm sorry about Timothy," Meg began. "I worry about the things that are going on, all the things he favors."

Neither of the others made comment, since there was really none to make, and she finished, with a small sigh, "However, one's children grow up and go their way. The best thing, Larry always tells me, is not to ask questions. You probably won't like the answers, and there's nothing you can do about them anyway."

There was a silence that Leah broke by saying, "Well, Lucy should be one comfort to you. I'll stand up for her any day."

Meg nodded. "I'm glad. She's as different from me as she can be, and still we have always been warm together."

From there the conversation went to neutral topics, Meg remarking that young Mrs. Donnelly was getting better looking every day, and Leah reporting that Mrs. Somebody Else had been in the shop for Florida clothes, when Paul, who was scarcely paying attention to such feminine topics, thought suddenly of something else.

"That man, Victor Jordaine, puzzled me in a way. Who is he?"

"Oh, he's somebody Tim knows. He's rented this huge house with elaborate gardens and an indoor pool. He'll probably buy it, he says. He must be enormously rich. I don't know how Tim knows him. He doesn't seem to be Tim's type, does he?" Meg gave a shrug. "But then—" She stopped for a moment and then said, "You know something? Maybe the reason I feel strange with the man is—well, he reminds me of Donal."

Paul couldn't remember when Meg had last mentioned her first husband's name, it had been so many years ago.

"Doesn't he remind you?" Meg asked now.

"Maybe. Indefinably," Paul replied. Both men had a certain kind of sharp good looks and an air of arrogant accomplishment. But otherwise the comparison was unfair to Jordaine, for Paul had despised Donal, had hated him for his Nazi sympathies and for the misery he had brought to Meg. About Jordaine he felt only passing curiosity.

"He's a big spender, all right," Leah remarked, explaining to Paul. "I met him here a while ago. He'd walked over from his place, and when he heard I was Leah of Léa, he was so interested that I was amazed. He knows about the best shops everywhere, in Europe naturally, but here too. And he's been coming in ever since to buy things for his ladies." Leah was relishing the account. "Lucy's funny, she's plays dumb and can draw information out of people in the sweetest, most innocent way. So she found out he's not married; he may have been, probably has been, but he either has a different woman in every city he visits, or else his affairs are very short lived, because he buys things in so many different sizes. He wanted to take Lucy out, but she wouldn't go, says he's not her type."

"I wish she would settle on a type," Meg complained, "and marry again. I keep praying she'll be as lucky as I've been."

Leah wasn't finished with Mr. Jordaine. "The things he buys! They're to die over! Some girl must have died over the last thing, I can tell you, positively the creamiest coat, as soft as butter and lined with black mink."

"Well, I didn't like what he gave me," Meg said. "No offense, Leah, you know that. It was very, very nice, but not for me. And it's really ostentatious to bring a thing like that, anyway, just because Tim invited him here to dinner. Good heavens, people bring a box of candy or a few flowers or something."

Leah wanted to know what Jordaine had given her.

"A pocketbook, a dark red lizard with a studded frame and a swan-shaped clasp. Very pretty, but nothing I need in my life. Frightfully expensive, I'm sure."

"Oh, I remember that bag! Was that for you? He'd bought about six different things that day. He was going to Rome for the weekend, he said, and didn't want to arrive empty-handed. It's fine if you want to return it, Meg. Money back, guaranteed." Leah laughed.

"No, no, I'll buy something I can have use for. I could use a nice sweater. I seem to live in them."

"You'll have to buy a lot of sweaters to equal that bag," Leah told her.

When the hikers returned, rubbing cold hands and stamping snow off their feet in the entryway, everyone reassembled for the last sociability before going home. Meg was commandeered to play the piano; some sang show tunes from *Oklahoma!* and *My Fair Lady,* while some just listened. Finally, Meg and Paul made everyone laugh with their silly song, "The Frigidaire Can Never Replace the Iceman." Meg explained, "We used to have a brown icebox on the back porch. The iceman's name was Elmer, I remember, and one day he . . ."

Paul was thinking, as she told her little story, how he envied Larry and Meg. To open your house to people in welcome, to see them depart well fed and merry, then to shut the door upon them and be alone together!

Outside as they got into Bill's car, he looked back at the house. The front door, on which hung a great wreath with a red

satin bow, had been closed. In each window, upstairs and
downstairs, there shone a candle flame. The cold was so intense that a branch snapped with the sound of a gunshot. But
the house was warm, a bright ship in an ocean of darkness.

He missed Ilse, half a world away. It was probably raining in
Jerusalem; a steady, cold, winter rain it would be, as on the
night when she had told him she wasn't going home with him.

Ah, well!

"A nice day," Bill said, as they turned onto the highway.
"Nice people, a lot of them."

"They're a varied bunch. Meg's family, I mean." Leah spoke
thoughtfully. "I suppose it's wonderful to have a large family. I
never had one, so I wouldn't know. But there's so much conflict
in Meg's crew that they're really better off as they are, dispersed all over the country. I noticed you and Tim didn't have
much to say to each other, Paul."

"No, not after Israel. I have little use for him. Or he for me, I
daresay."

"He's making his name known in this country, all right," Bill
said. "Oh, if that crowd would limit itself to speech, there'd be
no harm, maybe even a lot of good. I'm always for airing
opinions, the more the better. But when they get to ugly con-
frontations, I don't like it. This has to be a country of laws. I
don't like to see kids battling cops."

Paul was thinking again of Dr. Stern's son. *My grandson.* Had
Stern said where his son was? Could it be where Timothy was?
Well, whether or not, he hoped the boy wouldn't get involved
with him or anybody like him, wouldn't let himself be led off
course. But universities were large places, after all, and there
would be many other competing influences. One shouldn't
assume anything. Yet he wondered about the boy. A worry,
Stern had said.

Then Iris must have much to worry about, the boy, and Stern
himself.

Bill was passing the time on the ride home with casual remarks that Leah answered, which left Paul, alone on the back-seat, first to his thoughts and gradually to drowsiness. Then Bill's voice woke him.

"I don't know what it is. I can't put my finger on it, but Victor Jordaine just looked out of place, didn't he, Paul?"

Roused, Paul murmured, "Yes, I thought so too."

He was to have good reason to remember that.

7

At the very top of the sloping rows, from the farthest rear of the lecture theater, Steve looked down at a hundred unmoving heads. These, like his own, were turned directly toward the man on the podium.

The man was young, perhaps thirty or thirty-five. He had pink skin and a full, very blond head of hair. His features were long and Lincolnesque; his was a face that, once seen, would be hard to forget. Up until this day, the first of a new semester, Steve had seen Professor Powers only two or three times and only while hurrying across the campus. But he had not forgotten him, and had heard so much about him that he had made sure to enroll in one of his classes as soon as possible.

There was almost no sound in the hall now other than

Powers's full, pleasing voice, none of the customary accompaniment of coughs, squeaking chairs, and rattling papers.

"I was in Hanoi only a couple of months ago, and I can tell you that the spirit there is incredibly high. The courage of simple people! I was humbled by it, especially by the young. Look at your hands," Powers cried suddenly. "Yes, turn them over and look at them."

Puzzled, not understanding, but obedient, every student looked at his hands.

"In young hands like yours, in Vietnam and all over the world, the future is being formed." Powers leaned forward as though he would speak to, perhaps actually touch, everyone in the hall. "Well, so, you will say," he went on earnestly, "I'm young, I feel, I see what's wrong, but what can I really do about it? Johnson decides to bomb North Vietnam and kill a million innocent peasants, and what can I do about it except talk? But, ah, if enough people talk, if enough people change their way of thinking and their selfish values, they will ultimately change the world! Never doubt it. Never."

An unusual excitement was taking hold of Steve. Who could have thought there would be so much vitality in a course entitled "Contemporary Topics in American Literature"? It had been one thing to hear about this man Powers and quite another to hear him in person.

It was plain why he had such a following! He had warmth and energy and conviction. They shone through every word he had been speaking this morning. In a way, he could remind you of John F. Kennedy, although the resemblance was only external, for Kennedy had been basically just another American politician, while this man was enlightened. Even if Professor Powers were not famous, Steve reflected, one would know that he was a "kindred soul"; people carried certain airs about themselves that told you what they were, even without words. And this man —this man was *real.*

"It's a people's revolution in Vietnam," he was saying, "not a contest between rich world powers. If we would only leave them alone to make their own decisions, they'd build justice, economic, social, and—"

The buzzer sounded. Powers glanced at the clock and grinned. "Behind my schedule, as usual. I wanted to tell you about my study groups, but it's late, so I'll just say quickly that I like to keep an extra hour open on Tuesdays for in-depth discussion with any students who may be interested in extra reading, and so forth. It's totally unrelated to course credit, just pure pleasure. If any of you want to know more, drop by my office."

Steve made his way through the shuffle and bustle in the corridor and went outdoors. Avoiding the group of friends with whom he usually walked to the next class, he struck off by himself on a roundabout route to the science building. The midwestern winter, which had astonished him by its ferocious cold, had softened toward a January thaw this morning; a large drop quivered at the tip of each long icicle on the eaves and the sun was hot on his upturned face. Briskly, and yet removed in thought, he moved on the shoveled pathway between high banks of blue-white snow.

Round and round went his thoughts as he trudged. He was filled with an awareness of well-being that, during the past hour, had merged into exhilaration. In these few months at college he had been happy, anyway; the campus had become home. He had easily made new friends, male and female. They slept in their cubicles all down the hall, and whenever he had need to talk he had only to walk down the hall for the most intelligent conversation anyone could want. Or if he needed sex, there was always someone there for that. Here he was the freest he had ever been. Of course, if once the university should ever become truly free, people were saying—and Professor Powers had mentioned that too—and the political systems of the world rebuilt, ah, then! Then . . .

I'd like to talk to him, he said to himself. You don't find

people like him every day. Not where I come from, either in school or at home, that's for sure. And not even here, among all these brains. Not like him.

Professor Powers was alone in his office when Steve knocked and entered. From his desk he gave a cheerful greeting.

"Come in, sit down. Should I know you? Am I failing to recognize you? It's one of my shameful failings."

"I only had my first class with you this morning. Contemporary American Lit. I wanted to take it last semester but it was already filled." In his eagerness Steve's words tumbled over each other. Then he stuck out his hand. "My name's Steve Stern."

"Glad to know you, Steve."

Overcome with a need to show his admiration, he said shyly, "The main reason I chose my college was that I heard you were here."

"Really?"

"Yes. I was still in high school when I first read about you, how you were attacked for saying you hoped the Viet Cong would win. I know a lot of other people were shocked that you said that, but I thought you were right."

"That shows you were thinking more clearly than a lot of other people were."

Steve flushed with pleasure. "I like to read history and it makes you think about"—he wanted so much to say something impressive!—"about the future, I mean. And some of the things you said this morning—well, I've been thinking about them too, and I came to say I'd like to join your discussion group, and read some more and—and all that."

"Would you? Why, that's wonderful!" Pure pleasure shone in the professor's eyes, which were of a remarkable, blazing blue. "Well, then, tell me something about yourself. Steve Stern. Where are you from, Steve?"

"Westchester. That's just outside New York City."

"I know the area."

As it seemed necessary to keep the dialogue going, Steve added, "Then you know what it is. Just typical suburbia."

"Meaning?"

"Oh, you know."

"I know what I know, but I'm interested in hearing your thoughts about it."

He wanted to hear Steve's thoughts!

Encouraged, Steve set forth with a more natural ease. "Well, my last time home, for instance, I had to go to my grandfather's funeral. Just being there, watching the people, sort of crystallized things for me. Summed things up. You'd have thought it was an auto show. A line of Cadillacs and Mercedes and what-have-you all the way down the road. And the house filled with Republican types: Go in and bomb the hell out of Vietnam. I got fed up hanging around listening to them. Came to pay condolences, but couldn't shut up about their houses and stocks. Suburbia! Make money, spend money, that's what life's all about. It was a pleasure to get back to school." And Steve grinned, satisfied to see that his words were being well received.

"I know what you mean. I grew up the same way. My father was a self-made millionaire, and he never let you forget it."

"Well, my grandfather hasn't left millions, I'm sure, though by his standards he did all right."

All he did was make money and observe his obsolete religious rituals. There couldn't have been much else in his head. Mom must have known that. She's too intelligent not to know it. Yet—her tears. Real ones, too, no fake about them, like so many tears at funerals. She must really have loved him. *Honor thy father and thy mother as the Lord thy God commanded thee that thy days may be long. . . .* He smiled to himself. So well had he drilled for his Bar Mitzvah that the stuff would probably stick in his head for the rest of his life, and he'd never be rid of it.

Professor Powers said abruptly, "You're Jewish, aren't you?"

"Yes," Steve acknowledged. He hated being labeled; labels were not relevant to the new world, the new way of life that was bound to come.

"I could have been mistaken, of course, but most people named Stern are Jewish. I've been in Israel," he added.

"You've been everywhere, I guess."

"Hardly everywhere."

"You were in the South, I read. On the Freedom Ballot campaign."

"That was before your time. You must have been in junior high about then. Yes, we gathered together from all over the north. I lived with a black family, which infuriated the town. They put gravel in my engine and punctured my tires. One day a string of cars pursued me out of town. I was almost driven off the road going ninety miles an hour. I was shot at too. It was a bloody business. Murderous. I guess you might call it a small version of Vietnam."

These words took vivid shape in Steve's imagination. He had a sickening vision of a car skidding and reeling through the southern flatlands on a melting tar highway; men and guns followed. A head was blown away, and the gray, wet brains oozed. At the movies he dreaded scenes like those and always closed his eyes. He shuddered.

"Violence! In Mississippi or Vietnam, it's all horrible."

"Yes, but sometimes it's necessary," Powers answered soberly.

"I guess I have a special feeling about it from hearing so much about the concentration camps. My father's from Vienna."

"I understand. But it took violence to free the camps, you must remember."

"I guess that's so."

"Have you got a big family?" Powers inquired gently.

"A sister starting high school, a kid brother, and another brother only eleven months younger than I. He expects to come here next year because I'm here. Only, he wants to be a doctor. They're all strictly apolitical in my family."

Except Mom, maybe, he thought as he spoke. Mom was a liberal, which made her harder to deal with than his father was. With him you knew where you stood: nowhere. With her, the trouble was that she meant well; she would sympathize with your point of view and then suddenly jump away. Class interests influenced her, although she didn't know it and would deny it. People like her prided themselves on seeing both sides of a question fairly, but they always ended up by defending their own interests.

"Families!" he said aloud.

"I know what you mean. I have a brother with the State Department. He's at the embassy in Saigon. Real gung-ho on the war too. My father was a bootlegger; that's how he could afford to become respectable. He would have approved of my brother. He never approved of me or of my sister Agnes, because she's an artist and a lesbian. And I've got twin sisters too, a couple of clotheshorses. Them, he liked. Funny, isn't it?"

Steve was moved by the unexpected confidences. He was being treated like an equal, an adult equal, perhaps even a special adult. A person wouldn't talk this way to just anybody. You would have to feel some sort of a pull, an affinity.

And he said, "I know what you mean, Professor Powers. Though I can't say my parents don't *like* me—in their way they *love* me very much. But we don't speak the same language. And I can't say they've ever really taught me anything."

"Not uncommon. My most powerful influence came from a teacher I met in summer school when I was fourteen. He taught me more about the world in that one short summer than any ten other human beings have done in all the rest of my life, most certainly including my parents. By the way, I like to be called 'Tim.' No hierarchy, just pure democracy in my classes. Yes, one great teacher, that's all you need. Incidentally, you

must have met some good ones. Whose classes are you taking?"

Steve enumerated. "Mr. Hodges for Soc. One, Mrs. McCarthy in chemistry, LaFarge for French. They're all great. Then
Remington for ancient history. He—well." Feeling confident
now, he said boldly, "Decidedly not great."

Powers laughed. With laughter his face became radiant.
"Oh, the patrician! Brooks Brothers or J. Press. Old, old family. They haven't had a new idea in five generations. Don't let
him influence you!"

Steve joined the laughter. "Not a chance, Tim!"

"He's a big promoter for ROTC. God, we have to stop military recruiting on this campus! It's an obscenity. Business and
industry. What the hell, industry lives on war."

They talked. An hour passed before Steve became aware of
the time and stood up.

"Golly, I've taken up your afternoon. I'm sorry."

"Nonsense! I've enjoyed it. I don't know about you, but I
have a feeling that this has been a fortuitous meeting, and I'd
like to see you again. You are coming, aren't you?"

"I surely am," Steve answered gratefully. "And thank you.
Thanks a million."

"I can put you in touch with some of the brightest minds on
the campus, people you'll learn from. They're graduate students, most of them, people with tremendous experience. One
of the women, for instance, a sociology major, is just back from
her senior year in the Soviet Union. They'll make you produc-
tive, and I sense that's what you want to be, a doer. Not just a
talker, but an organizer, one who leads the way."

"Oh, yes! Oh, yes!"

The winter sun was tipping the horizon, its pale afterglow
seeping pink through the gray sky, when Steve walked back to
his room. He stood a moment to gaze at the splendor.

"A beautiful world," he said aloud. He was filled with a
wonderful new fervor. This man, so admired, so brilliant, this

leader, wanted him! He had treated him like an equal. He had
been simple and forthright about himself. Yes, this was the new
man, free of middle-class inhibitions, free and honest. To
someone like him you could confide anything, and he would
accept you.

Yes, it was wonderful. . . .

He paced his room, glancing every few minutes at the alarm
clock. From the window he could see the square where people
were sitting on the base of the Civil War statue, the crouching
soldier with the forage cap and the bayonet at the ready. There
was a Friday-afternoon letdown on the campus. You could see
it in people's posture.

He lit a cigarette, a Lucky Strike. It tasted like hay, like
nothing, but he wasn't about to smoke pot in his dormitory
room. Timothy had warned his people not to look for trouble,
so the floating ease of pot was kept for Lydia's place, which was
off campus. Lydia's place and other places. His hand was trembling.

Across the hall someone opened a door and music blared,
Bob Dylan concluding "Like a Rolling Stone," followed by
"Eve of Destruction," which was a bitter song that made you
sad, made you angry, and made you determined.

The clock clicked past the hour. Any minute his friends
would be here, and he would be swept along with them in
comradeship. He thought of the fighting priests, the Berrigan
brothers; men like them to be locked up in a federal peniten-
tiary! Three years behind bars in maximum security! And they
had known what they were risking when they raided the draft
board that first time, they had known and done it anyway.
Courage. By now Steve's hands were trembling so much that
he had to stub out the cigarette, but all the time his eyes were
on the statue below, where someone would be appearing to
signal readiness.

Timothy was to provide the borrowed car. He had friends

everywhere. An underground network, you might call it, and
Steve had been astonished when he learned how many so-
called respectable people, doctors, professors, and lawyers
who were the bulwark of the middle class, were already so
deeply involved and ready to risk so much to give shelter and
money wherever these were needed. Timothy knew people like
those from coast to coast. For that matter, he knew people in
Hanoi and Palestine and in Cuba, where he had taken a group
to go with the Vinceremos to work in the countryside and learn
about the new society. Next summer, without fail, he, too,
would go.

Presently, he saw Lydia rounding the corner of the science
building. Even at this distance there was no mistaking her
abundant, frizzy dark hair. It fanned out from her thin face,
making the face look even smaller. He wished, as he grabbed
his heavy jacket, that he could say she belonged to him. But he
must correct such thinking, for, as she reminded him even
when they had sex together—and it was very good sex—nobody here belonged to anyone else. Nobody in this world
ought to belong to anyone else. Sex was to be free, spontaneous, unashamed, and publicly acknowledged. It was simply a
need, like the need for food. And so, since Lydia had been
sleeping with Benjie and Mark, and probably, he surmised,
with Leo too, he had felt almost obliged to do the same sort of
thing. During the last semester he had spent nights with Jen-
nifer and Lori and would probably have to do it with Ellen,
although he didn't want to, for her pendulous, elderly breasts
and the remains of acne on her face repelled him. But she
wanted to, that was plain. Maybe it was her eagerness, too, that
turned him off. Yet it was wrong of him, wrong and typically
bourgeois, to judge a human being by physical appearance. He
was reminded of his sister Laura's overheard telephone conversations with her friends, such superficial conversations
about who was good-looking and who had worn what outfit
where. And he resolved while galloping down the stairs to

satisfy Ellen. They were comrades, and they would share. Who was he, who was anyone, to scorn another human being for not being beautiful?

"Hurry," said Lydia. "They're around the corner. Tim's got a station wagon, so we can all fit into one car."

There were seven of them. Lydia was the only woman. She was to be a backup driver for Tim, and besides, she, along with Tim, was the organizer of this undertaking.

No one spoke very much. They were all tense. The car left the campus and swept through the suburbs, past streets labeled "Churchill Circle" and developments called "Kensington Estates." Pitiable anglophilia, Steve thought. Ticky-tack. Absurd. There were twenty-five miles to go. They swerved onto the highway and through a succession of small factory towns, bleak, similar, and gray, a huddle of mean houses that needed paint, and a string of stores around the industrial heart, the factories clustered like a pile of cement boxes. The sun, which had been a pallid smudge under dirty clouds, now disappeared. The last remains of snow lay in grimy ridges on the shady side of the streets, while grit, along with scraps of paper, blew in the foggy air. A sudden gust shook the hanging signs above storefronts and sent a tin can skittering in a crazy dance across the curb and under the wheels of the car. It began to drizzle. The melancholy was almost unbearable.

"We're almost there," Tim said suddenly.

He turned off the main road and stopped on a deserted back street that contained only a cemetery, a church, and a small warehouse, boarded up. There was no one in sight.

"You all know what we have to do? Should I go over it again?"

No one answered. Everything had been so carefully rehearsed that each knew the instructions by heart, and yet, now that the moment had come, fear pounded in the chest, fear that in a crucial second all the instructions might just fly out of one's head. Timothy must have sensed this, because he began to speak very slowly and firmly.

"There's a briefcase for each of you in the back of the car. Each briefcase has four bottles of duck's blood." He paused and chuckled. "My cleaning woman makes Polish sausage. I paid her to make some for me, so she's been collecting the ingredients in my kitchen, enough sausage for ten families. Anyway, this is it. You go in, ask to see your own draft records, which you are entitled by law to do. Don't give your right names by mistake! So while they're looking, you get out the bottles, rush in and splash as many file drawers as you can. The clerks will try to pull you away, but let me repeat—I can't stress this too much—we do not want to hurt anybody. So temper your resistance. Let them pull you away rather than hurt anybody. That's clear, I hope. I will be waiting outside in the car with the engine running. Come out as fast as you can, because the second I see guards approaching, I'm going to drive off, and anyone who's left is left. That's all. We have to protect as many of you as we can. Any questions? Any comment?"

"You know," Steve said, "I've been thinking about the Berrigans, the way they stood there after destroying the files and waited for the FBI to come and get them. It seems somehow such an eloquent, heroic way of making a moral point."

"Well, but—" Timothy began, when Lydia interrupted.

"Eloquent, shmeloquent! They played that game once too often and ended up in prison. When you're in prison, you're no good to the movement, are you? Don't be a fool, Steve," she said sharply. "Save yourself if you can so you can work again another day."

Steve felt the reprimand. "Okay, I'm with you," he cried, making his voice sound jaunty.

Tim started the motor, and they drove into the center of town. The streets were deserted now in the heavy rain.

"We're almost there. The Selective Service office is in the

town hall, that far wing, the new wing with a separate entrance. Rather handy for us."

The men filed out. Tim touched Steve's arm.

"Good luck. You'll be okay," he said.

Courage surged in Steve's chest, and he went forward with Mark, who measured six feet four; yet Steve was the first to enter the lofty green-painted corridor, unmistakably official and governmental with a smell of marble. Steve's heart was pounding now, and there was a hot taste in his mouth.

He cleared his throat and was the first to speak when they entered the office.

"We would all like to see our draft records."

The clerk, a weary woman with gray curls, looked flustered.

"Is there any reason?" she began, when Mark came up beside Steve.

"All of us have got some problems, medical problems, and we've been worried. We're in school, and we're not sure where we stand or how to plan." He spoke persuasively with a pleasant smile.

The clatter of typewriters had ceased, and the few clerks who were preparing to leave, since the clock was moving toward closing time, looked up curiously.

The first clerk was dubious. "Well, I don't know," she began again.

It flashed across Steve's mind that this woman would not approve of them, since all except Mark were bearded. This woman would detest beards.

"Are these all friends of yours?" she asked Mark.

"Not exactly. But my attorney suggested that I ask to see my record, and somehow when word got around that I was coming here, these people asked whether I would give them a ride. So I did," he said with the same pleasant smile.

His manner, his clean-shaven cheeks and neat slacks, along with the word *attorney,* apparently impressed her.

"Well, all right," she said. "Write your names here, please, and I'll go to the files. It'll take a few minutes."

Steve moved outside of himself, outside of the time and the place, observing as if from a great distance. At any minute guards will come to challenge, he thought. Open the briefcases, they will say. But these were students, so it was logical for them to be carrying briefcases. Lydia had thoughtfully varied them, some new, some battered, and one was a canvas bag with books protruding. It was all quite natural.

The woman summoned them. They followed into a gray space with a concrete floor, green walls, and green metal file cabinets. She opened drawers and called names. Bailey. The B's were back here. Turner and Stankowitz, this way. She stepped for a second toward the door, the outer room from which they had entered, and said something to someone in that room, so she did not see that the men had opened the briefcases and the bottles. Then hearing the scramble of noise behind her, she understood suddenly what was happening and cried out. Other women came running, scurrying with furious, frightened cries, grabbing Steve's coat and Dick's shirt. Mark was opening more drawers and spilling the bottles. One dropped on the floor, its jagged neck broken off. Someone stooped to pick it up to salvage the dark blood. The blood was almost purple, thick and sticky, having congealed in the cold. Steve's stomach lurched. He had a vision of ducks flying in V-formation through the autumn sky. The women went running through the chaos to the telephone.

"Let's go!" cried Mark. They ran. They raced. The car's doors were open.

"Get the hell in!" screamed Lydia. "Quick!"

Tim gunned the motor and they went around the corner on two wheels. There was no one on the street in the heavy rain. It was almost dusk, and no one, as far as they could tell, had seen the car. Tim swerved so sharply that they all fell against each other. They were out on the highway and off it again. "Back roads," Tim said. "Through the farms . . ."

"Dick's missing," Lydia said, calmly enough.

"He braced himself against the door so that they couldn't follow to identify the car," Mark said.

"Oh, Jesus, now what?"

"He'll serve time," Tim said. "For malicious destruction of government property, interfering with the Selective Service process."

"How long, do you think?" Steve asked.

"Two years. Maybe three."

There was a reflective silence until someone said, "Tough. The college years thrown away. Lost."

"Not as lost as for the boys in Vietnam," Tim answered. "Not as lost as being trapped forever into this system. He went in with his eyes open, anyway, and he'll come out with his eyes open. You all did," Tim said, "and you all will."

Now that it was over, Steve felt a resurgence of confidence, riding back wedged in with his friends, these friends with whom he had just shared danger. He felt a wave of well-being, here in this snug car, safe on these country roads, field after vacant field going by, with here or there a lighted house, and the steady rain still falling, and Tim at the wheel. Tim had come through many days like these, he would lead them through more days, and be with them whenever it was plausible for him to be there. He was a leader. It was an honor to go with him. Steve's heart swelled.

"It would be best," Tim said as he stopped at the edge of the campus to let them out, "if you could find a way to disperse. Don't be seen together for the next few days. I don't foresee any trouble, but it's best to be careful. It seems unlikely that the clerks will remember you in such confusion. You don't look all that different from hundreds of others, but still, one never knows. If any of you can find a way to get off campus for the weekend or even to go home right now, tonight, that would be best of all."

Steve walked rapidly toward his room. Now that he had left the safety of the car and was alone in the dark, open space, he had an eerie feeling that some *thing* was about to pounce on him from behind. Imagine three years behind bars! He shuddered. "Those of you who can, go home," Tim had said. Of course, the perfect alibi. But how to explain this unexpected return to his parents? He would have to think of some excuse. Well, something would occur to him. The main thing now was to get to the airport fast.

They were all in the living room when the doorbell rang. The evening had grown late and Anna was preparing to go home when the loud peal startled the quiet and Iris sprang up.

She looked through the peephole. "Why, it can't be—it's Steve!" she cried.

Alarmed, Theo sprang up too, as Steve came into the room. He was disheveled, he looked exhausted, and his damp clothes clung.

"What—what's happened?" Theo stammered.

"Don't get excited. It's nothing—much. Had a little trouble, that's all, and it seemed prudent to get off the campus over the weekend."

A pang shot through Theo. "What sort of trouble?"

"We had—there was a little fracas at the local draft board. We don't think anybody will be able to prove we were there if we can show we weren't even in town."

"What do you mean by a 'fracas'?"

Steve hesitated. "Oh, you know. The sort of thing you must have been reading about in the papers."

Theo steadied himself. "You mean throwing blood and—"

Steve nodded. Laura and Jimmy stared at him, while Iris and Anna stared at each other. There was a nervous silence until Theo spoke again, his voice catching in his throat.

"Is this what you're doing! Is this what they're teaching in that place, this what you're learning?"

It was impossible to read Steve's expression. Regarding a spot on the wall behind his father's head, he seemed to have removed himself, or tried to remove himself, from the crisis.

"I'm waiting for an answer," Theo said and, when none came, continued, "You realize, of course, that your whole future is at stake. Right now. This minute. If you're found out you'll be in deep, deep trouble. Ruined."

Steve answered, then. "I know. I realize."

He cracked his knuckles. Theo hated the sound when Steve did that, but this time he took no notice. He is struggling to keep control, Iris thought, pitying her husband.

Oh, why this suffering? It was so peaceful here tonight, with all of us sitting at dinner. . . . Theo and Mama were talking. . . . And Philip played his new piece on the piano for us. . . . And afterward Laura played checkers with Jimmy. . . . And now the peace is shattered. . . . And what is to become of this boy?

Theo spoke. "What are you trying to prove? That you can do what you've done and get away with it?"

"I'm not trying to prove anything. I'm just trying to stop this filthy war. How many times must I spell it out?"

"Listen," Theo began, and now Iris recognized his "reasonable" approach, "listen to me. I myself believe this war is a mistake and for more than one reason. It's probably not winnable, to begin with. But in this year of 1966, fifty-six percent of the American people support the President. Johnson says he's willing to negotiate a peace, but not with the Communists in Hanoi. And he's probably right. Wherever Communists have won, in Hungary or in Cuba, terror follows. I tremble for the people if they win over there. But I am perplexed. Yes, I am. I don't know the answers, but I do know one thing. What you've been doing is not the answer."

"Try any campus. Talk to the faculty, and you'll find plenty of people who don't agree with you. People more knowledgeable than you are."

Theo flushed, tightening his lips against the response that was waiting to rush forth.

"That's as it may be," he said, after a moment. "But for heaven's sake, can't you see what you're being led into? Leave Marxism out for now, all that jargon that you and I don't agree on. Let's talk just about what you've done. How can you govern a country, any country, no matter what the system, if every citizen gets it into his head to decide what laws he will obey and what laws he won't? I accept the privileges of citizenship. If I'm ordered to go into the army, I have to go. I'll go whether I like it or not."

Steve raised scornful eyes to his father. "You're pretty safe. They're hardly going to reach your age bracket. Oh," he said almost gleefully, "there's a saying I came across last week. Somebody named Charles Edward Montague, I don't know who he was, but he wrote, 'War hath no fury like a noncombatant.' That sums it up pretty well."

"Don't be a smart aleck. You know damned well that I fought behind enemy lines in Nazi-occupied France. Don't insult me." Theo's voice rose as he repeated, "Don't insult me. Do you hear?"

Iris said desperately, "He didn't mean to insult you, Theo, I'm sure. It's just that we're all so terribly upset, let's try—"

"Iris, don't plead for him. I can handle it. This is no child's play, you know. What excuses will we have when the FBI comes to the door looking for him? Tell me, what excuses?"

Anna stood up, saying quickly, "I'll make coffee and a sandwich, Steve. You must be starved."

"No, I'm not hungry, Nana."

Anna had already reached the kitchen door, followed by Iris and Laura. Mama's as terrified as I am, Iris thought. It helps her to do something with her hands, especially in the kitchen. And, sinking in sudden weakness onto a chair, she let the other

two work off their fear, Anna slicing bread and meat, and Laura
rinsing a bunch of grapes at the sink. A cheerful domestic scene
it was, and a stranger, looking in at it, would have no idea of the
anguish just across the hall.

Tears sprang suddenly, and pretending to be looking for
something, Iris got up to open the refrigerator. In the turning
she was caught by her mother's eye.

"Laura," said Anna, "Laura, darling, it's awfully late.
Shouldn't you go to bed?"

Iris recovered herself. "You shouldn't have heard this tonight, Laura. It's too nasty, too frightening."

"I'm fifteen, Mom."

"But still you shouldn't."

"Don't you trust me?"

"Of course we trust you. But this is so serious, it shouldn't be
on anyone's conscience. Your dad and I will have to think and
talk, but you shouldn't be burdened with it."

Anna interposed quietly, "Laura knows what's going on in
the world. No one can hide it from her, and we shouldn't."

"Okay, Mom," Laura said. "Take it easy."

Iris kissed the girl's troubled forehead. "I love you, Laura."

When Laura went out, she cried to Anna, "Can you believe
this? Who could have dreamed that a child of ours would come
running home to hide from the law? Oh, can you believe what
Papa would say? And we were so proud of Steve, he was so—"

"Iris, Iris, don't cry, you'll make things worse. Where's a
tray? Pour a cup for Theo too."

Jimmy had gone upstairs, so that the father and son faced
each other alone. If Steve just wouldn't look so arrogant! Iris
thought. The very way he stands infuriates his father. He must
know that. It's almost as if he doesn't care, or even wants to
anger him. And she passed her hand over her forehead as if to
erase her thoughts.

Philip, who had been in bed, now came downstairs in his

bathrobe and stood at the door. The little boy looked curious and scared.

"Go on back to bed, son," Theo said. "I know you want to know what's going on, but you'll have to wait till morning, and I'll explain it to you then. You need your sleep. Go on, son, there's nothing to worry about," he added gently.

Then, as if a new idea had struck him, he turned back to Steve, crying, "Oh, I'd like to get my hands on them, these professors!"

"I told you," Steve said patiently, "professors had nothing to do with this. It was just me and some other guys. We do our own thinking. You don't know a thing about it."

"Don't I? Doesn't anyone who reads the papers know what's going on?"

Theo was sweating. Iris had never seen him so furious, never seen the veins stand out, so thick and darkly blue, on his temples. Nevertheless, he was still fighting against his own fury, and lowered his voice.

"When I remember myself at your age, never would I have dared—"

" 'The times they are a-changing,' " Steve said. "But you probably don't approve of Bob Dylan."

"He's a fine singer. He's making a fortune too. They all are, these entertainers. They sing about how they despise our money-grubbing country, but I see that they grub plenty for themselves and live pretty high. They ought to have their goddamn necks wrung so they'd never sing another note!"

"Have you said everything you want to say?" Steve asked now. "Because if you have, I'm tired. I'd like to go to sleep."

Theo glared. "Yes, you must be very tired. You've had a hard day's work. It can't be easy to tear up a Selective Service office."

The atmosphere in the room was as shiveringly cold as if the furnace had been turned off. Rain glinted on the bare glass wall that led to the terrace. They had all collected in the farthest corner, and Iris was reminded, miserably, of the crowd that gathers around an accident or someone fallen on the street.

Look at him, Theo was thinking, defying me, standing there in his dirty wet jacket and sloppy half-grown beard, a handsome boy like him—what's he trying to prove?

"Your sneakers are staining the carpet," he said.

"It's only water, and it's only a carpet. There are more important things in the world."

"Oh, really? Have you ever earned the price of a carpet? Why, you haven't even earned enough to feed yourself, and you dare to talk—to—to face us with that twist on your lips and —what's that on your pants?"

He looked down at a splatter of dark stains on his legs. "I guess it's blood."

"Blood, is it? That'll be a nice thing for me to think about next time your tuition bill comes! Very, very nice!"

Theo walked to the end of the room and drew the curtains. The heavy silk swished and the brass rings clattered in the waiting silence. When he came back, his face was drained pale. He spoke slowly and heavily.

"For the last time I ask you, will you leave these people you've been hanging around with before you destroy yourself entirely?"

"No. I can't do that."

Theo's fists clenched and unclenched themselves at his sides. "I ought," he said, "as a law abiding citizen, God damn it, I ought to turn you in. That's what!"

"Oh, no!" Iris cried out. "No, Theo! You don't really mean that. After all, it's not as if he had hurt anyone. He said, in fact, that they were very careful not to hurt anyone. You have to take that into consideration, Theo."

"No, Iris. Don't tell me what I mean or don't mean. Look at him with blood on his clothes, brought up in a home like ours—"

"Shit!" Steve cried. He was trembling. "I despise it. It's

narrow, stupid, selfish—" And he made a wide sweep with his arm to take in the whole room, his mother and grandmother, his father and brother, all the possessions so carefully collected for the benefit of our children, Iris thought, the books and pictures, the piano; he seemed with that violent gesture to condemn them all, even the innocent roses that Theo had sent for her birthday.

"You," Theo said. "Do you know what's going through my mind? That there's some sickness in the air and you've caught it. Even your language is sick. We don't talk that way in this house."

"We don't talk the same language at all in this house." Steve swung about. "I can't even stand a night in it. Nana, will you give me a bed for tonight? If you can't, I'll sleep under a tree."

"Don't be a fool," Anna said. "Go wait in my car."

When Steve had slammed the front door, the three stood looking from one to the other, as if an answer were to be found in each other's faces.

Iris spoke first. "It's all bravado. He's frightened to death." She appealed to Theo. "I'm sure, I could swear, he'll never do anything like this again."

"And I'm not sure at all," Theo answered.

"I'll drive him home. At least he'll be out of the way so maybe you can get some sleep, you two," Anna said. Putting her coat on, she added quietly, "If he's to disappoint you, you'll have to accept it. You can't get into another person's head."

"You're right, Mama," Theo said, deeply bitter. "You can't mold another human being to be his best. I see that now."

At the front door Anna spoke again. "Every life is a secret. Every life. You can only understand your own." In the dim light of the entry Iris saw her mother's smile, wry and sad. "And sometimes you can't even understand your own."

Theo walked around the room while he undressed, thumping his shoes on the floor and flinging his shirt over a chair, all of which was unlike him, who was ordinarily so methodical. All the time he kept talking.

"Yes, you work and try to build something solid for your children, and they reject you. But we must have done something right, because the others seem to have turned out." He grumbled, "Call themselves open minded! Meaning that everything they haven't thought of, everything that's older than yesterday or spoken by somebody over thirty, is garbage. And what's more, they're not even logical, because they want to make a revolution and still keep on living the free hippie life. You know how far they'd go, how long they'd last in Hanoi? Bah!" He sat down on the edge of the bed and put his head in his hands. "Iris, I don't know what to do. Maybe if I turn him in, it'll be better for him in the end. He'll suffer his punishment and learn a lesson."

Iris, who had been brushing her hair at the dressing table, now whirled around on the bench. She was horrified.

"Theo! You can't mean that. He'd never forgive you, never, for the rest of his life."

"It might be the best thing for him, all the same."

"And I—I would never forgive you either. He's only a child, and this will pass. Be patient with him."

"What? A child? I'm not going to coddle him, I can tell you that. I want to make something of him, not humor him."

"Didn't you agree with my mother a few minutes ago that you can't mold a person to your liking?"

" 'To his best,' is what I said. But that's only partly true. What I meant was—oh, for God's sake, let's have an end to this for tonight! I have to operate early. Set the alarm for five-thirty. I'll have to shower. I'm too worn out to do it now."

They lay together in the bed. It was her habit to rest her head in the hollow of his shoulder; he always said he liked to feel her weight and her warm hair on his chest. But now she slid upward so that their cheeks touched. And she felt the tiny flutter of his lashes. They turned toward each other so that their hearts met, fusing the double thud.

"Live hearts beating," she whispered, thinking aloud, and softly stroked his cheek.

"Iris. . . . Is the door locked?"

"Yes."

And she thought, when he moved upon her, when she received him, No matter what else comes, we have this always, this unmeasurable, pure sweetness and lovely trust, this healing.

Then came the moment's dazzle, the "little death," as someone, she couldn't remember who, had called it, and from it she woke again into life, into the silence, with the beloved hand on her breast.

It was a night on which, after making love, one should lie easily waiting for sleep in the warm bed, the warm room, safe from the rain that rushed at the windows and safe from the wildness out of doors. But one could tell that the wildness could break in whenever it chose. Somewhere at the back of the yard Theo heard a tree limb fall, cracking like a broken bone. It was probably the old maple in the corner; the bottom limb had long been rotten. Miserable night. At least Steve wasn't out in it, or in jail. Fool, young fool, ruining his young life! It was one thing to have ideals and to speak out, but not this way. Too bad somebody couldn't punish him enough to knock sense into him. Anna, maybe, Anna might talk to him as she had on the night of his Bar Mitzvah, which seemed a hundred years ago. But no. . . . He was almost a man now, and, anyway, this was different.

He twisted, turning lightly in the bed so as not to disturb the blankets and wake Iris. He listened. Her breathing was irregular, so she wasn't sleeping either. She was a wreck over this. Poor Iris. This was going to come to no good end. Their son was going to come to no good end. He saw that clearly. . . .

Iris could always feel when Theo fell asleep and when he

awoke. She moved to comfort him, but drew back; there were times when he needed comfort and other times when he needed to be let alone. How well she knew him!

What's Steve going to do next? The worry over him is even worse for Theo than it is for me. He would deny it, but the truth is he wants everything to be perfect.

Poor darling Theo. He wants to please me. He doesn't even flirt much anymore. And ever since that day a few years ago when he gave that nurse a lift in town, and I made such a jealous fool of myself, I've made up my mind not to notice it if he should.

A few cold tears slid down Iris's temples into the roots of her hair.

8

By the fall of 1967 Americans, despite their previous enthusiasm, were growing sick of the war in Vietnam, sick of the nightly television news, a landscape of burning villages, small people running, dank, infested jungles, ambushed trucks, and helicopters whirling to pluck the wounded out of the tropical hell.

It is a world in agony, thought Iris, not only on the far side of the Pacific, but in the east, too, where Egypt, Syria, and Jordan, helped by the Soviet Union, were almost daily marauding the fields and cities of Israel. No peace, said the Arab leaders who met in Khartoum, until Israel is driven into the sea.

It was an unending cycle of terror.

Chiefly, of course, it was Steve who weighed on her heart. He had seldom been home since the affair of the draft cards. On the telephone their dialogue was calm, but awkward. No one dared ask what he was doing, not only because he would probably not answer but perhaps also because it was easier not to know. At least he was still in college and keeping his grades up.

They never used Jimmy, who was now on the same campus, as a conduit. It was not fair, not a clean thing, to ask him to report on his brother. Once in a while, though, quite casually, Jimmy would tell them something, such as: "Steve left for a march in Baltimore today. I only told you so you wouldn't worry if you should read anything in the newspapers."

Iris asked once, "Wherever does he get the money? Surely his allowance isn't enough for all those trips."

"His crowd has money," Jimmy assured her. "I don't know where they get it, but they have it."

In February 1968 the Vietnamese had a national holiday. Tet was the anniversary of their defeat of the Chinese a century and a half before. It was astonishing that this battered people were not only still alive, but were able actually to launch an offensive against the Americans; yet launch it they did, right into the embassy compound in Saigon, and it took a night-long fight to rout them. There were those in the military who made light of the episode, but it nevertheless marked the beginning of the President's defeat. In March he decided not to run for another term, and America's youth, or a large segment of it, rejoiced.

In August the Democratic convention opened in Chicago. Preparations for it were ominous. The Illinois National Guard and the entire police force were in readiness to meet horrendous threats such as, for example, that "Yippies" were going to put LSD into the Chicago water supply. And so America's eyes were fastened even more avidly than usual to the television screen.

Theo and Iris were alone for the summer. Laura, by now a senior in high school, had gone to New Hampshire with a group to campaign door to door for McCarthy. Philip was at camp in the Maine woods. Jimmy was working as an orderly in a Chicago hospital. From Steve they had only a scrawled note giving minimal information: He was going west with a political science group for some sort of seminar and they would hear from him. By August they had heard no more, and it seemed as clear to Iris as if she had been told that he was no farther west than Chicago. But still, as she sat with Theo watching events, she did not speak of her anxiety.

They watched as, one by one, the "peace now" candidates lost and Humphrey won the nomination. They watched as chaos erupted through the city, as the police cleared Lincoln Park, where camping out had been forbidden. "Pigs!" yelled the young, the bearded, the long-haired girls in their uniform of jeans and shirts. "Commies!" screamed the police, striking with billy clubs. In Grant Park ten thousand rallied. Across from the Hilton Hotel there was a melee on the street. Bricks, eggs, stink bombs, and stones were met with tear gas by reinforcements of police. From upper windows fell bags of excrement and urine. And, facing the cameras, swaying as in a chorus or ritual dance, the young protesters chanted: "The whole world is watching! The whole world is watching!"

Iris, in tense absorption, was not even aware that her fists were clenched. The room was dark except for the great bright eye of the screen, and by its light she saw Theo leaning forward, straining to see it all. She wondered whether, like herself, he was searching for Steve in that frenzied crowd.

"The police are going too terribly far," she said. "It's brutal. They're only kids."

"That's true. Some of them have gone too far. And yet they're human and they're mad. These kids are out of hand. Throwing filth out of windows and dancing naked in fountains! They're supposed to be intelligent, they're college students. What sense are they making? What the hell do they want? We're having peace talks in Paris right now."

"I wonder," she murmured, "whether Steve is there."

"Well, he'd better not be dancing naked in a fountain, if he is." Theo sounded grim.

Not more than fifteen minutes later the telephone rang. Afterward Iris remembered that, with the first ring, she had been certain of an unwelcome message.

It was Jimmy. "Mom? Don't get excited. Everything'll be all right. But Steve was arrested this afternoon."

"Oh, God! Arrested? Where?"

"In Chicago. I'm there now. He called me and I flew in. I'm at the police station."

Theo grabbed the telephone and Iris ran to the kitchen to pick up the extension.

"It's a disorderly-conduct charge, nothing too bad, but they want bail. I haven't got enough money."

She heard the rage in Theo's voice. Whenever he spoke barely above a whisper, one knew he was enraged.

"I see. And if there's no bail?"

"Well, he'll be held. I don't know exactly." Jimmy's voice was audibly shaking. "You want to talk to him? He's here. We're at the sergeant's desk."

Then came Steve's voice. "Hello, here I am."

And Theo's: "What's this? What have you done now?"

"You know. You just heard."

"I heard, all right. What are you doing to yourself? And do you know what you're doing to your mother?"

For Iris had begun suddenly to cry, and through the open kitchen door Theo could see her.

"I'm sorry," Steve said. "But that's not the point right this minute. The point is, I need bail."

How could he be so cool? She imagined the police station; probably the only time she had been in one was the day somebody rammed her parked car, and all she remembered was a high desk of golden oak, so high that she hadn't been able to see its surface, and the glare of the ceiling lights. She saw Steve standing there now.

She heard him ask, "Do I get bail?"

"That depends on you," Theo answered. "On whether you'll promise to stop this stuff once and for all."

"No promises," Steve said.

"I see. No appreciation to this country that's giving you an education—"

"This country's not giving me anything."

"It's given you everything you have, damn it! Your freedom—"

"What freedom? To make money manufacturing napalm?"

Now Theo exploded. "Jesus Christ!"

Iris had to intervene. "Steve, don't argue with Dad. This isn't the time."

"You're right. They want me to cut this short, anyway, these fascists. Bail or not?"

" 'Fascists'! You're out of your mind to talk like that," Theo shouted.

In the background Iris could hear voices, ringing phones, and a sound like a chair scraping over a floor. Now she could see Jimmy standing at that desk; it wasn't fair that he should be in this mess, that he should have been called to this responsibility when he was only a boy himself.

"Steve," she pleaded, "don't say things you'll be sorry for. Talk sense and straighten this out right now."

"They want me to get off the phone, I told you."

"Very well," Theo answered. "I'll ask you one more time to give your word. Then I'll talk to the sergeant and find out what to do. Just give me your solemn word."

"I can't," Steve said.

Iris felt sudden panic. Was it possible that he was going to desert the boy?

"Call back if you change your mind," Theo was saying. "Now put your brother on the phone."

Jimmy's voice came through. "Dad, they want us off the phone. The place is jammed here, and—"

The receiver clicked.

Iris rushed back into the den. The sound on the television was shut off, but frantic motion was still bobbing and jerking on the screen, and Theo was standing with the dead telephone in his hand, staring at it.

"So here we are," he said.

"You're not going to help him? You're not?"

"You want to know something? I've gone as far as I can go. I've tried to be the best human being, the best father, I know how to be, but I'm no saint and this is my limit. I've reached it. Here. Now. This minute."

"You can't! What's to become of him? You can't!"

Theo was staring through the glass wall into the hot white summer night. "I remember his Bar Mitzvah, I remember it well. Right here in this room. I couldn't figure him out then, and I still can't."

"Don't bring that up, Theo. It's long past and forgotten."

"I haven't forgotten it."

"Locked up," she said. "Locked up."

"With a bunch of his own kind, Iris. Kids gone wild."

He looked ill. She watched him go into the kitchen and heard water running and the clink of a glass. Calm, she thought, keep yourself calm and let him calm down. Then surely he will call back and find out what to do.

When Theo returned with a glass in hand and sat down again, she was able to speak quietly, smoothing her voice as one smooths wrinkles in a skirt.

"It's an old scenario. Their ideals run away with them." And when he did not answer, she went on, "Such a confusing world right now, fearing the draft, growing up to face competition and overcrowding—"

Theo gave a stop signal with his hand. "Please. Spare me the pop psychology."

"It's not pop psychology. It's true. You grew up in a much more orderly world. I know there were wars—"

"Oh, yes, just a couple of wars and Hitler and—"

"I mean before that happened. You have to admit life was different. The father was the head of the household, the mother ran it, and the children obeyed. I don't say it was all better, but it was less confusing. Now things are fluid, with all the divorces—" She was prattling and she was pleading.

"We're not divorced, are we?"

"But there are other things. He's the oldest son. Maybe he expects too much of himself, maybe he's grown up too fast." She tried to speak before he should stop her. "It's very complicated. I've read—well, you're a doctor, I shouldn't have to explain to you—"

"Yes, yes, one can find an excuse for anything if one looks hard enough. Words. Fashionable words that say nothing."

While we stand here talking, Iris thought, what is happening in Chicago? In the heat of the August night she began to shiver.

"Ever since the Bar Mitzvah," Theo began.

"For God's sake, you're not going to bring that up again, are you?"

"I can bring up a few dozen other things instead, if you'd like it better."

"Thank you, thank you for that," she said with bitter sarcasm. "But never mind, you really don't have to drag up the past, last year and the year before that and the year before that. Just do me the favor of telling me what you're going to do tonight."

"I told you, I'm not going to do anything. If you think about it, you will see that doing nothing is the kindest thing I can do. I have one last faint hope that a touch of harsh reality will bring him to his senses."

"I can't believe you're going to abandon him! How hard, how hard you are!"

"Am I, Iris? Am I really a hard man? Think what you're saying."

"Right now you are. You refuse to see that even though these kids may be going about things in the wrong way, they are making a good statement."

"You make your statements with a ballot, not by throwing a bag of feces into people's faces. All they'll accomplish with these tactics is to tear up the country. And when there is no law and there is no order, what then? I'll tell you what: a rampaging mob and no one will be safe. Don't tell me about it. I saw the mobs in Austria. You didn't."

"This is different. Can't you understand?" She screamed now. "I'm going to Chicago myself! If you won't go, I will."

All at once a stream of energy surged through her, and she started upstairs for her pocketbook and a jacket. She'd sit at the airport and wait for the first plane out in the morning. Damn him! What kind of a father was he? Then, remembering something, she came back.

"I need cash," she demanded. "I haven't got enough."

For answer he turned out his pocket and emptied his wallet.

"Two tens, a five, and three ones. If you want them, take them," he said coldly.

"That's all you have? There's never any money in this house."

"Right. It goes out as fast as it comes in."

"That's not my fault. Who spends like a drunken sailor? I? This skirt is five summers old."

"Don't play the martyr. No one asks you to wear a five-year-old skirt."

It was idiotic the way this dialogue was veering away from the subject and out of control.

"Then I'll get the car and drive up to my mother. It'll take three hours to get to the Berkshires, she'll have money, and I'll fly from Boston in the morning."

"You'll do nothing of the sort. You'll leave your mother out of this. What can you be thinking of, scaring her to death, spoiling the first real vacation she's had since your father died—"

Theo grabbed Iris's arm, she pulled away, and in doing so upset the vase with her elbow. Water, splintered glass, and drenched flowers fell onto the pale carpet.

She burst into tears. It was not that she cared so much about the carpet or about any possessions, it was just—just the mess, the last straw. And she sank down on the desk chair.

"Oh, God, oh, God, what next!"

Theo went to clean up. Knowing exactly what to do, he fetched cloths from the cleaning closet and carefully sponged the puddle so as not to spread it. Then he gathered the glass in a newspaper.

"Anthuriums," he grumbled. "I hate them, dammit! I'm sick of everything, problems, kids, tears—isn't there someplace on this blasted earth where a man can have a little peace for a change?"

Iris tried to pull herself together. "For the last time I ask you, Theo, to be sensible. Pretend we're two sensible, ordinary people. Let's go to the bank first thing in the morning and fly out to Chicago."

He looked up from the floor. "Even if I wanted to, and I don't, I couldn't. I have two operations in the morning, and they come before the shenanigans of my idealistic son."

She jumped up. The chair caught on the edge of the scatter rug that overlay the carpet and crashed against the desk. The lamp swayed and fell.

"I can't stand this!" she screamed. "I'm a wreck!"

"I can't stand it either," he responded.

He went back to the kitchen to dispose of the broken lamp and the wet cloths. When he returned, she had sat down again, huddled, and staring at the dark circle on the carpet.

"I'm going out for a while, Iris." He spoke coldly, under control. "I think it'll be better for us both. We're just flying at each other."

"Go," she told him.

"I've got a pile of unsigned reports in the office. I might as well do them and get my mind settled if I can. There's no sleep in me tonight here, anyway."

"Go!" she told him again.

He slammed the door.

Even with the top down the night was sultry, and the rush of wind did little good. He squared his shoulders against the heat and tried to think constructively. Yes, he had done the right thing. Let the boy stew awhile, overnight or maybe another day, and then he would have his lawyer call Chicago and get the picture. Yes, that seemed best.

But God help the boy! God help them all. The last couple of years had been too hard, what with Steve's behavior and Iris's losing her father. They'd been so extraordinarily close. And he began to feel soft pity for her, with her tear-swollen face, curled up and defeated in the chair. Maybe he shouldn't have gone out. For a second he thought of turning the car around and going home, but then thought better of it. When people were overwrought, they brought up foolish grievances that had nothing to do with the problem at hand. Better for them both to cool off.

When he stopped the car in the parking lot, the long, two-story building was dark except for a light in the window of the cardiologist's office. Someone was working late, undisturbed by people or telephones.

Or something else might be going on. That secretary, the one with the invitation in her eyes, might well be having a good time with the doctor. He wouldn't be surprised. She must be a sight to see around one's office every day.

In the dead stillness of the deserted corridor his footsteps were loud. Behind him a door opened and a clear soprano voice called out.

"Hey, there. You slaving away tonight too?"

He turned and answered, "It's a peaceful place to work late."

She smiled. Her peach-colored mouth stretched into a glossy curve. Her white uniform, in all this soggy heat, was cool.

"You look as if you could use a cold drink," she observed.

"Oh, have you got one by any chance?"

"A thermos full of fruit punch. I made it myself. Nice and tart."

"Sounds wonderful."

"I was just about to put out the lights here, but you can take it to your place and return the thermos in the morning."

"That's awfully good of you, but I really don't want to take your thermos."

"Please. I don't need it overnight."

He had been in his office only a minute or two when she reappeared. She set the thermos down on his desk and filled a glass.

"There! Enjoy it. I'll be running off." She paused. "It's been a long day, hasn't it? This weather's awful."

In the lamplight her light brown hair glistened with blond streaks. No doubt they were made in a beauty parlor, but they were very attractive nevertheless. As she kept standing there, it seemed necessary to say something, so he asked whether she often worked at night.

"No, only once every few months when I get a yen to catch up with papers and billing. It's a terribly busy office. But they pay well, so I can't object to being overworked."

"They're lucky to have you, I'm sure."

He felt awkward making such a dull remark, but somehow she had tied his tongue. He had to keep staring at her. Even from the other side of his desk he could smell her fragrance; it was not one of those musky Oriental perfumes designed to be aphrodisiac, but faintly sweet like talcum powder, and this was infinitely more aphrodisiac. The crisp white cloth flared and clung to her in the right places. Beneath it she would be compact. She would be slippery, like hard rubber. He pulled his thoughts up sharply.

"I don't know your name."

"Alice. Alice Meredith."

"An old-fashioned name. You don't meet many Alices these days."

"That adds a little interest, don't you think so? Because I'm not an old-fashioned girl."

"I can see that," Theo said.

They regarded each other, he tilted back in his chair and she standing with one elbow resting on the bookshelf.

Not an old-fashioned girl. Definitely not. And he waited for what she would say next.

What she said next was: "You work hard, don't you? You look tired."

He thought, You'd look tired too, if you'd just left the scene I left at home. His spirits wilted all over again at the image of Iris weeping. God only knew what the next few days would bring; regardless of what he'd said, he would probably in the end find himself forced onto a plane and going through hectic, humiliating hours in Chicago.

"I hear they're going to make you chief of the surgical staff."

"That's the rumor," he said, trying to sound casual.

"You're very modest."

"I wouldn't say so."

"Well, that's what everybody says about you."

Back and forth the ball went over the net. He continued the game.

"Who says? Who's 'everybody'?"

"My bosses. People. Everybody."

"You talk to everybody about me?"

"Why? Do you mind?"

"I don't mind."

"I noticed you the first day I came to the building."

"I noticed that you noticed."

When, where, and how was this game going to end?

"You did? So why didn't you do something about it?"

This ball was in his court. It bounced and he missed it. Why, indeed? Tell her he planned to be utterly faithful to his wife? Certainly not.

"There was no opportunity," he replied.

"Opportunity? One makes one's own, doesn't one?"

"I suppose so."

He was thinking: She probably lives in one of those new garden apartments across the river. She would have a dinette and always something good to eat in the kitchenette. There'd be comfortable chairs, a good record player, and peace, no children, no commotion. That was the life of the unattached, the uncommitted. While he—he had a weeping wife, a rebellious son, and endless bills along with the need to be calm, well rested, and alert before he went to the operating room to take knife in hand. Calm! That was a good one. Calm.

There was a painful knot at the back of his neck. He reached for it, straining to knead it, pull it, and ease it away. Alice was watching him.

"You look all done in," she said. "Nerves have got you, haven't they?"

Embarrassed to be caught in weakness, he dropped his hand. "It's nothing. Just tension. In this business we all get it now and then."

"Why don't you let me do that for you? I'm very good at back massages. Honestly. I'm a nurse, after all. Hey, I can't do it through your jacket, can I? Now, loosen your shirt collar and lie back in the chair."

Her fingers were strong and supple. They gave incredible relief, as if she were actually separating the knotted nerves that had been aching from his shoulders down through his spine. He breathed deeply with the pleasure of it.

"Ah, thank you. That's good. Really good."

"If you'd lie face down, it would be better."

He saw that she was looking through the open door at the big leather sofa in the back room that housed his records and his library. His mind was divided. It was queer that he was able to understand so clearly how it was, that part of him saw exactly what was to happen, while part knew he must not let it happen. In the mesmerized part of his brain he didn't care, he had no will. Things were simply progressing according to an age-old pattern. Sunk into a dreamy haze, he got up and lay face down on the sofa.

She took off her clothes with practiced delay, tantalizing him almost to frenzy, with glimpses first of a long, flat back made rosy by the sun and marked with the creamy outline of a bikini, then of full, rounded thighs, perfect breasts, and a hard, flat stomach.

He turned over to make room for her, and she, now hurrying, slid to her place and clasped him. There was no lingering, there were no words, only a fierce and fevered, a devouring, haste. It was frantic, hungry, thirsty, and too quickly finished.

She smiled. "You were great," she told him.

He murmured something. It was said: Man is always sad afterward, but that was not true, because the afterglow could be a sweet contentment. It was not, now. He looked down into flat eyes without depth, and that mechanical smile. After all, they were nothing to each other.

He got up, arranged his clothes, and had to wait, concealing melancholy and impatience, while she dressed herself and painted her mouth, repairing the luscious, peach-colored lips.

Seeing him through her mirror, she explained, "I'm only going home, but you never know—you might run into someone important on the way. I feel absolutely naked without lipstick."

I didn't even like her, Theo was thinking. Then he started: Someone was knocking on the door. Alice paused with the hairbrush in midair.

"Who the hell do you think—" she began.

"Quiet, will you?"

The knocking, loud enough to be heard at a distance of three rooms, persisted.

Alice looked scared. "Who can it be, do you think?"

"I don't know."

Could it be, was it possible, that Iris would come here at this time of night? No, he decided. She wouldn't be driving around alone so late. She'd wait until he came home to say whatever she still had to say. It wasn't Iris. Presently the knocking stopped. They waited for five minutes, then ten minutes, and when it was not resumed, Theo was satisfied.

"It was somebody's mistake. Not a burglar. They don't knock. Probably a medical emergency. They saw the light on in a medical building and took a chance. Come on." And as she hesitated, "I'll reconnoiter. I'll call you if it's safe."

All that he could see in the parking lot were Alice's car and his own, both right near the entrance. So he went back to his office, put out the lights, locked the door, and followed Alice to the cars, telling himself all the while that he would make very sure never again to come back to the office at night. A situation like this could get to be sticky. Damn! He was angry, ashamed, and puzzled at the change in himself. He'd never used to think twice about an episode like this once it was over.

He waited until Alice unlocked her car and was about to open his mouth to say good night, when she turned and put her arms around his neck to give him a long kiss.

"You're sweet, and it was wonderful," she was saying, when they were blinded by the fiery headlights of a car that sped past them around the corner and, a second later, was gone.

"What a goddamn nerve!" she cried. "Well, 'night, now! I'll be seeing you around."

"Sure. Good night."

Not if I see you coming first, he thought. His anger at himself was mounting. All they needed in the family was another problem. How the devil had he let this happen?

·   ·   ·

For a long time after Theo had slammed the door Iris had cried. Cramped in the chair with her feet drawn up and a wet handkerchief balled in her hand, she began to feel disgust. She got up, ran cold water over her face, sponged her eyes, applied some makeup, combed her hair, and took stock.

They had both been beside themselves. At a time when they should have stood together, they had flown apart. She regretted now her own loss of control. Possibly, after all, Theo was right about Steve. He loved the boy as much as she did. It was almost eleven o'clock, and Theo was not home yet. A few hours from now he would have to be on his feet, alert and responsible. The strain of a night like this one was too cruel for the man. And she felt a compelling need to speak loving words, to let him know that they were together, that neither Steve nor anyone must come between them.

She called the office number, and when the answering service responded, understood that of course he wouldn't be picking up the telephone at this time of night. He had gone there for solitude. So she went down to the garage and drove to the office. In her mind was a picture of herself putting her arms around Theo.

There were two cars in the parking lot. The building was dark except for a dim light, as from a single lamp burning in Theo's office. He must be working in the library. There was a sadness in the thought of him sitting there so late, alone with his troubles. She went in and knocked at the door.

There was no response, and she knocked harder, then rattled the knob. It seemed strange that he didn't hear such a noise in this dead stillness. Fear struck her; he might have been taken ill; he might have been held up. Maybe she ought to get help somewhere, even call the police.

She went back to the parking lot. There stood his car, his new beige Mercedes. If it was a holdup, surely they would have stolen a costly toy like that. And what about the other car? It looked like a woman's car, of some inexpensive make, but sporty, and painted baby blue. So there must be someone else in the building.

She got into her own car, backed up to the far end of the parking lot under a dark tree, and turned off the headlights. Nameless fright kept her indecisive. She was timid about calling the police, yet she knew she ought to. Oh, God, if some terrible thing had happened— Yes, she must go at once to the police.

And at that moment the light in the office went out. A few seconds later Theo came walking from the building with a woman. She watched. She saw them speak together for a moment and saw the woman—young, slim, wearing a nurse's white uniform—reach her arms around Theo's neck and kiss him. She kissed his mouth. Iris's heart stopped.

And when it started again, pounding, she went crazy. She jerked the bright lights on, slammed the accelerator with her foot, gunned the engine, and swung around the corner on two screeching wheels.

Bastard! Bastard! On this awful night of their grief, he had been in that back room where the lamp had shone, where the leather sofa was, with her photo and the children's on the shelf behind him so he could see them while he lay on some filthy tart, thieving another woman's husband— Oh, he had their pictures everywhere, that one of Laura and herself in mother-daughter dresses, sprigged Liberty cotton, standing in front of a bank of pink azaleas when Laura was six years old, while he lay—bastard!

He could well have had this planned all along and only pretended he needed to work off his nerves at the office. . . . If her hands had not been gripping the steering wheel, they would have been fists.

So it had happened. And the suspicions against which she had fought, for which she had chastised herself so often and so harshly, had been justified after all.

"Jealousy," Mama warned, "is like poison in the veins." Well, let the poison pour, taste the green-black bile of it. Taste it.

Yes, I'm crazy now, she thought. But it's the cunning craziness of a woman who wants to hurt. No more weeping, no more weakness; this time let there be only strength and cold revenge.

Back in the house she went to the bathroom and locked the door. She ran a hot tub and lay down in it, not to wash herself, only to lie inert while her brain whirled and whirled. She was so numb with rage that she had not yet begun to feel pain. Later, she knew, it would come full force, but for now all she could think of was this need for revenge, how to hurt him without letting him know yet what he had done to her. That would come in good time, the right time. . . .

He was knocking on the bathroom door, rattling the knob.

"Iris? Are you all right? Why is the door locked?"

"Because I wanted to lock it," she said, clipping the words.

"Iris, I know you're still angry, but didn't you hear the phone just now? There's news."

"Yes?"

"About Steve. Somebody made bail for him. Jimmy just called as I was coming up the stairs from the garage."

She got out of the tub and wrapped a towel around herself. She wasn't going to appear naked before him now, when he had just come from another naked woman. And she unlocked the door.

"Well?"

"Jimmy says it was one of the professors, actually that guy Powers, curse his soul, except I suppose one ought to be grateful. I don't know, I'm all confused. But it seems he managed to arrange bail for a whole group of kids. Anyway, Steve's out and on his way back to school, Jimmy says, or will be in the morning."

"Thank God. What happens next? Do you know?" she asked, keeping her voice even.

"Jimmy—what a head he's got—made inquiries and found

out that Steve will have to appear back in Chicago. There'll be a fine and a warning and—"

The rest trailed away from Iris's ears. Details didn't matter. Steve was "out," and that was all that did matter.

Theo sat down and took off his shoes. "What a day! What a night! That Jimmy's a prince. I hate to see him dumped on so much because of Steve. He shouldn't have to be so responsible." Theo was close to tears. "Well, Steve's out of this mess, more or less, I suppose, for the time being anyway." He looked up at Iris, who was still standing with a towel wrapped around her. "You must feel a lot better."

"I would feel a lot better if my son's father, instead of a stranger, had provided for him."

He sighed again. "I'm sorry. Sorry about everything."

"Are you? What's everything?"

"Why, what do you think? That we have all this trouble. Sorry about being angry at each other tonight. But we'll get through. We'll be fine."

His smile made its appeal to her, the very smile that had touched her the first time she had seen it in her parents' house, the small, wistful smile that women loved.

"Why are you standing there? Come on, Iris, let's get to bed. We surely need the rest."

Stony and grim in her wrath, she mocked him to herself: Tired? Oh, yes, after the energy you must have used up tonight! Liar. Liar. You'll suffer, and you'll never know why, unless and until I get ready to tell you why.

She would not let him see her tears, although wild, passing terrors assailed her: that he had been having a long-term affair, that his lovemaking at home had been only a pretense all along, and even that he would one day come with guilt and sorrowful regret to ask for a divorce. Yes, it was quite possible that he would abandon her. It happened all the time.

·   ·   ·

"When do you plan to talk to me again?" Theo asked after the fourth day of silence.

"When I'm ready, I'll let you know."

"I had the firm here call a lawyer in Chicago. It's not so bad after all. Steve was with a crowd that was only marching, obstructing traffic, nothing more. There'll be a reprimand and a fine, which I'll pay."

"Congratulations," she said.

"Iris, this isn't like you. Why are you treating me like this?"

Coldly, she stared at the lips that that woman had kissed, then at the hands that had stroked the woman, her breasts, her— This was the start down the slippery slope, at the bottom of which lay hatred. It would end with hatred. Theo and Iris would hate each other. It was possible.

She wandered about the house all that morning. Pearl's face, by its very blankness, betrayed her curiosity. It might have been a comfort to confide in her, but Pearl was not the right one. Nobody was. Friends certainly were not, for Theo's reputation, if only for the children's sake, must never be compromised. And her mother must not be burdened. Besides, Anna would just have offered platitudes. Only her father, only he could have helped, and he was gone.

Too restless to plan anything for the rest of the day, Iris walked without aim into the yard. It was one of those rare mornings that bring a touch of sadness with them simply because they are so rare and will not last, with the porcelain-blue sky unclouded, the trees heavy in moist, glossy leafage, and the air cool in the stirring of a light wind.

Pearl called her to the telephone. "The doctor wants to speak to you, Mrs. Stern."

"I called," Theo said in a formal manner, "to let you know that the appointment is definite. I am to be chief of the surgical staff."

This was validation of his worth, a proud achievement, especially for a man still in his middle forties. This was cause for jubilation, and it was a grievous thing not to be able to jubilate with full heart.

"That's wonderful," she said with equivalent formality.

"That's all you have to say? In that flat voice?"

"I'm sorry you don't like my voice. I said it's wonderful. What else am I expected to say?"

"If you don't know, never mind. There'll be some recognition of it, some sort of announcement at the hospital dance. In the circumstances you ought to look especially good."

As good as your whore? she wanted to say, but said instead, "Most people say I always do."

"I meant, get a new dress. That's all I meant."

She bit her words off one by one. "Very well. I'll get a new dress."

The shop was in the summer doldrums, with fall things just beginning to appear, so that Iris had all of Léa's attention. Every chair and every hanger in the spacious pearl-gray dressing room held sumptuous silks, satins, and lace, tweed suits, dresses of French jersey, and hand-knitted sweaters.

Iris studied herself front and back in the mirrored walls. Black lace fell in wide, soft flounces from the low neck to the floor; shoestring ties and bows of pale blue satin were scattered over the skirt and fastened the puffed, elaborate sleeves at the elbows. Her reflection brought a smile to her face. She was flushed, and her widened eyes were bright with her pleasure, just touched with bitterness, in her own image.

"It's so becoming," Léa said. "But the lavender is lovely on you too. It's a hard decision, isn't it?"

"No. I'll take them both."

"Oh," said Léa, the sound forming in part an exclamation and in part a question.

"You seem surprised."

"No, not at all. I'm only pleased to have you back as a customer. You haven't been in for a long time, though I do see your mother now and then. How is she?"

"Doing pretty well. My father died, you know."

"I didn't know. I'm sorry. Your mother is a lovely person. Is she planning to move?"

"No, she likes her house."

This fashionable, shrewd woman asked too many questions. Her curiosity was the one thing Iris had never liked about coming here. Yet it was just her way—not very mannerly, but obviously she didn't know any better. And she did have the best clothes in the city, no question about that.

"I thought—so many widows move to Florida." And as Iris did not reply, Léa continued, "I'm thinking that a pale blue satin stole would be perfect with that dress in case it gets cool in the evening. Otherwise, it looks stunning just held over your arm."

"Why, yes," agreed Iris.

She was spending a fortune. The moss-green suit, the royal-blue jersey, three sweaters, the checked tweed jacket, the striped white silk, and the two evening dresses must amount to several thousand dollars. She wasn't going to bother calculating. Let Theo pay. He spent like a drunken sailor, anyway. God knew what he had spent on that creature, that whore.

"Come out to the front and look at the stoles. We've also just gotten in some stunning Italian bags."

On this humid afternoon in the city there were more sales-women than customers in front. Actually, there was only one other customer, a man who was making selections at a counter.

Léa draped the blue stole over Iris's shoulders. It framed a portrait of black eyes, red mouth, and white neck. "You see what I mean," she said.

"Yes. Yes, it's perfect."

At the full-length pier glass Iris examined herself. That mere cloth could make one look so different was astonishing. Her face and figure were, after all, the same as ever. But no, her face was not the same; something had energized it so that it gleamed; whether the something was anger, resolution, despair, or all of these, instead of deadening, it had mysteriously enlivened.

Then, in the glass, her eyes met the eyes of the man at the counter. He made no move to pretend that his glance had been accidental. She looked down, fingering the narrow, delicate fringe on the end of the stole. When she looked back up, his eyes were still on her. Only three or four seconds passed, yet within their space she realized two things: that the man's frank stare was approving and also that it was Theo's old familiar look, the one she had always pretended not to see.

She turned to Léa. "I'll take it, of course."

The man spoke. "If you'll allow me to say so, you make a picture."

"Why, thank you," Iris answered prettily. And she went back to the dressing room with a sense of having had a small triumph.

They were talking in the outer room. "You'd be surprised," the man was saying, "how much of a fad the American West has become in Europe. I picked up a rather nice little watercolor, a Navajo woman, this morning." The voice was full and rich with an indeterminate accent, not like Theo's accent, which was easily identifiable. "I owe a present to a friend in Geneva."

"A positive Santa Claus, you are." This voice, young and slightly saucy, belonged to the smart young woman named Lucy who was apparently a partner in the business.

"Yes, I didn't do too badly here today, did I? But seriously, when you travel as much as I do, people entertain you, and unless I'm in a place where I have a home, I have no way of properly paying back except with gifts."

"The question is, where don't you have a home? And now you're buying another one."

"Only a little mountain house. A Swiss retreat from cities

and Riviera crowds. Oh, don't put that scarf back. I'm taking that one too."

When Iris came out of the dressing room, the man was just leaving, and Léa was saying, "I'll have the white purse in tomorrow for you to look at, but in the meantime everything else will be delivered to you at the Waldorf. Good to see you as always, Mr. Jordaine. And you too, Mrs. Stern."

It seemed that Mr. Jordaine and Iris were going in the same direction. At the corner of the street, while waiting for the light to change, he remarked how pleasant it was to shop at Chez Léa.

"It just occurred to me, too, that perhaps my compliment to you was forward of me. I'm sorry if it was, because I didn't mean it to be."

"Oh, no—it was very kind of you."

That was a stilted answer, she thought, feeling awkward. Then, catching her reflection in a plate-glass window walking with this stranger, she felt more awkward still.

He was an attractive man, though, well built and well dressed. His thick hair was cared for; he had good teeth; his gold cuff links were in quiet taste. It struck her as funny that she should be evaluating these details of his person while he must be doing the same to her. And she was glad she had worn the black linen, her best summer dress, a fine display for her round, bare arms and narrow waist.

"The tropical summers of New York," he observed.

"Yes, I'm glad I don't live in the city."

"Where do you live?"

"Westchester." Flustered, not wishing to be rudely abrupt, she added, "I drove in. My car's parked near Third Avenue."

They both crossed Park Avenue and both turned downtown. His packages were being sent to the Waldorf, so obviously he must be staying there.

"I'm at the Waldorf," said Mr. Jordaine. "I had planned to buy a small place for my New York visits, because I spend a couple of months here every year, all told, but the deal fell through, so I've taken a place in the Towers. Have you ever seen the Towers apartments?"

"No, we—I—don't know many people in the city. We—I—mostly stay close to home. With four children, one doesn't—" She stopped. Clumsy, clumsy, she thought.

But he appeared not to notice, continuing easily, "As far as I'm concerned, the Towers are all anyone could want. I shall probably make this place my permanent New York home."

Iris wished she could think of something interesting to say, something sparkling, while at the same time she wondered why it mattered whether she said anything at all, because in a minute or two they would be at the Waldorf and she would go on without him. Too bad! It was exhilarating to be striding down Park Avenue like this. If Theo could see her . . .

Then she thought of a response. "A home when you're not in Switzerland?"

"How did you know about Switzerland?"

"I could hear you from the dressing room."

"Really? It's a good thing I wasn't telling any secrets."

All at once words came. "Secrets are safe with me anyway."

Now, wasn't that an odd thing to have said? Without prior thought it had popped out, sounding positively coquettish, even a trifle suggestive too. She felt herself blush.

They had reached the front entrance of the hotel and paused. Mr. Jordaine looked down at Iris for a long moment.

"I believe that," he said seriously.

"Why, how can you tell?"

"I read people rather well. You're an honorable person."

The moment prolonged itself, and then he said, "I don't know about you, but this heat's given me a terrible thirst. If you have a little time, I'd like to invite you in to have a drink."

Iris's heart jumped. She wondered whether he had meant a drink in his apartment. Some women dared things like that even after a ten-minute acquaintance, she knew. Yes, and some women got themselves murdered by psychopaths for their daring. But in this case such a thought was ridiculous. This man was obviously a gentleman, a courteous European gentleman. Still, she certainly was not about to go upstairs with him.

"The bar? Peacock Alley? Iced tea? Whatever you choose." He smiled. "If you need a reference, you can call them at Chez Léa. They've known me for years."

She felt foolish. "No, of course I don't need one. And iced tea will be lovely."

"I guessed you'd pick tea," he said, following her to a table.

"I don't care much for liquor except wine with dinner."

Her heartbeat was still rapid. She could hardly believe what she was doing, sitting here with this stranger, ordering tea and cake. He faced her across a bowl of fragrant white flowers. People were moving around the room. The fragrance and the motion made her faintly dizzy.

"Well, this is an unexpected encounter, isn't it?" he began.

"Very. It's nice here, so cool and dim."

"A chance to recharge before you go home to the four children."

"They're all away for the summer. Two are grown, anyway. One son's getting ready for medical school in a year or so."

"One wouldn't guess it to look at you."

She tried gaiety. "Oh, yes, I'm an old lady."

"Hardly. Especially in that dress you just bought. I hope you're going to wear it someplace where it will be appreciated."

"It's for a dance at my husband's hospital. He's been appointed chief of surgery."

The dress was probably too splendid for the occasion. It would raise eyebrows. Let them rise. Let the men stare as this man had—and as he was doing now.

"You're not used to being admired," he said surprisingly.

"What makes you say that?"

"Your shy way of putting your head down. Shy. Almost demure."

"Is it? I don't know. I wasn't aware." And as if to prove otherwise, she looked straight into his face.

He returned the look and she, too embarrassed to turn away again, held on; eyes looked into eyes.

"You haven't told me your name," he said.

"Iris."

"It suits you. An elegant and rather formal flower."

"But I'm not formal at all."

"It must be the shyness that makes you seem so. By the way, I'm Victor."

If only she could think of something else to say, not some stupid remark like "That's a nice name!" But she never talked to a man alone, not for more than two minutes, and then only to a friend's husband who would likely say something about the fifth-grade teacher who was a horror, or about the new real estate assessment in town.

"I hope you don't mind my calling you 'shy'? I mean it as a compliment. It's a supremely feminine quality."

This remark gave her an opening. "If it's not carried too far."

"I'm sure you wouldn't do that. All you need is a little time to get to feel at ease."

"You're right," she admitted.

"You're not comfortable with so-called witty types and cocktail-party conversation, wisecracks and double entendres."

"Oh, I never liked cocktail parties. In fact, I hate them."

He nodded. "I know. One-upmanship. Who's who. That's what they're all about. You come home tired out from it all. I know I do."

And he went on to relate anecdotes of his cocktail-party experiences. He was not only amusing and discerning, but so straightforward and friendly besides that Iris began to feel completely relaxed. Leaning back in the chair, she accepted a

pastry and exclaimed spontaneously, "This is really delightful."

"I'm glad," said Victor Jordaine, "because you were very
reluctant, you were afraid to walk in here with me."

She looked down at her hands, at her glittering rings and
tanned, graceful wrists. And this sight, for some reason, encouraged even greater self-confidence, so that she felt a return
of that first small triumph when he had admired her at Léa's
place.

"You can imagine," she exclaimed almost gaily, "that I don't
do this every day."

"Or any day at all?" When she did not answer at once, he
went on, "Jealous husband, I suppose?"

"Oh, yes!" If Theo knew . . . If Theo only knew.

"Well, this is all quite, quite innocent. I'm alone, I was
thirsty, and a drink is ten times more enjoyable with a charming
woman sitting on the other side of the table. You can feel
perfectly free to tell your husband when you get home."

It was not quite, quite innocent. If it were, she would not be
having such a flow and ebb of complicated feelings. And this
man, who seemed to be almost clairvoyant in his judgment of
her, was surely aware of them.

"All right, then, don't tell your husband."

"I didn't say I wouldn't."

"You looked it. So maybe it's just as well if you don't. Hus-
bands and wives can have a way of making unnecessary trouble,
can't they?"

"Are you married, Mr.— Victor?"

"I was divorced six years ago. But we're still friends. We have
dinner together whenever we both happen to be in the same
city at the same time."

"I know people do that, but I can't imagine it. If I—we—were
divorced, I would hate him." A lump came unexpectedly into
her throat. "I would have to hate him."

Jordaine was interested. "Really? That's awfully old fashioned, if you'll excuse me for saying so. People are more honest today. Why wait till hatred sets in after years of stifled misery, till the bitter end, when you can't stand each other another minute? Go while the going's good, I say."

To her utter horror and shame Iris's eyes filled. She blinked hard, but he had seen.

"Oh, oh! I'm sorry. I've upset you. I'm sorry."

Feeling humiliated and ridiculous, she wiped her eyes. "It's all right. Silly of me."

"Not silly at all, if you're in trouble."

"No, really, I don't know what came over me." And since some explanation seemed to be called for, she made one. "We had a—a quarrel. And since we don't have them very often, they have this kind of effect on me, that's all."

He gave her hand a light, quick pat, saying quietly, "There's nothing to be ashamed of."

"You're very kind," Iris told him, meaning it.

"Well, I've seen a lot of life, I've been around, and I know when things hurt."

This is really an extraordinary man, she told herself, so very kind, so very understanding.

"So let's talk about happy things, Iris. Tell me about your children—if you want to, that is."

Here, except for Steve, was safer ground. There was no sense getting emotional all over again, which would surely happen once she got started on Steve. So, skipping the two oldest, she gave an account of Laura, being careful to make it brief so as not to be a bore, and then one of Philip and his talent for the piano.

"I started teaching him myself, but he's too good for me, so he goes to music school instead."

"You must be pretty good yourself."

"I never got anywhere with it. I only play for my own pleasure. I love the piano."

Jordaine's eyes lighted. "I just got an idea," he said. "I

happened to see something in the paper this morning about a piano recital tomorrow at Carnegie Hall, or maybe it was Lincoln Center, I don't remember. Some South American, I think, some fellow who won the Cliburn contest in Texas. If I can get tickets—oh, I know I can—would you like to go with me tomorrow night?"

This was a dare, and Iris had never taken one. She recalled that as far back as grade school, whenever a challenge had been offered, like going up to somebody and saying something outrageous, she had always been the one to hold back. And also she thought of this very day's noontime resolution: If Theo can, why not I?

"Yes, I'd like to," she said.

Filled in turn with excitement and misgivings, she woke several times that night. All morning, at the market and at her desk, this inner conflict continued, but as the day wore on, her feelings stabilized themselves, and it was the sense of excitement that swelled. Desired by a most desirable man, she felt as youthful as a girl. She was too stimulated to eat lunch. At three o'clock she got out her clothes, a red-and-white print with a ruffled neckline, and thought, as she faced her clear eyes in the mirror, that she must remember to wear portrait necklines whenever possible; they shaped her face into a heart and gave her a romantic charm. Then she fastened her best gold bracelets, sprayed on perfume, and went downstairs to start the car. It was just after four o'clock.

At the very same time Victor Jordaine was entering Chez Léa.

"Ah, there you are," said Leah. "And here's the bag. It came in this morning. Look how it's made. The finest, absolutely the finest."

He gave a quick glance at a small white lizard pouch, delicately grained, smooth as silk, and framed with a narrow, gilded filigree.

"It's handsome, but I've changed my mind. I'll take it in black after all. Gift-wrapped, naturally. Your special wrap, if you have one."

"Of course. I'll get a card for you."

"Not necessary. I'm delivering it in person."

Evidently Jordaine was in a hurry. He walked restlessly around the shop, looking out of the window and glancing at articles in the showcases while his package was being wrapped. Yet when Leah handed it to him, he lingered.

"How will this go with a black lace gown?" he asked.

"Why, beautifully," she replied. "Goodness, you must have bought this in every color there is."

He said, almost mischievously, "I bet you can't guess who's going to get this one."

"The size-four dancer?"

"Lord, no. Her taste runs to spangles. She wouldn't appreciate anything like this."

"I give up. Who?"

"How about the lady who bought the black lace dress yesterday?"

Leah stared in astonishment. "You can't mean Mrs. Stern."

"I do mean Mrs. Stern."

"But you didn't know her, did you?"

"I didn't, but I do now."

"Mr. Jordaine! Do you mean you picked her up?"

"That's a vulgar expression, isn't it? We left here together, struck up a conversation, and I'm taking her to a piano recital tonight."

Frowning, Leah twirled a pencil. "I don't understand," she said.

"Don't look so shocked. What's wrong?"

"She's married. She has four children."

"So! What are you, an evangelical from Arkansas?"

"Hardly. But I've known her, I know a little about her." Leah spoke rapidly and earnestly. "You can see she's an innocent, a babe in the woods. She's been totally sheltered. That's why I don't understand."

"That's what makes it more interesting. She has the kind of dark good looks that appeal to me. Somber. Mysterious. And when you combine that with innocence, it's almost like having a virgin."

Leah drew back. "Mr. Jordaine, for God's sake, have a heart. She's probably just had a fight with her husband, or—"

"A shrewd guess. There was a fight, and not a small one, either, I'm thinking."

"I don't know what to say. It's so out of keeping for her, it's so—"

"Oh, it's not so unusual."

"You think it is unusual, or you wouldn't bother to tell me about it."

"All right, so it is. A bit of an adventure, that's all. Piquant."

Leah's voice, just above a whisper, shook with anger. "Mr. Jordaine, I'm going to say what I think, and if I lose a good customer, so be it. What the devil do you think you're doing?"

Jordaine laughed. "I didn't force her. Anybody'd think I was planning to rape a fifteen-year-old girl. Well, I'll be on my way. You may be seeing me again, or you may not."

"Good riddance," said Leah.

"Chopin," said Iris, as the crowd streamed from the concert hall, "makes me want to waltz." And she took a small, swaying step on the sidewalk.

Jordaine, with a hand on her elbow, guided her across the street.

"So you enjoyed it," he said. "I'm glad."

"It was wonderful. Such joyous music, and yet so sad. When you think of Chopin and George Sand on Mallorca, so in love, and then you remember how he died, so sick and so young, it's bittersweet. I suppose I sound corny. Do I?"

"You sound charming. Don't people tell you that you have a beautiful speaking voice?"

"Sometimes."

Actually, Theo always said that her voice was the first thing he had fallen in love with. And where was Theo now? "Working" in the office again as he had been "working" the other night? So, walking late here with this man under the mild pink summer sky, while the music still danced in her ears, she felt not only animated, but also blameless.

"You belong to the waltz era," Victor remarked now. "You have the grace that so many women seem to have lost. I see you in a smaller, more quiet world than this one, perhaps in an Old World university town, studying piano or teaching."

"I was a teacher, and you're a good guesser."

"It's not guesswork, it's insight. I've gotten to know a lot more about you in this short time than you think I do. So you were a teacher?"

"Yes, and I loved it. What I'd really like is to get my master's or even a doctorate and go back to it."

"Why don't you do it?"

Hesitating, Iris said only, "It's not as simple as that."

"Meaning, I suppose, that your husband doesn't want you to." When she neither affirmed nor denied that, he said, "That kind of attitude is going fast, and it should. This is 1968."

She turned to him eagerly. "Then you approve?"

"Absolutely. Your mind belongs to you, and you have a right to use it in any way you want to."

He was defending her. Even her mother, a person "on her side," had weakened her ambition and diluted it with reminders of her primary obligation to Theo, so that as time passed she had thought less and less about her ambitions. Now this stranger, with these few words, made her grateful.

They arrived at the parking garage and, in the hot glare of the overhead lights, stood waiting for Iris's car to be brought. Jordaine handed her a package.

"I want you to have this," he said, looking serious.

Indeed, she had noticed that he was carrying a small glossy parcel, but it had surely not occurred to her that it could be a gift for herself. And suddenly, recognizing Chez Léa's wrapping, she was embarrassed.

"Please, you shouldn't. Really. Really, no," she protested.

"Why not? It's my pleasure. Don't hurt my feelings," he protested in turn.

She was confused, thinking: I've had no experience; at my age it's absurd not to know anything; perhaps it's not impossible that he's fallen in love with me, but on the other hand, I may be an idiot for even considering the possibility.

His hand was still extended, holding the package, so she was forced to look up at him. He had a commanding face with vigorous lips and a jutting forehead over thick eyebrows. He was not a handsome man, but he was certainly an impressive one. Never, never marry a too-handsome man, he's a magnet for women. . . . She bit her lip, hurting it.

"Don't look so distressed! Here, I'm putting this on the backseat and that's that. When shall I see you again, Iris? You said you were coming into the city to the dentist."

She must somehow have mentioned that.

"The day after tomorrow."

"Then let's have dinner. We really have no time to talk. Take the train in next time. It's safer than being on the road in a car alone at night."

When she was in the driver's seat, he leaned through the window and kissed her lips.

"You smell of roses," he said.

"No, it's jasmine."

"Whatever, it's sweet. And you're sweet. I'll meet you at the Waldorf, at the front desk, day after tomorrow. Make it six, an early dinner, so we can have a longer evening before you have to go home."

All the way back on the parkway, through the verdant tunnel

under the trees, her mind reworked events. Something was happening between herself and Victor Jordaine, but what it was she could not know yet. And she understood that she really wanted to evade the knowledge, that what she did want, with every heightened sense, was to enjoy the novelty and the dark, delicious secrecy.

The house was quiet. As soon as she reached the top of the stairs, however, Theo, still dressed in business clothes, came out of Jimmy's room.

"I haven't been able to sleep. Where the hell have you been?"

"That's no way to talk," she answered, raising her chin.

"Listen here, Iris, I've had a week of this, and I'm fed up with it. Where the hell have you been?"

"Where've you been? That's another question."

"Right here. I came home and had my solitary dinner. Pearl said you left here at four o'clock. And you were gone yesterday too."

"So? You told me to buy a dress, didn't you?"

He glanced at the package under her arm. "You weren't shopping until midnight."

"I went to the movies."

"You're mighty dressed up for a movie. What did you see?"

"Don't badger me, Theo. I won't stand for it."

"Iris, you—" He stammered. "If you'll stop this ridiculous feud, I'll come back to our room. I don't understand—you've never acted like this before."

"There's always a first time, isn't there?"

And giving him a look of triumph, leaving him stunned, she went to the bedroom and locked the door.

If he could know, she told herself, that I can do whatever he does whenever I may want to, how it would shatter his assurance! But he will know, and he'll be shattered. And then, then we'll be equal.

·　　　·　　　·

On the appointed day Iris chose to wear red. A most delightful dress which made her look, so Theo had said, like a slender,
scarlet exclamation mark. The dress had been bought at his
direction one day when, out together, he had seen it in the
window of a local shop. It was ironic that his taste was to
enhance her in another man's sight. Thinking so, she felt an
ache of grief, and decided that this must be a form of masoch-
ism, hurting herself because she wanted to hurt Theo. And yet,
she was enjoying it all, the very act of dressing, the fastening of
pearl-and-diamond earrings before the dressing-table mirror.
Birds twittered in the branches at window level. The cool day
was magnificent, and the evening lay ahead.

The lizard purse still lay in its box. Having been brought up
to recognize certain guidelines with respect to the giving and
receiving of presents, she was feeling some doubts about it.
Obviously, it was expensive, no ordinary gift that one accepted
as if it were a box of chocolates. Yet it was equally obvious that
Victor was a very rich man, so quite possibly this gift meant no
more to him than a box of chocolates would to someone else. It
would be unforgivably rude to refuse a box of chocolates,
wouldn't it? But on the other hand, she argued, there was no
reason he should be giving her anything at all. That being the
case, she must return it to him.

"I'm leaving my car at the station," she told Pearl, "and
taking the train to the city."

"Will you be here for dinner?" There was unmistakable disapproval on Pearl's dark face.

"No, not tonight. I'll be quite late coming home."

That for Theo! Let him keep wondering for another few
days. Thinking so, in haste and distraction, she forgot to take
Jordaine's gift. Well then, next time, she thought, startling
herself with her easy, positive assumption that there would be a
next time.

The blood pounded in her ears; a tiny fear leapt in her chest
and lodged there until she stifled it.

·   ·   ·

The wine went to Iris's head and her face burned.

"I get so red," she apologized.

"Never mind. It's becoming. Are you having fun?"

"How could I not? I'm living dangerously."

"For the first time in your life, I'll bet."

"I'm drunk," she said.

The champagne bottle resting in its nest of ice was almost empty.

"Not at all. You're feeling a pleasant glow, that's all."

That was true. All around them, in this luxurious, cushioned space sparkling with flowers, sat couples equally sparkling and luxurious. She wondered how many of them might be clandestine couples, like herself and Jordaine. If any were, they certainly didn't seem bothered by it, for they were filling the room with their chatter and bright laughter.

Victor was observing her with a mixture of interest and amusement. "Talk some more. I like to hear you."

"What about? Anything special?"

"Just about yourself. Your family. After all, there's nothing more fascinating than people."

She had been telling him, or actually answering his questions, about her ancestors.

"Jewish," he had said.

"Oh, yes. But you're not."

"No. We're from every corner of Europe, a little Italian, some German, a touch of Greek—you name it. Tell me some more about your father," he said now.

She sensed that in part he was simply interested in knowing, because he had a sophisticated curiosity about things, and that in part he wanted to ease the conversation for her. Also, she remarked to herself, he had the subtle perception to understand that she did not want to say anything about her husband.

"Well, my father—I loved him very, very much. He was kind and wise. He wasn't educated, just self-taught. He made himself, really, starting with nothing. He was a builder. Some of the best prewar apartment houses in the city were his until he lost them during the Depression," she finished ruefully.

"An interesting business, building."

"Oh, I think so. One can actually see and touch one's results. And what do you do, Victor?"

"No one thing. I'm an investor. International investments. That's what keeps me moving about. More coffee?"

"No, thank you."

"What I want is a brandy. I've got some fine old stuff in my place, so let's go up. You may like one too, when you taste it."

Startled, she questioned. "Go up? But I have to get my train."

"Why, it's only eight o'clock. People are just starting dinner. There's plenty of time. I want you to see the view from up there. It's a spectacle."

Obediently, Iris followed. Odd thoughts popped like small explosions in her brain. I follow because I have the habit of obedience. No, it's because I can't be rude, can't eat the marvelous dinner and then walk away. No, I follow because he will be furious with me if I don't. . . . But why should I care whether he's furious or not? No, I follow because I have embarked on this cruise and must stay on until it ends.

All the way up in the elevator, a little cage like a jewelry box, she trembled. They stood so close that she could smell his shaving lotion, which was spicy, tart, and aphrodisiac. Or more likely, it was all the champagne running warm inside that weakened her limbs.

She was still trembling when they entered the apartment. Through swimming, dazzled eyes she saw a vast and lavish room, all white and emerald. The carpet was a snowfield, and there were white flowers on tables with marquetry tops. An illuminated cabinet of some rare wood, as long as the end wall, was filled with shining objects. There were large, vivid paintings, among which she recognized a Matisse.

Jordaine was studying her reaction. "Like it?"

Extravagance like this was beyond her experience. It was assuredly too ostentatious for her taste, but she was nevertheless impressed and could only nod, murmuring, "I've never seen anything so splendid."

"I had everything brought from Europe. Come, see the view."

Below lay the city and its rivers, the whole set forth like spangles on a dark cloth. She stood for a few moments as overawed as if she had never been this high above it or seen it this way before, although she had done so many times. He was breathing heavily just behind her shoulder, and his body seemed to be exuding heat. If she were to turn around, she would be pressed against him, and she dared not move, but stood there still looking down at the long northward reach of Park Avenue, while waiting for whatever was to come next.

Then he put both hands on her shoulders and turned her about so that she was pinned against him thigh to thigh.

"You're afraid," he said.

"No. No, I'm not."

"Yes, you are. You're afraid because it's forbidden."

He put his mouth down on hers, a soft, persistent mouth, hot with the fruity smell of wine. His persistent, skillful hands moved over her softly . . . softly. . . . All was drift, all was flow.

His voice was hypnotic: "More. More." Her head sank down on his shoulder. Her knees refused to hold.

After long minutes he broke abruptly away, saying, "Go into the bedroom. I'll wait. But hurry."

He opened a door and again she followed. Here in another spacious room was a vast bed covered in pale flowered silk. A tall rococo mirror in a gilded frame faced the bed. In a corner one lamp was lit, drawing an arc of pink light upon the wall; the only other light came from the sky-glow at the windows, where the curtains were drawn back.

She stood quite still, looking at the bed. Her eyes moved to a bedside chair on which a woman's robe of finely pleated pink chiffon had been laid. She understood that she was expected to undress and wear it till he should come in and take it off.

She bent down to remove a shoe, but the sight of the robe stayed her hand. Then she looked back at the bed. Its long, low headboard took the shape of a giant's grimace, and this illusion frightened her. Was she losing her mind? What was she doing in this place, in this bed?

And as if she had been injected with some stiffening potion, all the heat and all the softness left her body; cold and rigid, she kept standing there, not moving from the spot, just staring.

This couldn't be Iris in this place. . . . She was frozen, unable to move or think except to sense vaguely that she must get away yet not knowing how to get away. Her mouth was dry, her palms sweating. She felt terrified and, at the same time, ridiculous.

There came a knock at the door. When she did not answer, the knock was repeated. Then the door opened, and Jordaine stood naked in the doorway. The sight repelled her. It wasn't plausible that only a few minutes before, in the other room, she could have desired the man. Yet it was so.

"What? What's the matter?" he demanded.

Her lips quivered. "I—I can't. I'm sorry. I'm awfully sorry."

"What do you mean, you can't? What the hell do you mean?"

Her eyes filled with tears of shame. "I don't know. I made a mistake. I thought—"

"Yes? I'm really interested. I'd really like to know what you did think."

"Don't be angry. Please don't."

"I said—don't you listen?—I said I want to know what you thought this was all about."

"I thought—I guess I didn't really understand myself."

Jordaine's mouth twisted into a sneer. "No, I guess you didn't," he said in a nasal voice rough with contempt. "I didn't know there were women like you anymore. You're a hundred years behind the times. Oh, I sized up your type, of course I did, but it's a matter of degree. You! You belong in a goddamn museum."

Iris gave him a look of piteous fear. The man was in a fury. He was blocking the door, and she was trapped. When he took a step toward her, she recoiled.

"Ah, get the hell out, you little fool!" he cried. "What do you think I'm going to do to you? Rape you or beat you up? No, I don't need that sort of publicity. Get the hell out, I said, and be quick about it."

When she fled, he gave her an extra shove through the outer door so that she stumbled and struck her cheekbone on the opposite wall. Then he slammed the apartment door behind her.

Once out of the elevator, she ran as fast as her three-inch heels would allow. Park Avenue under the gold, squared-off top of the Pan Am Building was busy with strollers and prosperous-seeming people climbing in and out of taxicabs, going about their various, sensible affairs. Only one drunken derelict came weaving sadly out of a side street; he and I, she thought, are both out of place in this scene.

Incredible as it was, for her wrath at Theo had not abated, she was nevertheless running home to his protection. It was only because of him that, at the moment of decision, the man who had been until then desirable had become an impossibility. It was only he who, from the day she had met him, had ever appeared in any of her erotic dreams. Chastity or naïveté, call it what one would, she was addicted to Theo. And in her trouble she needed only him.

Her heart began a violent beating that seemed to resound in her ears. How would she be feeling now if the thing that had begun tonight in that fantastic white-and-emerald room had gone to completion? And where else might it have led? She imagined herself facing her sons and her young daughter. . . .

Humiliation stung. And it all came of having a conscience. It came of having parents like hers. Imagine either one of them . . . No, it could not be imagined.

But it had happened to her! So quick, so easy it was to do what one had no original intention of doing. Yet hadn't I secretly had the intention? she asked herself. I had been playing about with the idea of vengeance, of *showing* Theo. . . .

No, she dared not be as angry at him as she had been only a few hours ago. And never, never would she tell him about today; in *him*, because he was male, there would be no forgiveness. Fair or not, this was simply a fact of life. But as soon as she got home, she would talk to him quietly, reasonably, and in the end, once having told him the reason for her cold fury—even lovingly. Not right away, but soon. Yes, she would tell him, I will put it all past if you will do what is right from now on. Yes, she would say that.

The conductor was calling her station. The train stopped with a screech of iron, and she stepped down into the hot smell of cinders that had lain all day in the sun. Half a dozen people got off, found their cars in the almost empty parking lot, and drove away. Iris's car was at the far end, the last one, parked under a light pole. When she saw that Theo was standing next to it, she speeded her steps, prepared to give greeting, until, coming nearer, she saw that he was in a high, serious temper.

"Where were you, Iris? I've been worried sick. I have to know."

The words "have to" affronted her. "You don't 'have to' know anything about me."

"I'm your husband, Iris, angry or not. Last night, the night before last, then the night before that. Anything could have happened to you! What's going on? Come, get in the car and let's talk about it."

"I'll get in the car because it's too long a walk home. That's the only reason I will, not because you ask me to. What are you doing here, anyway?"

"I took a cab to the station. I was going to wait here until the last train came in and then I was going to call every person in the city who might have a clue for me. All of this because I refused to fly out to Chicago! Okay, you've made your point." Even in the sickly light from the lamppost Theo's face was dark with distress. "Now, tell me, where have you been, running around all dressed up with your jewelry on, alone at this time of night?"

Where I've been, she thought. I wouldn't have been there if it hadn't been for you in the first place; it's your doing; you drove me to it.

He was waiting for an answer. But she was cornered and utterly unable to think of one.

"Have you been meeting a man?"

She gave a short laugh. This was such a reversal! It was also the triumph she had envisioned, and yet there was no sensation of proud triumph, only this queer, bitter comedy.

"What the hell are you laughing at? Have you?"

"I'm going to let you worry about that so you'll know how it feels, how I've felt."

He groaned. "Oh, my God! Are we going to dredge up ancient history again? How long is it—seven years, eight years?"

"Try one week," she said.

She met his eyes, fastening his startled gaze with her defiant one, until at last he lowered his.

"You were at the office," he murmured.

"Yes. I went there to tell you," she said in a breaking voice, "that I was sorry we'd had words and how much I loved you. Then I saw you come out with her, I saw you kiss her, I saw—"

"Oh, my God," Theo said again.

He reached for the hand that lay on Iris's lap, but she drew it away.

"Will it do any good if I try to explain what happened?"

"Not much. I'm just as well off not knowing the details of your love affairs."

"Oh, Lord. That was as far from being a love affair as—as— Listen to me, I haven't ever had a love affair since we were married. I've done a few stupid things, and this was the most stupid of all. She came in—"

Iris clapped her hands over her ears. "Don't tell me! I don't want to hear what you did. Do you think I don't know? 'My wife thinks I'm working late, isn't that a good one?' Yes, the two of you laughing away at your fool of a wife! 'She's a fine little woman, my wife, and I don't want to hurt her, but you and I are different, darling, you give me—' "

"Wrong, wrong! I never spoke two words to her before that night, much less talked about my wife. I haven't seen her since, and I don't intend to see her ever again. The woman's a zero to me. Zero. Do you hear?"

"Now you're going to tell me that I didn't see what I saw."

"Yes, you saw it, but it meant nothing. She—"

"Next you're going to tell me nothing happened in that office where all the lights were out and—"

"I could lie or try to, anyway, but you wouldn't believe me, so here's the truth: I don't know how it happened. It was one of those crazy things, five crazy minutes, after which I hated myself."

She had a clear, blinding picture of those five minutes, of him whom she knew so well, of him avid and searching, of his secret ways. . . . And now this woman, a woman whom she might so easily encounter on the street or in a store, a woman unknown to her, Iris, but who would know who Iris was, had the same intimate knowledge of the man that the wife had. It was unbearable. Unbearable!

"Oh, you disgust me!" she cried. "I can't stand being next to you on this seat. You're foul, you're rotten!"

She opened the door. Theo slid over and grasped her, but wrenching her skirt away, she got out and slammed the door behind her. And a terrible cry filled the air, a cry like nothing Iris had ever heard in all her life, and she turned to see him bent over on the seat, bowed almost to the floor of the car, clutching his hands.

Then it flashed. He was reaching to pull me back when I, not knowing, slammed the door on his hand.

She ran around the car and got into the driver's seat stammering, "What? What?"

The words coming through gritted teeth were barely audible. "My fingers. Hospital."

In her terror her own teeth chattered. She drove like mad, watching the road and watching Theo. He was holding his head down to keep from vomiting or fainting; she knew that, and remembered, too, that the fingertips were the most sensitive parts of the body. He was stifling his moans. Macho, male pride in bravery, it was, and this cut her to the heart.

He went stumbling into the emergency room. A nurse came forward, greeting him in surprise: "Dr. Stern!" and then saw, with horrified, comprehending eyes.

They took him away into the depths of the hospital, into places unknown to Iris. As if she were paralyzed, she sat unmoving on the straight wooden chair. In a kind of fog she was aware that people were running and gathering, that people were being telephoned for on Theo's behalf. All of this was out of her hands. There was nothing for her to do but wait. She was aware in an odd way that she was not having coherent thoughts. People were coming and going—a drunkard, a man with a bee sting, a baby with a fever—in a thin, steady stream. She couldn't think about them. She couldn't think clearly about Theo. She wished there were a place to lie down in, a hidden place where there wouldn't be any guilt about not thinking.

After a while a nurse came over to her.

"They've taken the doctor to the operating room, Mrs. Stern. It'll be awhile."

Iris raised her eyes, which had been closing.

"What doctor?" she asked.

"Why, Dr. Stern," the woman said gently.

"Operate? I thought—"

"The damage is quite extensive. Dr. Bayley's come in. Mrs. Stern, do you feel all right?"

"Yes. . . . Stupid of me . . . not knowing whom you were talking about, I mean."

The woman took Iris's elbow. "Come. You can wait in one of the doctors' offices upstairs. Can I get you a cup of coffee?"

"No. No, thanks. It wouldn't go down." Operating. Not just bleeding and bandages. "Is it so bad, then?" she asked, following the white back through corridors.

"Oh, I'm sure they'll know what to do. Dr. Bayley's outstanding in microsurgery. I'm sure you know about him."

Iris didn't. Now every nerve in her head was waking up. Microsurgery meant attaching parts that had been severed.

"Dr. Bayley's outstanding," she repeated.

"Oh, my, yes!" The nurse gave Iris a keen look. "Are you sure you're feeling all right?"

"Thanks, yes. I'll just sit here."

"I'll tell them where to find you."

From a soft beige chair Iris looked at beige walls. These modern medical offices must come ready made, all of them the same, with the walnut-finished wood, the textbooks, the beige curtains, the diplomas, and the family photograph in color. This family had three children, all girls in pinafores, a chubby mother, and an Old English sheepdog. There was a world clock on the desk so you could know at a glance what hour it was in Singapore or Helsinki. Here in this town, it was half-past midnight.

A long time ago, or maybe only a short time ago, she had been sitting in a dining room at the Waldorf-Astoria. Diamonds, silk, and flowers. . . . Now here. The hospital smell, smell of sickness and disinfectant, seeped everywhere, even into this clean beige cubicle. Upstairs where Theo was, in a white place that gleamed with steel, the smell would be stronger. She felt like vomiting and, remembering what she had been taught, put her head down between her knees.

Long hours passed and she was still sitting so when the door opened and two men came in, doctors in white, looking official. The young man was Dr. Bauer, still as friendly and unassuming as, when an intern, he had tried to thank her for her kindness to him and his shy young wife. The older man, red and burly, must be the famous Dr. Bayley.

Jed Bauer introduced them. "This is Dr. Bayley, Mrs. Stern."

The burly one held out his hand. "Dr. Bayley." He sat down. He got to the point.

"We have a very unfortunate situation, Mrs. Stern. Your husband's lost three fingers. That's the worst news. The better news is that I've been able to reattach two of them. The index finger is lost up to the first joint."

Iris did not speak. The clock said quarter to nine in Helsinki, where the sun was long up and people were going to work. In the beige cubicle, silence rang.

"A heavy door. It must have slammed full force," Jed Bauer said into the silence.

Bayley ignored that to interrupt Iris, who had opened her mouth to ask a question. He had anticipated the question.

"The two I attached, if all goes well, will be minimally useful. That's to say he'll be able to hold a fork, drive a car, et cetera."

The time in Singapore was—well, no matter, it was already the next day there, once you crossed the international date line. He'll hold a fork, et cetera.

"And his work? I don't suppose . . ." Her voice trailed off into a stillness that no one broke.

The men looked at her, pitying her brimming eyes, her leaking nose, and her desperate hands. Then she buried her face in a handkerchief. After a moment she asked whether she might see Theo.

"He's not really awake, but you may go in."

She looked down at the beloved sleeping face. It was white and clearly cut, perfect as white stone. His great swathed paw was white too, enormous in bandages, with his forearm resting on a pillow. She had a sense of unreality.

Jed Bauer was waiting when she left the room. "Come, I'll drive you home."

She answered mechanically, "I can drive."

"No. Dr. Swensen will follow in his car and bring me back."

When he stopped in front of the house, Bauer handed an envelope to Iris.

"There's something here to help you through the night. Take one right away."

"I never take things like that," she told him.

His rebuke was kind. "Mrs. Stern, there are a few times when it doesn't pay to be strong and proud. This is one of them."

She went upstairs through the dead, silent house and obeyed the doctor. Then she pulled off her clothes and threw them on a chair. The shoes, the red dress, and even the sapphire ring were thrown. The last thing she saw before she dropped onto the bed and turned out the light was the glossy box with Léa's filigreed purse, gift wrapped.

9

It was given out quite simply that a terrible accident had happened, which was of course the truth. Sympathy from every side was unending. A shock wave passed through the local medical community; far from being chief of surgery now, Theo Stern was finished with surgery forever. Worst of all for Iris was the unspoken commiseration, for naturally it was known that she had been the one to slam the door.

"I can imagine how you feel," said a friend, embracing Iris with tears in her eyes.

The family, including Anna, who was still at the Berkshire inn, had been told something, about half of the truth, Theo having insisted on doing it that way. There was no sense spoiling their summer, he said, when there was nothing that they could do about it. And Iris understood that he was unready to face them and their sorrow for him.

While he was still in the hospital, she had knelt beside his bed so that her face was level with his.

"I beg you, I beg you, not to hate me too much." She had barely been able to speak. "Yet, how can you not?"

Frowning, he had turned his head away. "Foolish, foolish talk. Hatred! All foolish."

"I swear by my life that I wish it were my hand. Believe me. Do you believe me, Theo?"

"Yes. Yes." He winced, and she knew he was trying to hide his pain—only, which pain was the greater, the physical or the mental anguish, she could not know.

Later, when she went home alone and lay all night without closing her eyes, she knew which must be the greater. For what was he to do? With all his bright future wiped away? Only blemished years could lie ahead. Blemished, aimless, and gray. She wept, and wept harder to think how insignificant had been last week's tears, even her tears over Steve.

When she brought Theo home, they had still not spoken very much.

"Can't you see I don't want to talk?" he said.

"Only tell me one thing," she implored. "Tell me you understand how sorry I am for this, for everything I said, for everything I did."

"I understand," he said wearily. "Now, for God's sake, enough."

He wanted to go to the office to "put things in order," he told her, by which he meant to cancel appointments and transfer current patient records to someone else. When he came home, he sat on the terrace turning the pages of the newspaper with his left hand. After a while he dropped the paper and sat there staring out over the lawn toward the pool where nobody swam now. Between the oblong of still turquoise water and the pink brick pool-house stood lounge chairs and umbrella tables waiting for a gaiety that was not coming. These were the play-things and this the setting for success and confidence.

He looked too desolate sitting there alone, and Iris went out with a book to join him. After a while she ventured to pierce the heavy silence, saying, "Theo? Tell me what I can do for you."

"Do?" he echoed.

"I thought," she said timidly, "maybe you'd like to talk, to say what you're thinking."

"Thinking? How to stay sane," he replied.

She did not answer. The lump in her throat lay like a tumor.

But she tried again with less personal subjects. In the dining room she read aloud a letter from Laura and one from her mother, who, having no idea of what really had happened, had now stopped offering to come home.

"Mama says Bernstein was marvelous as ever at Tanglewood," she reported.

Theo only nodded. He scarcely ate. She was trying not to see the bandaged hand that rested on the table. And then she had to look back at it, couldn't take her gaze away from it, and felt the agony in her own fingers.

Step by step, over and over, she retraced events. It was as if a machine inside her head had been programmed to perform a certain set of movements, complete them, and repeat them. It started with Steve's arrest, and then the woman. . . . And all the red-hot rage in Iris settled on the woman; she could have killed her; it was the woman's fault, the bitch, that this awful thing had happened to Theo, and her fault that Theo would never love Iris again. For how could he love her? She had crippled him.

She walked into rooms and forgot what she had gone for. All night alone in the wide bed, for Theo slept in Jimmy's room, she had miserable dreams of loss.

The dog runs out of the house and races down the street among speeding cars, my little children plead and call and I am helpless. Or: Theo and I are on a train that halts on the tracks for repairs; I get out to walk a little, when the train starts up again; it races past me and I run after it, but no matter how fast I run, I cannot advance and the train goes out of sight, with Theo on it.

She would wake in a sweat. In the mirror heavy eyes pouched within dark blue circles accused and stared. And always in the evening, confined to the dinner table, facing the food that neither of them wanted, there was the grim silence broken only by desultory, meaningless remarks that neither of them wanted to make. The gloom was palpable. They were in a drifting boat going nowhere. She became numb.

And one day there came a thought, stunning and chilling in its clarity: If I weren't here, they would all be better off. Jimmy is on his way, Steve will sink or swim, Laura is one of the happy blessed, and Philip—well, somehow Theo will pull himself together and take care of him; one child isn't much to care for.

Immediately came the reaction to the thought: It is bizarre, unclean, and you don't mean it anyway, Iris. Stifle it. Get out of the house, into the light, and it will go away.

She found an errand to do in a department store, but forgot what it was. She stood at a counter behind a cluster of old ladies, trying to remember. The old ladies were animated, widows probably, out to lunch and window-shop; later they would go home to their tidy small apartments where old family photographs stand on top of television sets; they'd make tea in their kitchenettes and feed their cats, sufficient unto themselves.

When she still could not remember, she went to the car wash. They had a young girl there vacuuming the cars. She looked like a cheerleader, all-American, lean and competent and healthy. She was whistling. Uncomplicated, Iris thought, untroubled. My Laura is like that, thank God. And my mother is too. Lucky Laura, to be like Mama. Lucky Mama.

In the front hall when she got home there stood a pile of packages, dress boxes from Léa. The very number of them, piled to waist height against the wall, was obscene. What could she have been thinking of? Yes. The less said about that, the better. Yes. So then, what to do with them? They had all been altered, for her sleeves had always to be shortened, therefore they were unreturnable. There was nothing to do but take the boxes upstairs and unpack them.

Linen, silk, and cashmere rustled out of the tissue paper, mocking Iris with their creamy extravagance. Hanging them all out of sight at the back of the closet, she wondered how they were going to be paid for. Last came the black lace with its sprinkled bows and fairylike blue stole. For a few minutes she stood looking at it with hatred, as if it were a living enemy; then she removed the price tag and called downstairs to Pearl.

"Come up. I have a present for you."

The woman was astonished. "You're sure you want to give this away, Mrs. Stern? It's brand new."

"Yes. If it doesn't fit you, give it to your niece. She goes to dances, doesn't she? And here's a bag to wear with it. It's lizard, lined with satin. And the clasp is a swan, see? Beautiful, isn't it? The best quality."

Iris prattled as though she were persuading Pearl to buy the things, and she saw that Pearl, aware that something was very wrong, was covertly searching her face but did not dare the intimacy of a direct question.

"Maybe you'd like to take the afternoon off so you can show it to your niece. Do, go ahead. There's nothing more to be done in the house today."

When Pearl had left, the afternoon stretched ahead. There was nothing to fill it, or rather there were things, there always had been, but what was lacking now were the will and energy to do them. For a moment she thought of straightening her bureau drawers, for hers, unlike Theo's, were never as neat as they should be; but then, how trivial a thing was a bureau drawer!

In the drowsy heat the house slept with window shades

drawn down against the sun's glare. From room to room Iris walked, through Laura's pink nest where the bed was heaped with stuffed animals, to the full toy shelves in Philip's room, to Jimmy's neat space now marked by Theo's occupancy—journals of medicine on the night table—and then to Steve's, with whom it had all started. No! No, that was not fair, not honest, not true. Whatever it was, it must have started long before Steve.

Downstairs she wandered, inspecting idly, really just glancing and not caring. The Norfolk pine on the terrace was wilting for want of water; it didn't matter. Someone had put a sweating glass on the piano and made a ring on the ebony finish; it didn't matter. Pearl had left the kitchen in serene order; that didn't matter either. This was how a home, how a family, fell apart, all the calm safety and solid comfort gone, melted like a sugar cube in a glass of water.

The door between the kitchen and the garage was open. Two cars were there, Theo having taken a taxi to his office, where he would sit all day doing—what? Iris had no idea, perhaps just staring and thinking, as he did at home.

Maybe she ought to drive somewhere, go up into Connecticut on back-country dirt roads, find a pond, sit down, and look at the water. It would be something to do. She took the keys from the hook on the back of the kitchen door and got into the car. She was so tired. For a second she glanced at the car's right-hand door, the instrument of the crime, then started the engine. The fine costly mechanism softly hummed and thrummed.

"Always open the car's windows and the garage door," Papa said long ago when he was teaching her to drive. "Carbon monoxide is odorless. It kills without warning and only takes minutes."

"Only minutes?"

"Yes, you feel sleepy without even realizing it, while the gas creeps."

An easy death without blood or pain. And yet to die so young would be a pity. I'd have to think a lot more before I'd do it, she thought. I don't know.

When she laid her head back on the seat, a beam of sunlight, shafting through the corner window of the building, struck into her eyes. And through the dazzle, behind the closed lids, came pictures, all of Theo's face: coming out of the office with that woman that night, contorted in shock as he grasped his muti-lated hand, bent over hers as he approached her in the act of love—his face.

The motor hummed; vaguely she felt its subdued, vibrating thrust. The shaft of sunlight quivered, moving through the summer leaves, through the drowsy day. Sleepy . . . sleepy.

When finally they removed the oxygen tent, Theo was able to speak to her, answering her question before she asked it.

"It was the gardener who found you. He came by to get lime for the lawn, heard the motor running, and looked in."

So small, she was, lying there. She had never seemed so small, nor her eyes so beautiful, and sad.

"Why? Did you really want to do this?" he asked, imploring.

"I thought about it, but I didn't want to."

He thought perhaps he understood, but he wasn't sure. And now that she wasn't going to die, he felt free to be angry. Did they not have enough troubles without adding this? But he said nothing, only sat there looking at her sad eyes.

Suddenly she cried out, "You haven't told the children or my mother?"

"No. I knew you wouldn't want me to."

"And if I had died?"

"I would have said it was an accident."

"Ah," she whispered. "Thank you." Then she said, "It was an accident."

"If you say so."

"I'm very tired, Theo."

"I know." He stood up. "I'll be back in an hour. You rest."

Out in the hall he remembered that he hadn't kissed her, hadn't said any loving words. But if he had done so, he would have started to cry, and he couldn't let that happen. It would have been like shoving a toboggan down a hill; after that first push it has its own gathering momentum.

When he had passed the nurse's station, he felt them looking after him. Probably no one believed the story that Iris had fainted in the car; they would have connected the event somehow to his fingers, which were now throbbing again under the bandages. And they would be right.

Ah, to hell with them, with the whole damn world. . . .

On the fourth morning he took Iris home, where she went straight to her room and lay down. When Pearl brought up a tray of food, she took a few mouthfuls and pushed it aside.

"Mrs. Stern looks awful bad," Pearl told Theo.

"She'll be all right in a few days. She'll get her strength back," he replied, that being an expected, stock reply.

But he was a physician, and he knew that it would not be so simple for Iris to "get her strength back." How tortured she must have been! He supposed he would never know whether she had really intended to die. Possibly she herself did not really know. Then he wondered where she could have been on the night of the accident; he tried to reconstruct the two or three minutes from the time she alighted from the train to the slamming of the door; he could remember thinking that she had been all "charged up." Where, where could she have gone in her new red silk and her jewelry? And he concluded: probably out with one of the women she knew who lived in the city, maybe that two-time divorcée Joan Somebody. They would have gone to an expensive restaurant and commiserated with each other about how rotten men are, and Iris would have told what she'd seen that night at his office. God Almighty, if he could only undo it, or if he could only make her see it as the worthless escapade it had been!

She was having a hard time being near him. She could not meet his eyes. Not that it was comfortable for him to meet hers either. Fortunately the house was large enough for them to avoid each other for hours at a time. Only in the dining room at their stilted meals that could not be omitted—for were they each to take a plate and hide somewhere apart?—were they forced to confront each other.

"Why do you look away from me?" he asked abruptly one morning later that week. "You keep turning your head toward the door."

She answered very low. "It's because I can't bear to see your hand."

He said nothing. She's overcome with double guilt, he thought. But it wasn't his fault; he'd told her ten times that he didn't blame her for the accident.

"No, I can't bear it," she repeated.

"Then don't look at it," he said with exasperation.

"How you hate me!" she cried.

"Iris, I've told you—"

"But I know. No matter what you say, I know."

"Damn it, Iris! What do you want of me?"

She didn't answer, and he sighed, deeply and audibly. They finished their coffee and got up from the table.

Theo despaired. He would be better off at his office, morbid as it was there, helping the secretaries close down. It was early yet, and he went out to the yard where the monthly crew had come to clean the swimming pool. Locusts were already drilling in the heat, but the baby-blue water shimmered like ice. He stood for a moment watching the men, and it crossed his mind that they were thinking, and would probably say when he left, what a lucky bastard he was to live the easy life in a place like this. Then, remembering that he hadn't paid the company for last month's service, he walked back to the house. The mail had been put through the slot and lay on the hall floor. He bent to pick it up, but now, one-handed, could not manage the slippery catalogs, struggled, and swore softly.

"That's all right, Doctor, I'll get it," Pearl said from the kitchen door.

What must she be thinking of us? he asked himself. Iris upstairs like a recluse and I like this. The blind leading the blind.

In the living room with the mail spread out on the coffee table, he began to sort through ads, appeals, and bills. As always, there was a plenitude of bills: Philip's orthodontist, a fat insurance premium, and college tuitions soon due. The nine or ten major operations that would have tided him nicely over the next month or two were now not to be. In the pit of his stomach fear gathered and made a knot.

Last in the pile was a bill under the heading of Léa. He ran his eye down a vertical line that filled one page and part of a second. Lace evening gown . . . cashmere suit . . . satin blouse . . . He reached the bottom line and gasped. More than ten thousand dollars worth of clothes! It had to be a mistake.

He ran upstairs with the bill in hand and burst into the bedroom where Iris was sitting at the window, not reading, just sitting with limp hands in her lap.

"What the hell can this be?" he demanded, waving the bill. "Is it a mistake? Somebody else's statement?"

Iris shook her head. "You wanted me to get an evening dress," she said, faltering.

"For a coronation in Westminster Abbey, for God sake? And all the other stuff—what is this?"

"I'm terribly sorry, Theo. I realize I shouldn't have done it."

" 'Shouldn't have done it'! That's all you have to say? 'Shouldn't have done it,' " he mocked. "You haven't by any chance gone entirely crazy, have you?"

"Perhaps I have, Theo."

He groaned. "Jesus! Where is it all going to end! One thing after the other—"

"It's not so bad, Theo. The things haven't been worn. I'll sell them. They're all in my closet."

"What, run a tag sale in this house? Put an ad in the paper?"

Her eyes filled. Tears again, the ultimate defense and the ultimate weapon too. He was furious.

"What I want is an explanation, Iris," he yelled. "Where's this thousand-dollar evening dress? I'd like to have a look at it."

He opened up the closet door, rattling hangers over the clothes pole.

"You can't. Everything else is there, but I gave that one to Pearl."

He was stunned. "You—what? You gave it to Pearl?"

The tears spilled over and rolled down her cheeks, yet she spoke very quietly.

"I can't explain. If you can only accept how terribly sorry I am—"

Theo had suddenly no words. He just looked at her, at the tears and the sturdy body gone frail. It might even be possible, as absurd as it seemed, that a smooth saleswoman could have talked her into buying all those things, that she simply hadn't known how to say no, any more than she had ever known how to say it to her son Steve. And an enormous weariness drained him.

Her small voice queried, "What are we going to do, Theo?"

"I don't know what you mean."

"I mean your work, your life. I keep asking what's to happen now."

"What do you want? Shall I sell shoes? Be a waiter? No, a waiter has to have two strong hands so he won't drop soup down the customers' backs."

"Then we have nothing to talk about."

He was filled with rage, an aimless rage at the evil, wretched fate that had rained down on them, but he was suddenly too exhausted to give it vent.

"I think I'd better go to my office," he said, adding, "I'm not meeting a woman there either."

"I didn't say you were. I didn't think you were."

"Maybe it would be easier for us both if I were to sleep at the office too. You can reach me there if necessary. The phones are still connected."

At the same time an inner voice admonished him that this was cruelty. But immediately a second voice responded, saying, "Cruelty! Look at yourself! It's you who are the first victim. Feel sorry for yourself!"

"It's better for us both," he said again.

"I understand. You don't want to stay in this house with me." She lifted her head in a conscious gesture of bravery. "Well, that's all right. I don't want to stay in it with you either. You expect me to pay for your hand with my heart's blood for the rest of my life, don't you? And I can't do it. There'd be nothing left of me. There's nothing much left of me as it is."

"Ah, go to hell," he said softly. "I'm fed up with this drama."

"I'm in hell already," she answered.

He stood a moment on the threshold looking at her. She had returned to her first position, drooping at the window. Even her hair drooped, rumpling her collar. Then he felt a twinge in his fingers like the slice of a knife running up past his elbow. And all of this because she had caught him that night! To hell with her, to hell with everything. Everything!

Feeling this huge disgust, this hopeless doom, he spun around and without another word left the room. A short while later, carrying a suitcase, he left the house.

Here in the office these last few days he had been able to huddle undisturbed. Yet when he tried to read or tried to think, he had no success at either. When he thought about his children and how he was to provide for them, he was beside himself. As for his marriage, it would come to no good; he saw that clearly, impossible as that would have seemed only days ago.

Hours passed. A fearful heat wave burned the afternoon outside, but in the room it was cool and dim. He turned on the little radio for some music and lay back in the swivel chair. "It will all come to no good," he said aloud, aching, and closing his eyes, let the music sweep over him.

10

The heat wave had engulfed the city, but in the restaurant the air was chilled, and Leah drew her flowered jacket closer. All during the lunch Paul had had the feeling that she was vaguely abstracted, which was quite unlike her. Twice he had even had to repeat himself. But as if he had noticed nothing, he continued to scan Ilse's letter.

"It came just this morning, and I knew you'd want to hear it. Listen to this. 'We've all seen your students in Chicago. What a year this is! We've seen it all, the Sorbonne riots in May and the students in Italy going wild. It's amazing to think that these kids could actually boot Johnson and de Gaulle out of their jobs. Here in Israel we've escaped all that. Our students know their government is fighting for its life, for their lives, and they're not about to tear their government down.' "

When he ran his eyes ahead to the next paragraph, Paul read silently, skipping through it.

"Dearest Paul," it said, "I'm still in love with this place and still in love with you. I can't believe it's already been four years. . . . Quite unselfishly, I wish you were here because we need men like you. . . . But sometimes, too, I confess, I need your strength for myself. There's so much evil abroad again. I think we're seeing only the beginning. . . ."

"She says," he resumed, "that we're seeing only the beginning of a bad time. Oh, this is interesting, where she writes, 'I have acquaintances who are in a position to know about things that don't reach the newspapers. People don't want to believe that a growing, worldwide terrorist network exists, really worldwide from Japan to Cuba to everyplace. It's financed, that's known, by some of the richest men in Europe, but they're hard to identify. The people who went to Paris, for instance, to incite students to riot are the same ones who sent that shipful of weapons to Beirut, that ship that we Israelis caught before it could land. They've sent thousands of students to Cuba from all over Europe, along with Palestinians who go for guerrilla training. The pity of it is that a lot of these kids are idealists like the ones who're protesting your Vietnam war. They don't know they're being used, misled at the top. They should come here, or somewhere, and work, make themselves useful. Excuse me, I get indignant. I think I'm back in the apartment at the end of the day telling you everything on my mind, while you so patiently listen—' "

He did not read aloud the rest of the sentence—" 'with that wonderful wise, loving smile of yours—oh, when, oh, when will you come to me?' "

"Sounds like Ilse, doesn't it?" he finished.

"Aren't you going over to see her? You really should, you know."

"I'm waiting for her to come here."

"She won't. Once Ilse gets an idea in her head, she keeps it."

"I can't go through it all again," Paul said, as always, giving *it* a double meaning, that he wasn't going to endure another parting with Ilse and also that he wasn't going to talk about it again now.

He folded the letter, paid the luncheon bill, and put the American Express card back in his wallet.

"Well," he said, starting to rise, "I'll be on my way. Thank goodness for air-conditioned cars. I'm going up to Greenwich to see one of my favorite old clients. She's over ninety and sharp as a tack, but it's too much to ask her to come to the city in all this heat."

As Leah made no move, Paul sat down again. He glanced keenly at her.

"Is there something you want to tell me? Maybe I'm imagining things, but I seem to sense that there is."

"There is. I've been sitting here all through lunch debating whether I should say it or not."

"Say it. You're not ill or anything?"

"Nothing like that. Remember a man named Jordaine who was at Meg's a couple of Christmases ago, good-looking in a swarthy way, obviously rich? You talked to him for a while."

"Victor Jordaine," Paul told her promptly. "We couldn't figure out what Timothy, of all people, was doing with him."

"Ah, yes, you never forget names, do you?"

Sometimes, naturally, he did. But Jordaine's was a name that had stuck because of the incongruous connection with Tim Powers.

"So, what about him? I remember that he's one of your best customers. You were telling about his women. It sounded like a harem."

Leah, looking distressed, lowered her eyes. "He was a customer. I doubt he'll be back. We had some words."

"Really? What about?"

"About your—about Iris."

"I don't understand," Paul said.

"It's hard to explain, but . . ."

There was a hammering in his chest. "Explain," he commanded impatiently.

"Well, here goes. He took a fancy to Iris. They met accidentally in my shop and she walked off with him. He came in the next day to buy a present for her and said things I didn't like. Plainly speaking, I told him she's an innocent and he should leave her alone. He laughed."

The place where the hammer was at work now burned. "I don't understand," he said again. "What would he want with Iris?" And he thought without saying, A quiet type, no beauty, lovely only to a certain discerning kind of man.

Leah shrugged. "A game. Something new, a change from his usual expensive tramps and tarts. A respectable suburban housewife, and Jewish besides, to make it different. Piquant, shall we say? A challenge. And she happened to look very pretty."

"What do you make of it? You're smart. Is the marriage on the rocks?"

"I shouldn't think so. She was buying a dress to celebrate her husband's being made chief of surgery or something."

Paul straightened the grimace that must be contorting his face. "Are you sure of all this, Leah?"

"Of course I am."

"All right. Stupid question."

An innocent, Leah said. Perhaps she wasn't such an innocent. He knew nothing about her, after all. Yet, the way her husband had spoken . . . Paul remembered every word: A good wife. Old fashioned. Quiet.

"I'm sorry I told you," Leah said. "I'm going to kick myself all the way home."

"It's all right. It was natural to tell me."

"Maybe. But cruel in a way, since there's nothing you can do about it."

He recovered himself. What was he doing worrying about a grown woman with whom he had no contact and never would have, simply because she happened to be his daughter? It was senseless. The whole business was. And he saw again, quite distinctly, that man's lifted, cynical eyebrow and the easy bold-ness under surface courtesy. None of these went with what he remembered of Iris.

He put his hand out and touched Leah's. "You're a good girl to care. You always were. Forget it, as I shall."

"Oh, I hope you will. I'll still feel like a heel, though."

"Forget it, I said. Say hello to Bill for me. I'm off to Green-wich."

Nevertheless, he drove the car with only half a mind. He wished that Leah hadn't told him. He wished Ilse's letter hadn't been so filled with tension. He wished he could learn once and for all to mind his own business.

Yet he couldn't help his thoughts. They went inevitably far back and made connections. How Anna had paid, and was in her most secret holy of holies probably still paying, for her mistake, or transgression, or whatever you wanted to call it! He hoped it wasn't going to be repeated in a second generation. Of course, these days they had the pill. . . . But Anna and he had been in love, while *this,* Leah said, was a pickup. And at the ugly word he flinched. Flinched, too, at the memory of his own suspicions about Stern. Well, it would be just one more Ameri-can family going down the drain, a family with four children.

This was usually a pleasant drive, with the traffic very light so early in the afternoon and the road curving nicely under a ceiling of trees. But today it was too bright, the brightness too piercing. It disturbed him; he wanted to draw a curtain over it, a curtain of gray mist or rain. Leah's message had changed the day.

Long before the exit to Greenwich he left the parkway, having no idea where he was going, knowing only that he had lost patience to cope with the formal old lady, the tea table heavy with old silver, and the courteous repartee that went with them. He decided to stop at the first drugstore and telephone a proper excuse. Somewhere in Rye he parked the car in a shady spot, made the call, bought a can of cold Coke, and went back to the car to drink it.

I'm off my head, he thought. If Ilse were here, she'd certainly let him know he was. However, she wasn't here, more was the pity, but Theo Stern was here. . . . His suburban office couldn't be more than a short drive away. And through some queer power of suggestion he felt a twinge in his shoulder, which he knew was ridiculous of him because the shoulder never bothered him in the least. But, plausibly, it could, couldn't it? And a look at it wouldn't be amiss, would it?

He straightened himself in the seat while he labored to straighten his thinking. Let the intellect rule the emotions. Ask himself what he hoped to gain. Answer that he only wanted to *know,* that was all. Once he knew whether that marriage had fallen apart or not, he would be able to put it out of his mind. He swore he would. But how would he find out? Very likely he wouldn't. On the other hand, there might be a clue, a chance remark. It was worth trying. If he didn't try, his speculations would torment him. He knew himself.

And he went back to the telephone booth to look up the address.

The office door was locked, but the sound of music was plainly audible. Paul wrapped on the glass again, listened to the stately lament of the Verdi *Requiem,* waited, and rapped a third time. Abruptly then, the music stopped and Dr. Stern came to the door. The man looked dazed, as though he had been sleeping, and he had a heavily bandaged hand.

Startled, Paul said awkwardly, "Excuse me, I was in town,

and I thought the office was open. I wanted to make an appointment to inquire about my shoulder. You operated on it."

Stern's face was so blank that Paul, disconcerted, lost his initiative and backed away from the door. "But you've had an accident. I don't want to disturb you."

"It's all right. Come in. What seems to be the trouble?"

At this point Paul would have refused, if Stern had not asked him again what the trouble was.

"It's nothing much, I'm sure. But I thought I should be cautious. You may not remember, I had two wounds there. . . ." His voice trailed off, and he felt foolish.

"I remember you very well, Mr. Werner. I'll have to look at you here." They went into a room with a magnificent carved desk, an Oriental rug, and full bookshelves. "The examining room is dismantled," Stern said with a bitter twist of his mouth, so bitter a twist that Paul dared not ask a question.

When he removed his jacket and shirt, he felt light fingers moving over the scar.

"I see nothing," Stern said, "unless perhaps a touch of sunburn."

"Ah, yes, I've been on the beach."

"Then that must be it," Stern said. "There's nothing to worry about."

It seemed necessary for Paul to be saying something while he put his shirt on and knotted his tie.

"I've friends on Long Island who invite me to swim. I guess I'll have to watch out for sunburn. And I'm really sorry to have bothered you for no reason."

"No bother. I have plenty of time. In fact, I have nothing but time."

Paul took the opening, for it seemed to be an opening. Besides, it would not even be decent to ignore the man's injury.

"Your hand," he began. "I hope it will heal quickly. You must be in a hurry to get back to work."

"I shall not be going back to work."

The cold, flat tone shocked Paul, so that his glance went automatically to Stern's suffering face. It looked twenty years older than the lean patrician face he remembered.

"I'm not what you saw before, am I?"

And Paul could only reply, "I'm sorry."

"I'm having a bad time. I've lost the use of three fingers."

"Terrible!" Paul exclaimed, knowing the response to be entirely inadequate. Yet after all, there were no words suitable to so great a ruin as this one.

"Smashed it in a car door last month," Stern said.

And he sat down, indicating with a gesture that Paul might sit, too. Apparently, he needed to talk about his tragedy. He must have been sitting here brooding all alone; there were no ringing telephones or clattering typewriters sounding from any of the inner rooms. In this room the blinds were half drawn, allowing a gloomy green light to be filtered in through the trees.

Paul's eyes moved to the diplomas on the wall behind the desk and to the brown textbooks. *Restorative Maxillary Surgery*, he read. What was he doing here? The purpose for which he had come was now forgettable. If there had been any other human being in the office, he would have gotten up and left, but it seemed heartless to walk away from anyone so beaten, just as it would be to leave a sick stranger alone on a street corner without knowing what he was going to do or what was going to be done for him.

"A crazy accident," Paul murmured, needing to fill the waiting silence, even with nothing more than a platitude. "They always say that home or your own car right near home is where most things like that happen."

"So they do say."

The gloom mounted. It was so palpable that Paul felt its chill on his skin. Then suddenly he began to see what was taking shape in his own head: that this event would have profound effect upon Iris, and that possibly it could in some way have to do with what Leah had told him a few hours before. He shivered and asked abruptly how the accident had happened.

Stern sighed. "It's this war in Vietnam. We have a son, a marvelous boy, exceptionally bright, filled with potential, ideas, ideals—well, fiercely independent, and that's the sad part of it: he's become a radical, a rebel, and we can't reach him."

When he paused as if he were trying to draw a clear thread through his story, Paul interjected, "You told me about him when I was in the hospital."

"I did? I don't usually air my worries like that."

"There was a blizzard and you were held up, so you sat in my room for a few minutes and we got talking."

"I'm not a garrulous man," Stern said with a troubled frown, as if it were important that Paul be aware of that. "It seems you've been the victim of one of the rare times when I talk too much."

They would be rare times, Paul recognized. This was an unmistakably proud and private human being, one who would reveal himself only when under some extraordinary stress.

With a reassuring smile he said, "I don't mind listening." And it seemed to him that he had told Stern the same thing that other time too, but he couldn't be sure.

"So, as I said, he's always been fiercely independent, but now he's older, and things are worse. He got himself arrested at the convention in Chicago."

"These are confusing times, very hard on the young. It's not like the Second World War when we knew what we were fighting for and what against."

His remark was lame, a liberal's cliché, Paul knew, and scant comfort for a parent.

"That may be," Stern said rather sharply. "I happen to think we are fighting there to keep scoundrels from eating the world up, piece by piece. Anyway, we quarrel over the boy, my wife and I. She likes to say he just needs to find himself. What's this business about 'finding oneself'? Don't they know who the hell they are? I've no patience with it."

"Well," Paul said gently, "sometimes one doesn't really know who one is." And he thought: Who am I? A banker, and a fairly shrewd one, who increases wealth and preserves it; also a philanthropist who takes pleasure in giving it away; a dilettante of art and music who feasts on them both but produces none himself; sometimes a politician scheming on behalf of the underdog; a lover—or was one—

"Anyway," Stern resumed, "he was arrested. My wife wanted to go to him at once to help him, but I thought, and actually I still do think, he must live with the consequences of his actions. How is he to learn? Ideals are one thing and I understand them, but behaving like a hoodlum is another. I saw enough of hoodlums in Vienna."

Paul groped mentally for the connection between the son and the hand, to which his gaze now moved. Stern, following the gaze, understood.

"So we quarreled and one thing led to another. Led to many things. . . ." He got up and raised the blind. "It's dark as a cellar in here. I should have thought of it before. Is the light in your face? No?" And with his back to Paul he said, "She slammed the door on my hand."

Paul was stupefied. She—Iris—did that!

"It was an accident, purely and simply an accident, and I have told her over and over that of course I know it was, that any fool would know it was."

An accident. Relief washed over Paul, and his heartbeat, which had accelerated, slowed again.

"But she feels such guilt—" Stern's voice broke and he stopped.

The breaking voice and the impressive tallness—the phrase *fine figure of a man* flashed through Paul's mind—were painfully incongruous. On Stern's behalf he felt humiliation, and knew he should not be a witness to such profound and intimate grief.

He ought to find something kindly to say, make some suggestion—but what?—and leave. However, he did not.

Suddenly Stern turned about and, erect as a military officer,
came to stand before Paul.

"I should apologize for this behavior in front of a stranger,
and I do apologize."

"We all have to talk sometimes," Paul responded. "And it's
easier to talk to a stranger. You know what they say about the
stranger in the airplane, whom you'll never see again. It's
doubtful that you'll ever see me again."

"The man in the airplane. Yes, I see. Or perhaps if one has a
father or an uncle, someone half again as old as oneself. Not
friends, though, certainly not in communities like this where
everybody knows about everybody else and what they don't
know, they invent." He paused. "If I were Catholic, I would go
to a priest, wouldn't I?"

Yes, wrap one's trouble in a package, hand it over, and maybe
get it back a little lighter. When I had Ilse, Paul said to himself,
I could do that. And he spoke very softly to Theo Stern, repeating, "I'm willing to listen."

Stern sat down in the swivel chair. There were two creases in
his cheeks, which were too young to be creased like that. And
Paul wondered whether in time they might go away.

"She found me with a woman, here in this office. It was the
night Steve was arrested and we argued, and I came here to
have some peace. The last thing I wanted was a woman! I curse
myself. The damned woman. She'd been waiting for me, waiting for weeks. I'd known it every time we passed in the halls. I
was at loose ends that night, distraught about everything. I
didn't know what to do with myself. So—so it happened. You
know how it is. The last thing I wanted to do was to hurt Iris."

Paul felt the sting of wrath. "The last thing" he wanted was a
woman. Now the last thing he wanted was to hurt Iris. Which
was it? Yet he began to see his way through the tangled tale: Iris
must have been getting even. The incident at Leah's place . . .

Of course that was it. Ah, what was wrong with the two of them! They must have spoken unforgivable words to each other, words that each of them deserved. But the hand was a cruel price to pay all the same, all out of proportion to the crime. That talent! Swept out with the trash, gone forever. Poor devil! And Paul's anger ebbed away.

The low voice with its hollow, tired tone continued. "She was in a frenzy. To tell the truth, she's always been jealous, though she tries to hide it. And this was just too much. Of course it was. I knew that. It must have been unbearable for her. I know how I would feel if she ever—"

So Iris was yet another sufferer from that consuming sickness, jealousy. Well, she must have reason enough! How often in the years of his youth had not Paul tortured himself with the physical image of Iris's mother and the man she married, the image of that man in possession of her! So the old passion ramified, not dead yet, only sleeping its long sleep.

On a shelf behind Stern's bowed head stood a photograph of Iris, alone this time, unlike the family picture that Paul had seen in the other office and memorized. Her lovely eyes gazed gently into space; the smile on her lips was very faint, unwilling almost, as if in reluctant response to the photographer's command: a little smile, please. There was nothing of her mother's kind of radiance about her. Yet in her dignity she was the fitting counterpart to the mature and handsome man who sat here now.

Paul opened his mouth to speak. "Perhaps—" he began, when Stern's voice, rising as if he had an announcement to make, interrupted him.

"She tried to kill herself. At least it seemed that way, although she claims she didn't. It was carbon monoxide in our garage. It's possible she didn't mean to do it. I think maybe she doesn't know herself. Maybe in a way she did, and in another way she didn't. That's possible too."

Paul's mouth was dry. "And so—how is she?" he whispered.

"She's all right. She was found in time."

"And where—where is she?"

"At home."

Suicide. . . .

"You're quite sure there's been no—no brain damage?"

Stern, looking surprised, replied, "Quite sure."

Paul heard himself saying next, "I don't understand. It's terrible. Terrible."

There came a few seconds pause, during which the two men saw into each other's eyes, and Paul knew that his feverish reaction had been inappropriate.

Hastening to correct himself, he said, "I'm just so shocked that I don't know what to say. You've had more trouble than anyone should have to bear."

Stern gave a small, hopeless shrug. "I've seen terrible things in my time, in my work. One has to bear them. There's no choice."

A wind must have risen outdoors, because the leaves were shaking, so that the light in the room began a nervous motion, distorting Stern's face, which receded into shadow, and emblazoning the bandaged hand that lay on the desk.

"What will you do?" asked Paul.

"I've been trying my damnedest to think. I've left home and come here to think in peace. But to tell the truth, I haven't been getting anywhere."

Only then did Paul remark the partly emptied suitcase lying open on the floor next to the desk. He spoke quickly.

"You're not planning to stay away from home, are you?"

Stern, passing a weary hand over his forehead, said only, "It looks that way."

"I see."

How human beings punish each other! How Iris must have suffered to want, no matter how fleetingly, to die! This man, too, bewildered and wretched. . . . But along with his shock and pity Paul was aware, too, of anger at the colossal, blundering mess that these two seemed to have made.

Intelligence over emotion, he reminded himself then, and said more quietly, "I should think, if you were to leave each other, it would only compound your trouble. You have children—"

At the word *children* Stern winced and, stammering some in agitation, cried out, "Oh, God, yes, that's part of what's destroying me! Education, travel, all the things I wanted to give them, are going down the drain . . . have gone already. I don't even know where I'm going to find college money for the next semester."

Paul's gaze swiveled almost automatically around the room, his experienced eye making rapid, astonished evaluations: on the wall near the door a rather good small neo-Impressionist landscape, on the opposite wall a grouping of very fine nineteenth-century bird prints in hand-carved frames, in the corner a tall, bronze, Art Deco torchère, on the desk three delicate Japanese ivories, and on Stern's left wrist a heavy gold Patek Philippe watch.

These silent calculations were marked by Stern, who interrupted them to say "You're trying to make sense of what I just told you."

"Frankly, yes, although of course it's no business of mine."

"Some might say I have a tendency toward extravagance. I know my wife thinks so." The short laugh lacked humor. "But a few dollars more or less don't alter the basic fact that it's expensive to live. I gave a great deal to charity, especially and understandably to refugee relief."

"Understandably."

"Often I ask myself why I should be alive when so many others died."

As at that other time in the hospital Paul was drawn to Stern. Regardless of the difference in their ages and in spite of all strong disapproval, here was a spirit that answered to his own.

Yet he could not refrain from saying "Yes, of course one gives, but not to the point of impoverishment."

And Paul thought: I have absolutely no patience with people who live beyond their means. It's my banker's mentality. But he tried to keep from sounding reproachful when he spoke.

"Have you put nothing away at all?"

Stern shook his head sadly. "Very little, I'm ashamed to say."

Irresponsible! A man with a wife and children giving to strangers, no matter how deserving; spending on charming, silvery landscapes. . . . And Paul drew a mental picture of the house in which Iris must live. If the office was like this, then the home must be a treasure box. What was to become of her, unused to want as she was, burdened with God knew how many varieties of guilt, over the rebellious son, over the severed fingers, over—and Paul shut his eyes as if to shut out the recollection of Jordaine's ironic face. What was to become of her?

As if his fears had transferred themselves to Stern, the latter said slowly, "The pity is that none of this particular trouble is Iris's fault. She seldom spends an unnecessary dollar. And this has been such a hard year for her anyway. She lost her father and took it badly. She was so close to him, much more than to her mother. I don't know why. Iris is a very complicated human being, not that we all aren't, but she—" He stopped.

The minor key in which these rambling words were spoken, with their hint of more sorry confessions, made Paul suddenly recoil. He, who had come here in what he had really expected to be a vain attempt to learn something, any little something, was now afraid of being told too much.

He brought the dialogue back to the immediate. "There must be something you can do, some way you can earn a living as a doctor without using your hands. Maybe you could teach your specialty."

Stern shook his head glumly. "No. To teach surgery, one must be able to demonstrate it."

A fly, unnoticed before, had suddenly began to buzz around the room, darting and alighting, repeating its path in aimless circles. Paul, drawing the inevitable analogy to human affairs, controlled his frustration and tried again.

"Well, then, is there anything else you could teach? Excuse me if I ask the wrong questions, but I know so little about medical careers."

Stern, with a totally discouraged expression, was following the fly's frantic arabesques. "No. Nothing," he said.

"But there has to be some solution for you. You do have general medical knowledge. I should think you might practice as an internist."

"Mr. Werner, it is years, years, since I studied about the heart or the stomach. What do I know about them?"

"There are books. Isn't it a matter of refreshing your memory?"

At that, Stern, who was already sitting erect, made himself taller in the chair.

"That would be a deception at best and a shameful fraud at worst. Without the right training, I'd be a second—no, a tenth —rater. If I can't be perfectly qualified, and I mean *perfectly,* at the top of my field, I would rather be nothing. I would rather open a hamburger stand!" he cried. And with an agitated sweep of his good arm, knocked the telephone off the desk.

Paul, as he picked it up, said silently to himself, It's a devilish business, dealing with a perfectionist. Aloud, he asked quietly, "So then it's to be a hamburger stand?"

It took a few moments before Stern answered.

"I have thought—but no, it's quite useless, not worth talking about."

"Perhaps it isn't useless."

"Well, in my work I've had occasion to make repairs after cancer surgery, usually on faces, so in a way I became emotionally involved with cancer patients. I sometimes thought it was a specialty I might have studied if I hadn't done what I did."

"You'd like to be an oncologist?"

Stern shrugged. The gesture was becoming familiar, and Paul waited.

"I would need a two-year residency at a minimum, and I can't afford it."

"I thought they paid residents nowadays."

"Not enough for my needs! Four children and a wife, no matter what happens between us. And three are in college next year. No, it's no use."

Something indefinable within Paul, prompted perhaps by a rage against fate, a rage going far back into his own past with its mistakes, wanted to deal harshly with this muddled man, with this entire muddle.

"Families rally in times of trouble," he said. "Wives go to work."

"Oh," Stern said bitterly, "that would be the least of my problems. Iris has been nagging for years about going back to teach. But what she could earn wouldn't be a drop in this particular bucket."

Ignoring the last, Paul persisted. "Nagging? Why nagging?"

"Because I didn't want her to. I wanted her at home, running a proper household. No one can be in two places at once."

Very mildly, Paul chastised him. "You're living in a past age, or one that's passing fast." But when Stern, raising his eyebrows, said nothing to that, he added more softly, "You're thinking that I have no right to reprimand you, and you're correct."

"I asked for it. It's I who've imposed on you with my troubles."

What a charade this is! Paul said to himself. A dishonest game on my part, filled as I am with pity and self-pity, posing as a kind, disinterested old man. I should be ashamed, and I am.

Neither spoke. Obviously, Stern was waiting for Paul to get up and leave. But Paul was not prepared to leave.

"So it devolves upon money in the end," he remarked.

"Most things do, in the end."

"I will give you what you need to become an oncologist."

The words fell into the stillness and hung there.

"I beg your pardon," Stern said.

"I said, I will give you what you need."

"I don't understand."

"You look at me as if I weren't quite right in the head. But I assure you, I am."

"It makes no sense. Why should this total stranger make an offer like that?"

"I'm not a *total* stranger. You forget, I've known your wife's family—"

"Not really, Mr. Werner. You were acquainted with my wife's mother, I believe, a long time ago. So I still don't—"

"Haven't you ever heard of people helping other human beings who happen to need help? And I like you. You're a fine doctor, and it happens that I can afford to help you. That's all there is to it."

Stern was giving him a long, steady look, a physician's look of appraisal.

"I don't know why I have the feeling that there's really more to it, Mr. Werner. As I think about it, too, I'm sure your shoulder doesn't hurt either. Tell me, why did you really come here today?"

The odd thing was that quite suddenly a reversal had taken place, and Stern's was now the dominant spirit in the room.

Beneath this unexpected scrutiny Paul floundered. The best answer he could produce was not good enough; he knew it even as he gave it.

"It was an impulse. An eccentric one, you might say."

Stern was obviously not satisfied with the answer.

"Extraordinary . . . a puzzle. Like your very generous offer, which of course I can't accept."

Ah, but this man was difficult!

"Why can't you?" demanded Paul.

"An enormous loan like that? It's not lack of appreciation, no. But there's such a thing as self-respect. Pride."

"Of which you have too much, if I may say so."

"Maybe. But I know what I can do and what I cannot do."

"Apparently, you can let your family suffer. Your wife, who came close to killing herself. . . . Is your pride more important?"

"It's not fair to put it that way, Mr. Werner. You're making it black or white, and that's so simple."

"If you won't take my help, why don't you go to your wife's mother?"

"She's all alone. Why, I would never take from her! My father-in-law left her very comfortable, but not comfortable enough to invade her capital. I couldn't deprive her of her little luxuries. She's up in the Berkshires now, going to the concerts at Tanglewood. No, never."

"So that brings you back to square one. Back to me."

A powerful impulse drove Paul to stand up and, with his hands clenched in his jacket pockets, walk to the window. The situation was completely mad. And he was horrified to feel tears rising in back of his eyes; this was the first time his eyes had been wet since the day he flew out of Israel, leaving Ilse behind.

"Things are coming back to my mind," Stern was saying. "Disjointed incidents. I know there are things you are not telling me."

"Not so."

"Iris has a vague memory of meeting you two or three times while she was growing up."

"That means nothing."

"Except that—well, to be blunt about it, when you came to that dinner a few years back, and afterward came to me as a patient, she said it was clear that you were always turning up. She said you stared at her and it gave her a nasty feeling."

"That is a brutal thing to tell me," Paul answered, still not turning around.

"I'm sorry. I didn't mean it to be. But I believe you appreciate honesty. And you must admit there is something unusual about all this."

He is pushing me, driving me to the edge, Paul thought. How easy it would be, what relief, to come out once and for all with the truth! But that would be insane.

"I'm thinking frankly that there must be some connection. Did you perhaps have business dealings with Iris's father that ended badly? Or was there some rivalry, maybe, over Iris's mother when you were all young? I suppose I sound like a private investigator, but there's something hidden."

Paul did not answer. His heart was hammering.

Stern's voice, although courteous and quiet, was absolutely relentless. "Unless of course I am completely crazy. But I don't think so."

Now, now, all the years of repression, of secrecy and denial, took their vengeance. And Paul, losing the control that had for so long kept him from doing the unthinkable, whirled about to reveal without shame his wet eyes and trembling mouth, out of which came the unsayable.

"Iris is my daughter. Now you know what's hidden."

Then he walked away to the opposite end of the room to stare at a row of books without seeing them. Again a long, long silence followed. Behind him he heard Stern making loud rustling noises with the papers on his desk.

At last Paul broke the silence. "Damn queer things you hear if you live long enough! That's what you're thinking, isn't it?"

"I don't know what I'm thinking. I'm just hearing your words in my head. I'm wondering whether I heard them correctly."

And then a fearful panic seized Paul. He felt ill, so faint that he almost lost his balance and had to brace himself with both hands on Stern's desk. In God's name, what had he done? In God's name . . .

When he leaned forward, his face came to within a few inches of Stern's open mouth and shocked, dilated pupils.

"You heard them correctly. And if you ever repeat them, I'll kill you and then kill myself. Do you hear that?"

"My God," Stern whispered.

"Because I couldn't live with the damage I'd done. I don't know what came over me. The first time in all the years. All the years!" he cried.

He sank back into a chair with his face in his hands. From some inner room came the single chime of a clock marking the half hour. A horn sounded in the parking lot. He'd lost control. He'd given to this stranger, this unknown quantity on the other side of the desk, the ultimate power to destroy. Iris . . . Anna. . . .

He heard a chair scrape, heard the shuffle of shoes on the rug, and felt a hand on his shoulder.

"Paul. Paul. Look up. I want you to have a little brandy, but I can't manage it with one hand."

When he looked up, he saw the concerned expression of the *doctor,* the professional command. Obeying, he seized the bottle and the glass that Stern had placed on the desk and poured a drink.

"I needed that," he managed to gasp when he had taken a mouthful.

"Take more," Stern said. "It dilates the blood vessels. Your pressure must be shooting up to the top."

"Yes. I'm dizzy. I'm scared."

Stern's hand grasped his shoulder again, firmly this time.

"Listen to me, you'll be all right. And you're not to be afraid, not about a stroke because you're not going to have one, and not about what you've told me. Look into my eyes. I swear to you, Paul, as God is my witness, I will never tell another human being, no matter what may happen—no matter what, do you hear me?—what you said. I swear it."

The deep, troubled eyes were intelligent and compassionate.

He is honorable, Paul thought. Yes. I have to believe him. I must. Yes.

Yet he had to say more. "You understand what the truth would do to them both?"

"Oh," Stern said quickly, "to anyone at this point in life. But Iris"—he shook his head—"Iris would be shattered. No one knows that better than I do."

"You will want to hear the story."

"If you feel you can tell it."

Stern resumed his seat and Paul, under his quiet gaze, felt the slow lessening of panic.

He began. "It's simple enough. I was engaged to be married when Anna and I fell in love. I didn't have courage enough to break the engagement, so I broke Anna's heart and my own instead. A few years later we met quite accidentally, and Iris was the result."

"That's it?"

"That's enough, isn't it? But," Paul added quickly, "there has been nothing between us since. I want to make that clear. She was loyal to her husband. He never knew."

"All the years I've been in this family . . . It's incredible. Anna, with her beauty and serenity . . . I could have sworn it was a good marriage, that she was happy." Stern was bewildered.

"Maybe she was. One makes oneself content. There are different ways." Paul's voice roughened and stopped. Here in this room he had stripped himself naked and exposed the forbidden. For an instant he felt as though he had merely dreamed of doing it, that it was merely an expression of his worst nightmare.

"He was a good man, a very kind father. Iris adored him," Stern mused as if he were reminding himself aloud of things forgotten. "It's astonishing, although it shouldn't be, I suppose, how much is hidden in people's lives, even in one's own, like my old life on the other side of the ocean. Is anything what it seems to be?"

"Fortunately for us all, yes."

"I don't know what to believe. I accused her of seeing another man that night, and then I thought how ridiculous that was. She's not a woman one would ever suspect, but now there's this about her mother. . . . I don't know anything. Maybe I never did."

Paul felt a great weight. At last he had gotten what he had never dared hope to have, the freedom to talk and learn about Iris, and now he did not know what to do with it.

Then something struck him again, and he had to ask "So I made her feel nasty, you said?"

"An exaggeration. 'Uncomfortable' would be more accurate."

"Those few times we met in all the years! I suppose I must have been overeager."

"Iris is very acute. She sees everything, the most subtle things."

Yes. The world crushed such people. Meg had been like that. If you loved such people who could not rescue themselves, you had to rescue them as once he had rescued Meg.

"You will get together again, I hope?"

"I don't know." And Stern's lips tightened into a pale, unbecoming gash.

Paul, who had spent his business life in negotiations, had learned to feel when an atmosphere was changing and the subject must be dropped. On the subject of Iris, Stern had abruptly closed up. He ventured, nevertheless, just one more remark.

"Whatever there is between you, whatever, my advice is to have it out in the open. Tell the truth to each other, hold nothing back." He finished wryly, "I know I'm a fine one to be giving advice like that, but I'm giving it all the same."

His energy had returned. Typical of him, he wanted now to

get down to solutions, to wherever a solution was possible. From his inner pocket he withdrew a checkbook, pin seal with gold corners. Many years old, it was his mother's last birthday present. It was a trifle ostentatious and not what he would have bought for himself, but he would keep it, nevertheless, until it should wear out.

"I have always wanted to do something for Iris, and I've never been able to. I have never spent ten cents on her. Do you know what that can do to a man? I want to give you whatever you need to get back on track. Just say what you need."

Stern had a doubtful expression. "I don't think you understand. We're talking about supporting a family during two years of study—" he was saying when Paul interrupted him.

"Let's not waste words." In this total reversal of mood he was feeling a curious kind of joy. "What is your average income?"

"I'd have to figure that out," Stern answered, hesitating.

"Not exactly, of course, but an approximation."

"I can't even say that offhand."

It was hard for Paul, who kept exact accounts, to hide his astonishment. "But how then do you know what you can afford to spend?"

Somewhat ashamedly, the other replied, "I suppose I don't really know. It gets spent as it comes in, and there always seemed to be just enough."

"Just enough," Paul repeated, feeling distaste. Then he checked himself. He must hide the distaste, must not seem to be lording it over this man with the power of his checkbook, and weakening his dignity.

"Would you object to letting me see your bank statements for the past three or four months? That would give me some idea of what we're talking about."

"Not at all. You'll have to get them. They're in the file drawers in that closet."

And so, while Stern read at the desk, Paul spent the next two hours in the study of money, which, like the analysis of blood, reveals in a different way the life of the owner. When he had finished his notes and conclusions, he was left with both indignation and wonderment, both of which he curtailed.

"You understand," he said gently, "that I can't maintain you in this style. I'm afraid you'll have to make some changes. Painful changes."

Stern nodded. "Go on."

"The house. You spend a fortune on the gardens, it seems."

"They're very beautiful."

"They must be. And the real estate tax is enormous."

"It's a large property."

"And the country club. It's very pleasant, I'm sure, but the cost mounts up, doesn't it?"

Stern sighed. "Oh, yes, it mounts up, all right."

"And the rented villa in the Caribbean. And—"

Paul hated what he was having to say. It was like undressing a human being in public. But really, this flow of cash, out the minute it came in, was outrageous.

"It will be a new way of life," he said, and softening his manner with a smile, added, "I'm sorry to have to make this gift with so many strings attached to it."

"Not a gift," Stern said, "a loan. I'm accepting it only because I'm desperate. My children—you understand?" And again he drew himself up taller in the chair.

So proud. So proud, Paul said to himself. This is killing the man.

"All right, then," he agreed quietly, "a no-interest loan."

"No, no. Prime rate."

Paul smiled. "You're a stubborn cuss, aren't you? But I can be stubborn too. Since you won't take my gift, you'll have to take my interest-free loan. I'll send a quarterly check, but if anything should come up and you run short, I want you to let me know. Will you give me your word that you will?"

Stern nodded. Paul, seeing that he was overcome with emotion, got up. Dusk had fallen, so he lit the lamps. In the mild glow Stern's eyes shone wet, and Paul, who had not minded showing his own tears, bent over his checkbook and turned considerately away.

So proud, he thought again, but I can't help liking him. And aware that Stern was still unable to speak, he said lightly, "Well, I'd best be going. Good luck, and God bless you all."

He laid the check on the table, then pressed the other man's left hand and went out.

All the next day Paul's mind knew turmoil. Much had been clarified, that was true. But the trouble that was central to everything still lay smoldering like a hot coal. What was to become of Iris? And almost squinting with the effort of recalling her face, he imagined her abandoned in some ornate, overlarge house, sick at heart, floundering to explain to her children, then dismantling her home to move out. And would it be she who would live in that smaller house he had prescribed for them, or would it be Stern himself? Possibilities, all pitiable, all wretched, presented themselves to Paul; what he saw chiefly was a repetition of her mother's disrupted life, or worse. Far worse.

"You're a hundred miles away, Mr. Werner," said old Katie when she brought his eggs to the breakfast table.

"So I am, so I am."

Actually, he was thinking that somebody should be giving Iris some emotional support. She should not be alone with her pain. Her mother should be with her, her mother, who knew them both, must be the one to bring the husband and wife together. Or must try, at any rate. Paul frowned. Perhaps nobody could do it, but somebody ought to try. Definitely.

Absentmindedly, he buttered toast and ate the eggs. Stern would never appeal to Anna. He would never appeal to anyone for help. There was something too rigid about him; one didn't have to be a psychology major to see that. Or to know that it's the rigid branch that breaks first either. Well, thank goodness the money would keep the branch from breaking off; he'd be able to keep his children going, to reestablish himself. But that still left Iris.

And, just as on the road to Westchester he had abruptly veered off and gone to Stern, so now Paul shoved his chair away from his unfinished breakfast and stood up.

"Katie," he called, "I have to go out of town. I may be gone for a day or two, or I may be back very late tonight. So don't be alarmed if you hear me."

The Berkshires, Stern had said. She'd gone to the concerts at Tanglewood. She would be staying, then, somewhere close by. With a whole lot of persistence he should be able to find her.

He couldn't help but think of Ilse again while he threw some clothes into a bag. Would she, prime rescuer that she was, understand what he was about to do, or would she tell him again that he was "playing with fire"? Dear Ilse! He wanted to believe that she would understand.

But whether or not, he was on his way.

11

At the front desk a pleasant young man told him that Mrs. Friedman had just gone to read on the side lawn. He walked out again into a green-gold afternoon, the middle period, when all is somnolent, even the birds gone out of sight and hearing. The only sounds were the long-drawn late summer rattle of locusts and the chirp of crickets from the meadow beyond the split-rail fence that divided it from the lawn. People were talking under the broad shade of maples.

At the far end of the slope he saw her sitting with a book propped on a small rustic table. As she was partly turned away, he could not see her face, but he recognized her at once by her posture; there was something Edwardian, he had always thought, about the grace with which she moved or sat, about the long fluid lines of her legs and her neck and the very folds of her skirts. "Her serenity," Theo Stern had said, only yesterday.

His steps were soundless on the grass and he took his time to reach her because part of him wanted to flee. And then he astonished himself by hearing his own whisper: "I knew her when she was eighteen."

As if she had sensed that she was being observed, she turned and saw him, rose from her chair and sank back. An expression of alarm came over her face; her eyes widened and her lips parted, so that he had to speak quickly.

"Don't be upset, I haven't come to bother you anymore. . . . That's past. May I?" he asked, indicating the second chair.

"Please do."

"I've come for Iris's sake. No, don't be afraid. It's nothing bad."

She said somewhat sternly, "What do you know about Iris? What can you know about her?"

He saw that her breathing was rapid; the strand of pearls around her throat moved in and out.

"I only know what I heard from her husband. I went to his office yesterday for a checkup. You probably don't know that he operated on my shoulder a while back."

"I knew," she said, still sternly, "and I wondered why you had chosen him out of all the many you could have gone to. I tried to hope it had been a coincidence." And when he did not answer at once, she said, "Or else I thought you were playing a dangerous game and it made me very, very angry."

"Anna," he said, "I hope you won't stay angry. I have never made any trouble before, have I?"

"No."

"Well, then, I'm not going to make any now."

She gave him a long, quiet look and, apparently satisfied, asked him what he had come to tell her.

Confronted now with the actual moment of truth, he realized he had not sufficiently prepared himself. He had a quick flash of himself as a spy or diplomat, juggling his words, trying to keep separate the things he must tell one person while concealing them from another, all the time guarding against any fatal slip and disaster.

"As I told you, I went to the office. I found Dr. Stern alone there in a bad state, severely depressed. He's hurt his hand. He said you knew."

"Yes. He caught it in a door. But I didn't think—he didn't say it was anything much."

"He didn't want you to know how bad it was. He's lost three fingers. He won't be able to go back to work. The office is being closed."

Her hand went to her throat in a gesture of dismay.

"And the truth is," Paul continued, feeling, as he spoke, the full brutality of what he must say, "it was Iris who slammed the door."

"Oh, God," Anna whispered. And over her face there passed a look of piteous fear.

Paul spoke softly, rapidly now, to get it over with. "Of course they both understand it was a horrendous accident. But she"— and he thought again of himself as a diplomat or juggler who must keep all the balls in the air without letting any one touch another—"but she is filled with guilt in spite of it. It has torn them apart, it seems. He has left the house and is living in his office." He slowed down, having gotten safely past the attempt, if such it had been, at suicide. "They need help badly. Someone must talk to them, and of course, I—obviously . . ." He put out his hands palms up, almost in supplication. "That's why I'm here. I would never have come otherwise, you understand."

"Oh, Iris. Oh, Theo," Anna said. She looked fully at Paul. "And he will never work? That will kill him. What will he do?"

"He will study for two years." It was a relief to have something positive to say. "He wants to become an oncologist."

"I see."

"But it will entail big changes. He has no savings." And as her forehead creased in surprise, he asked, "I suppose you had no idea of that?"

"None at all!"

"Well, it seems that the money went out as fast as it came in. I have offered to lend him whatever is needed until he can get on his feet."

Almost imperceptibly, Anna's back stiffened. "That won't be necessary. I can help. I will go to him now."

"Anna, he won't accept anything from you. You are, after all, alone now." And in the sudden realization that something of the sort should be said, he said it: "I was sorry to read of your husband's death."

With a slight nod she acknowledged his sympathy. "Thank you."

He continued, "Forgive me, but although you are obviously not in want of anything, you are still not—"

"Not a rich woman, you're trying to say? No, but—"

"I, however, happen to be a rich man. I have never done anything for Iris, and you know how I have always felt about that."

She interrupted him with a low, frightened cry. "You haven't, have you? Haven't said anything to Theo—"

"No, no!" He was juggling again, balancing the words in thin, in very thin, air. "Of course I haven't. It's a business deal. Grateful patient, and all that, you see. It's unusual perhaps, but entirely plausible." And Paul managed a smile, as if to bring Anna along with him into a neat little conspiracy. "I had a hard time convincing him, I can tell you. As low as his spirits are, he's stiff-necked with pride."

"He always was. Although I am very fond of him," she said quickly. "He has been a son to me."

Ah, yes. Maury dead at twenty-three. I know, I know, Paul said silently.

"And a good husband and father. Oh, but Iris! Where is she?"

"At home. She sits in her room, he said. They have nothing to say to each other."

"It's so strange that he told you all these things."

"Not really. I'm old enough to be his father. I'm a stranger, and he needed desperately to talk to someone. It's always easier to talk to a stranger."

"That's true."

She gazed out across the lawn. A small wind stirred the leaves above her head, so that for an instant the sun broke through the dense shade and, dazzling in her eyes, revealed tears brimming on her lashes. He stared and blinked; he had forgotten that her lashes were gold.

She took out a handkerchief and wiped her eyes. "I have to go to them," she said.

"That's why I came, so that you would."

"And it's that bad between them?"

"It seemed so to me."

Then neither spoke. She was looking away again across the lawn. He was free to examine her. Her sheer cotton dress was the clear cool yellow of a crocus. Her hands lay gracefully in her lap. In this summer of 1968, this noisy year of shaggy hair and unwashed, sandaled feet, she seemed to have been left over from another time.

But her speech was quite current and modern. To Paul's surprise, she mused.

"There's something childlike in Iris. An innocence." And even more surprisingly, she said, "I'm no psychologist, but, you know, I always thought perhaps it was Joseph who kept her that way. I don't know. Before she was married, she wanted to teach slum children. She has great feeling for people whose lives are hard. She has talent. But he wouldn't allow her to go into those neighborhoods. They were what he came from, he said, and there was no reason for her to return to them."

"Her husband mentioned that she always wanted to go back to teaching. I gather he didn't approve either."

"I know." Anna frowned. As she seemed to be thinking, Paul waited until she spoke again. "It's odd. Has he no disability insurance?"

"I asked the same. Yes, but the wrong kind. The policy doesn't say that he must be unable to practice his specialty. As long as he can earn a living at anything else, selling cars or whatever, he's not covered. It was the insurance agent's careless, stupid mistake."

"And Theo's," she acknowledged sadly. "He was never a businessman. It's too bad he would not let Iris handle these things for him. She has a head for them. But he never would let her."

A waiter came with a pad and pencil. Anna asked, "Will you have some tea, Paul?"

His name was round on her lips. It echoed in his head. Paul. . . .

"Please. I'd like that," he replied, wanting only to prolong the time.

When the tray came she poured milk into his cup. She had remembered that he drank tea like an Englishman. He would have liked to comment upon her memory, but the remark would have been too intimate, and he did not make it. So he stirred and kept stirring the milky tea, while he watched her hands move over the tea things, the pot and the little plate of cakes. A fine ring glittered on her finger. Her husband's gift. He wondered how her hands would feel, touching him with love. Her skin was still silky; he could tell by her neck and her chest, where the pearls lay just above her breasts. Her body would still have kept some of youth's strength. Then he braked his thoughts. He hadn't known such thoughts were still in him after so long. And he felt a rise of something that was almost

anger. If it had been Ilse in Anna's position all those years
before, she wouldn't have had such scruples! She would have
come to him with their child, no matter what. It's true she had
left him for Israel. But a country wasn't a child, after all. Yes,
Ilse would have come to him. Still, maybe that wasn't being fair
to Anna. . . . How could he really know what she had felt for
the man she had married? It was all too complex. He mustn't
let his mind wander.

Anna was speaking. "Things began so well for them. And
now this folly, this ruin. I remember the day they were married."

Yes, Paul thought, I remember it too. Ilse and I were hidden
on the sidewalk, watching them drive away. That was the day I
rid my soul of you, Anna.

He steadied himself, saying gently, "Perhaps it needn't be
ruined after all. Perhaps you can reason with them."

"They're stubborn, both of them. Theo even more so." She
seemed about to add something else, but stopped.

From behind a hedge came a clear, exultant cry and the ping
of tennis balls. *Ping! Ping!* they went. And he thought how
queer it was that they two were sitting here in this place on a
summer afternoon, having tea together.

"You see," she said after a minute or two, "in a way, Theo
still lives in prewar Vienna. He was a very rich boy. He grew up
in elegance. They had a mountain lodge in the Arlberg, and his
mother took the children with her to a suite in a Paris hotel
while she ordered her clothes twice a year. He loves beauty and
order, perfection in everything, while Iris . . ." Anna gave a
small rueful laugh.

Paul waited until she resumed. "He wants to run a family like
an operating room, too. Luckily for him it works with the children, all except one."

"I know. He told me."

"Steve was an unusual child, gifted, really. He could do
anything well, from tennis to chemistry. He read the newspa-

pers and formed his own opinions, often"—and here Anna gave the rueful laugh again—"often not his father's opinions. And so there were sometimes tensions."

That fine, proud man with his Old World memories, and the young man of the sixties, young man in a hurry and sure that he's right, Paul thought; it was easy to see how those two might clash.

"He thinks Iris has been too indulgent of Steve, but that's not so. She has a wonderful way with children. She understands them. They loved her as a teacher. She's very competent, and they've asked her again and again to come back."

"And she would like to?"

"Oh, yes, if it were up to her—"

"Then you must tell her to do it," Paul said promptly. "We have one life and we must do what we *want* with it," he added with emphasis.

"It's not always possible to do what we want to do," Anna said, in a low voice with his same emphasis.

For the first time since they had started speaking, she looked straight into his eyes. He returned the look, but it became suddenly too difficult for him, and he turned away from it.

Then she, too, turned away, saying, "She has never been sure of herself, Iris hasn't. I used to think she felt different in the family, unsure of her place, for no reason that I can figure out, because I never . . ." She did not finish.

"Of course not," Paul said.

"And somehow it carried over with Theo. I know it, but I never knew why."

He spoke soberly. "It is just one of many things one never knows."

The sun had fallen behind a great sailing cloud, dimming the day as if in accord with the fall of their voices. With effort Paul reenergized himself.

"So you will go to the rescue?"

"I shall leave tomorrow morning. I'll say I got bored being away so long."

"Then I've done what I came to do."

"You have, and I thank you. I'm sorry if I wasn't very cordial when I saw you coming toward me."

"Understandable." He stood up and gave her his hand. "I shall of course be wondering and hoping that peace will follow all of this. No doubt I'll be hearing from Dr. Stern, since"—and here Paul gave a small, self-mocking smile—"since, after all, I am his creditor."

Her hand was alive in his; he felt the narrow bones and the padded, warm palm. He dropped it quickly and walked away.

Before driving off, he turned to look. She had moved from the chair and was standing with her back to a hydrangea bush. We called them snowballs, he remembered. The last thing he saw was the blooming white bush and her arm raised in farewell.

Their talk, interspersed with long, strained, apprehensive silences, had been going on for an hour or more, and it was now past midnight. A band of eerie light from a lamp at the library window lay on the grass. Beyond it the darkness was a comfort, making their faces almost invisible to each other and making it easier to say things that would have been almost unsayable under revealing light. And Theo, after his habit of feeling an event from the utmost depth of being while at the same time watching it as an inquisitive onlooker might do, thought with painful irony that this prosperous pair, sitting on a terrace on a quiet summer night, would make an attractive advertisement for lawn furniture or a fashionable drink—except that the hand so conspicuously resting on the chair's arm would have to be airbrushed out of the picture.

"I suppose it could be possible for me someday to see your hand without flinching," Iris said.

Thinking, This must be the hundredth time since the accident that she has said it, he answered patiently, "I don't know how many ways I can tell you that it will be."

In a way, to a very different degree, he was reminded of his own avoidance of that woman at the office; he had been using another entrance ever since because he couldn't bear to look into her face. And this thought led him to Iris's aborted adventure and her poor little humiliated admission, which two weeks earlier, would have brought him to a jealous fury and outrage, but now brought him only to pity and sadness. Perhaps that was because of what he had learned about her, although surely it was not pitiable to have Paul Werner as a father—had the circumstances been the right ones. Down these twisted, connecting paths his mind traveled.

Iris spoke again abruptly. "I'm looking up at the roof. I should expect it to have caved in from all that's been happening beneath it. But there it is, still solid, as if it didn't know or didn't care."

"It hasn't caved in," Theo said, still patiently, "because we are not going to let it. I've told you, and I will tell you again, I've already inquired about a residency in oncology. I'm well known in the medical world, and I'm almost sure to get a good one. In a few years we'll be on our feet again. This family is going to hold together. God help us, it is."

"And the money for all this?"

"Oh, I had some put away." He made his voice light and casual. "And the bank has agreed to a loan. When we sell this house and tighten our belts, we'll pull through."

"You've seemed so hopeless. You wouldn't talk about anything. Now where have all these ideas suddenly come from?" she asked, wondering.

"I needed some time to think, that's all."

His confidence increased with the words. It was like what is said about a smile: The more you do it, the more you feel like doing it. The more confident he made himself sound, the more confident he felt.

She sighed. "So you have it all planned out."

"One has to try." Theo made acknowledgment, thinking, It was not I; I was floundering, I was dying in that chair when he came in. A quiet power, the man had had. One would never think of him as old; there was a kind of shining to him. I've been surreptitiously searching ever since for what there may be of him in Iris. They're both dark and aquiline, but then, so many people are. And one finds what one wants to find. I think also of Anna, and I feel a vague aching. Yes, they would have gone well together. Yes, I can see that. For with all his solid virtues, the husband was far less the man for her than Paul Werner would have been. I am a romantic at heart; God knows, that has been my trouble.

And as he sat there in the stillness, his mind went on puzzling. Without meaning to or knowing that she was doing it, had Anna treated this unwelcome child in some way differently, more kindly, perhaps too kindly, to compensate? He had to remark the contrast between the mother and the daughter; yet was it a fundamental one, or only the natural contrast between a foreign woman, reared in want, and another reared softly in America? It is too complex for me, he thought, and anyway it is all done and over with and cannot be altered.

Iris's voice came with unexpected emphasis, making a declaration. "My mother said I must do what I want now."

"What is it you want?" he asked.

"You know what. You've always known, although you never understood how much I wanted it."

"Perhaps I didn't."

"You never understood a lot about me."

"I thought I did, Iris. Haven't I always been loving to you?"

She made a small sound that might have been a swallowed sob. "That morning after I came back from the hospital, I woke up early, and the first thing I saw from the bed was the oak at the window. It was so beautiful, so alive. . . . And I thought, Oh, I don't want to die. I never did want to."

"I believe that," he said softly. "Listen, you will do whatever you want with your life. Go to work, get a master's degree, even a doctorate, if you will. Everything will be different, I promise you."

"My mother said, and I see she's right, that you must speak out, you must insist. It's strange that she didn't always talk that way. It was as if something or somebody had opened her eyes, and so she opened mine too. I've been so jealous of you, Theo, and she always used to tell me I must never let you see it. I can't imagine what changed her."

Iris moved in the chair so that the beam of light from the window crossed her face, and he saw in it an earnest, passionate expression that was completely unfamiliar.

"All my life I was a second choice. I was nothing compared with my brother. Mama was so proud of him. And even Papa . . . I used to feel that he was giving me all that lavish love to console me for being less of a person than my brother was. Then you came with all your women and the wife you lost in the Holocaust. And I knew you longed for her. Liesel . . . she was so beautiful, people said."

A bird, uttering a single cry, left in the stillness an echo of its alarm. And Theo wanted to flee, to go into the safety of the house, to sleep and think no more. But "You must be truthful with each other. You must hide nothing," Paul had said.

So he answered steadily, "I didn't long for her in the way you put it. It wasn't what you think. I've never told you."

"Secrets, Theo! Don't keep secrets. Tell me now."

He lay back on the chair. It was queer that, with this sudden challenge, his hand, which had not bothered him all day, should start throbbing again. Psychosomatic. He had to clear his throat before he began, as if the very words themselves, words never before spoken to another soul, had sharp, rusty edges.

"You see, there was something that happened in the week I was to leave for America to arrange to bring the family over.

Somebody sent me two dirty, anonymous letters about—about her. They said she was meeting a man in her chamber-music group, a violinist. I knew him, of course; I knew them all. He was young, poor, and good-looking, rather touching in his shabby jackets. I couldn't believe it. Those dirty letters—and my wife. I was ashamed to mention them to her. And maybe—no, not maybe—I was also afraid. Suppose there was some truth in them? I began to reflect. We had had a very short engagement because her parents had pressed for a quick marriage, which had delighted and also surprised me. And so, when this happened, it came to me that possibly they could have been in a hurry to get her away from an unknown musician with small prospects, and safely into a marriage with a doctor of good family and with the best prospects. Wouldn't it have been only natural? I knew enough, as young as I was, about the way the world works. So I tortured myself, while at the same time despising myself for having such vile suspicions.

"But I had to know. And so I waited down the street from the place where they had their rehearsals and watched them come out together carrying their music. I followed them quite a distance into a poor district of the city and saw them go into a house, very probably his house. I felt—I cannot tell you how I felt . . . so angry that I suppose I could have killed, but at the same time sick and exhausted from the shock. For a while I waited on the street, but then it became too shameful, too degrading, to be standing there like a spy, and I turned about and went home.

"It was much later, almost dinnertime, when she came in. I had been busy the last days winding up affairs, so she was surprised to see me already home so early and quietly reading. I asked her about her day. She said she had taken the baby for a walk and gone shopping. I said I thought I had seen her walking toward the Ringstrasse—where I had not been all that day. 'Could it have been you?' I asked to trick her. 'Why, yes,' she said, 'I bought you a heavy sweater to wear on the ship.' I asked

her, feeling sicker and uglier with my lie, to let me see it. 'Oh,'
she said, 'they didn't have your size. I'll have to go back and
pick it up tomorrow. Why didn't you stop if you saw me?' 'I was
on the tram. And what was your day?' I asked, smiling. 'Well, I
went to rehearsal. We worked on the Mozart, which made us
very late, and here I am.' She looked straight at me with clear,
honest eyes. But when you are lying, it's usual to affect simplicity and candor. Oh, I wanted to say much more, but I was afraid
to. I didn't want to believe, you see. I wanted to find some
excuse for her. Besides, I told myself, there was no time because I was going away; it would have to wait until we had both
left Vienna behind. Perhaps there was nothing serious to it
after all. . . . Musicians are often loose living. . . . And she
would never be seeing the fellow again.

"So then I left, and I shall never know."

A long, heavy silence fell, as when a fairy tale has bewitched
an audience of children, or a dream has revealed things ancient, hidden, and astonishing.

Theo, having come to the end, now waited for Iris to speak.
But his unburdening and the very cadences of his voice had
touched her too sharply for immediate speech. As if through an
old-fashioned stereoscope or through a telescope, she was seeing another Theo, very young and rather tender. She had never
been in Vienna, but had seen enough pictures to form one of
her own: He was standing on a street of old houses with narrow
windows; it was a raw gray afternoon in March, and he was
facing the wind, looking up at one of the windows. Rejected
and grown somehow smaller, "Can this be happening to me?"
he would have been asking himself. Had he felt just then as I so
often have? Iris wondered. And she saw him differently from
any way she had ever seen him before, not diminished, only
more vulnerable and not very different from herself. . . . Not
very different from the self who, in precarious balance and for
petty revenge, had weighed her own worth by the cheap flattery
of a stranger.

"I'm sorry, Theo," she said at last. "I'm very sorry." And she thought, For the first time we have seen each other really naked, underneath the skin.

He raised his voice. "I mourn for the little boy I lost, my first child. I don't know how he died. And sometimes I think that has something to do with the anger I feel toward Steve, because Steve is alive and ought to do better with his life. Strange, isn't it?"

"Not really," she said, because in a way she really understood. Yet at the same time she said to herself, It's your pride too, Theo, quite apart from the child you lost. It's because you're ashamed that Dr. Stern's son should be one of the bearded rebels.

And then she told him, "I am always more worried about him than I am angry."

"I know. Don't you think I worry too? Perhaps, though, I should worry a little less, and you should be a little more angry."

"You must have seen in yesterday's papers some more about that professor he has attached himself to, that Timothy Powers. We have to get him away from those people, Theo. Don't you see that we have to?"

"But we can't do it. No one can change him or help him until he wants to change."

She did not agree, but seeing no sense in going back again over trodden ground, did not argue the point, just said with irony, "He certainly shatters our middle-class respectability, doesn't he? When I think of the things that have happened to us in these few days to shatter this image we've had of ourselves!"

How abrupt the descent, she thought: Theo's affair at the office that night; her own absurd fiasco with Jordaine; her own attempt, or what surely looked like an attempt, at suicide.

Theo had been having a different thought. "This is a community where appearance counts for almost everything. Retrenching won't be easy for you or for the children, I'm afraid."

"We'll manage," she answered firmly.

The moon had broken through clouds and the garden was suddenly illuminated. At its far end the long row of arborvitae stood like black spears, unmoving in the windless night. The ground shone like opals, and the pool was silver. Theo had designed a small, perfect haven, expecting to stay here forever. Glancing over at him, she saw that he, too, was feeling the enchantment of moonglow and with it the wrench of loss. How often had she looked at the richness of this home and found it a worry, an unneeded burden! Yet now that it had to be given up, she was not as accepting as she would have predicted.

Enormous changes awaited them, and the very physical effort to make them all was daunting, or could be if one let it. She was not going to let it. For the first time in her life she was looking into a future of confusion and struggle; she was tired already, and yet sure of being able to cope with it.

At least there would be no parting. She was suddenly too weary now to analyze her immediate emotions toward Theo except to feel a deep relief. He had come back refreshed and as if renewed after those few days at the office, when she had thought all was lost between them. Something extraordinary had happened to him. It was mystifying. . . .

A cooling ripple of wind shook the air and stirred the leaves.

"It must be near dawn," Theo said. "Let's go in." At the door he leaned down and kissed her cheek lightly. "It'll be all right, Iris. Trust me."

"Yes," she told him. "Yes, I will. And trust myself too."

A beginning had to be made.

12

Then the long climb began. After the house was sold, the darkest day came when the movers arrived. It was then that reality took final shape. There is something about the dismantling of a house, Iris thought, especially when one is not leaving it because one wants to and is going to a better place, that is unutterably sad; it is a hundred little deaths as one object after the other is hoisted on indifferent shoulders and carried out. There went the enormous piano, once Theo's treasure and now Philip's, which was to be squeezed into a living room where it would take up almost half the space. There went the portrait of a dark-haired woman that Theo had brought home to surprise her on one sunny anniversary, their ninth, she remembered; he always insisted that it looked like her, although she herself had never seen any resemblance. Cartons of fine English china were carried away, wedding presents and gifts from Mama, who for some reason could never resist china; it would surely find no place anymore in the Sterns' house, not only because there would be no room to store it all, but also because they would no longer be living the life for which such things were intended. Since the new house had only a crawl space for attic, they were to be stored in Anna's house. It made absolutely no sense to Iris that these things which, with the exception of the piano, she had never particularly wanted, now seemed to be protesting as though they were alive, at being taken from their home.

Theo had walked out to the rear garden and was standing alone with his back to the commotion going on inside. She knew he must be memorizing the scene: white rhododendrons —he had specified white because of its coolness against dark grass; the small reflecting pool in the corner, overhung with a lavish weeping willow; it had been a thin wand, only shoulder high, when he had brought it home and placed it exactly where it ought to go, turning the earth for it himself; she could still see him making his decisive calculation, predicting the height that it had now attained. Other eyes after today would watch its long, limp branches sway in the faintest summer wind, Iris thought, knowing that he was thinking that too; but those other eyes would not see it in its loveliness as he would. Yes, that was sure, for these new owners were not the kind of people who would stand still to contemplate a branch moving in the wind. And she felt Theo's loss as her own.

Two men had come around to the back and were picking up some furniture that stood at the far end of the garden beyond the pool. These were fine teakwood chairs, a table and a gracefully rounded bench, all weathered into a soft silver gray. They had come from England and were Theo's choice. On sunny, chill fall days, he had liked to read on that bench while wearing his sheepskin jacket.

"You'll freeze out there," she had always said, and he had always replied that he liked the cold on his face as long as his shoulders were warm.

Defeated, he asked now as she came toward him, "Why are we taking those things? We've no room for them. Ought to sell them, that's all."

"No. We'll make room. I'll figure out a way."

It had taken only a few months to sell the house and go through the formalities of the closing. Iris had expected some money to put by, the difference between the value of this house and that of the new one, which was merely a cramped imitation Tudor with nooks, corners, leaded windows, gables, and false Elizabethan beams, standing in a small yard on a street of similar houses at the old, unfashionable end of town. Within walking distance of the train station and the shops, it was a world away from these quiet, open spaces. But to her astonishment there was nothing to put by, for a few years before, Theo, without telling her, had mortgaged this house.

"Why? Why?" she had demanded, keeping her anger and dismay under control.

"Because," he had explained, "everyone said it's smarter to invest than to let money lie idly tied up in a house."

But he had not invested; instead he had spent. She saw that he was ashamed, and spoke of it no more.

Action was the thing. There was a shortage of teachers in the community, and Iris's application was accepted almost as soon as the words were out of her mouth. A full-time position would be available for the coming fall, while in the meantime she was kept busy working as a substitute.

"Well," Theo said now, "this is it. Are we ready to go?"

"Ready," she answered.

So they drove away. The new owners came for the keys, exchanged polite good wishes, and watched the Sterns go down the drive for the last time. Theo went first, following the van. Iris went in the station wagon with the dog and Laura's cat.

"But this place was never really ours, was it?" She spoke aloud to the animals on the backseat. "I never knew that all the time it actually belonged to the bank."

She would miss it nevertheless, the Japanese calm of the glass walls that brought the summer indoors, as well as the white shine of winter, blue on the crusted drifts and powder on the holly.

And, too, she thought wistfully, I prided myself on being so practical with all the built-ins. I never thought about moving, did I, and not being able to take them with us?

Fortunately, Anne had several unused bedrooms and had given them enough bureaus, cabinets, and bookshelves to furnish the new rooms. She had provided curtains too, beflowered "cozy" prints that went with the nineteenth-century furniture that Iris disliked and Theo admired.

A little cluster of neighborhood children stood on the sidewalk watching the van being unloaded as Iris drove up. Among them she recognized some of her "own" sixth-graders.

"My mother's bringing over a pie, Mrs. Stern," called one of the boys.

Theo will hate this place, she thought, as she watched him maneuver his Mercedes into the narrow garage at the end of the short driveway. In the yard next door half a dozen children were whooping on a swing set. He would surely hate that too. And she had a mental picture of him reading on his English bench in his private corner back of the quiet pool.

Pearl was in the kitchen. She had offered to stay and help straighten out the house, after which she would look for another position. There was no room for her here, nor was there money to pay the rather handsome wages she had been earning. Now, with sleeves rolled, she was scrubbing the kitchen counters. She looked up and smiled.

"They left it nice and clean, Mrs. Stern."

"It's a bit different from the other one, isn't it, Pearl?"

Dim and dingy, with worn linoleum and old-fashioned

wooden cabinets, it was a contrast to the airy space where Pearl had rolled dough and tossed salads on marble countertops.

"With a coat of paint it'll be pretty," Pearl said, giving stout comfort. "Yellow would be nice."

Weakly she made herself agree. "You're right, Pearl. It'll bring the sun in."

And Pearl, still comforting, continued, "Dr. Stern, now that the bandages are off and he can move his fingers, he's more like himself."

"That's true."

"And working again in the hospital."

For Theo had begun a two-year training program in oncology at a New York hospital, an undertaking vast enough and new enough to be daunting.

"That's true." And suddenly, overwhelmed with everything, Iris's eyes filled and she put her arms around Pearl. "Oh, we are going to miss you," she cried. And then, laughing a little, "And I don't mean your cooking, either."

"I know, I know that, Mrs. Stern."

The back door opened and Laura appeared, carrying her schoolbooks. She stood staring about the kitchen.

"It's so queer to be coming home here," she said slowly.

"You don't like it, Laura, I understand."

"Well, Mom, what do you expect me to say?"

Iris's throat ached with the effort to sound brave. "I expect you to say we're going through a bad time, but at least we are together." She thought: You can't know how bad a time or how close we came to not being together. "Come. I'll show you the upstairs," she said.

There were three small bedrooms and a fourth much smaller one, intended to be a sewing room in a time when people still had dresses made at home. This was to be Philip's. Jimmy and Steve were away and could share a room whenever they might be here. Neither would be likely ever to live at home again. God alone knew where Steve was heading! As for Jimmy, at the rate he was going with his girl, Janet, and far, far too young as he was, he would probably be married before long. Well, she was a fine girl and one had to be grateful for that.

Laura would have her own room, of course. The furniture had already been placed there. Between the bed, the desk, the bookcases, and the armoire, which, they both saw at once, had been gashed in its passage up the narrow staircase, there was barely room enough to walk. Dark shades at half rise threw greater gloom over the walls and the brown floor. Laura took one long look and sat down on the bare mattress.

"Oh, Mom! It's horrible," she wailed, forlorn and in tears.

"It isn't the greatest," admitted Iris. And she had a flash of self-revelation, rather humbling: Oh, wasn't I proud and pleased with my superior self for not caring about "things"! Well, but I had always had them, hadn't I? Yes, I could well afford the luxury of not caring.

"And all because you slammed the door on Dad's hand," Laura cried.

Iris felt as if she had been stabbed, but she answered only, "Don't ever let him see you crying, do you hear? Now, hang up your clothes, straighten the room, and do the best you can," she said as she went out.

She stood at the window in the upstairs hall looking down at the street. The moving van had driven off and here, finally, they were. All, all was changed. The change had already sobered her children, so swiftly had it overturned what had seemed to be an unchangeable, established order. Iris wondered with irony whether "we are simple enough for Steve at last?" There was no more country club with its pool and no more backyard pool of their own; they'd have to go to the Y to swim, where Theo now took his exercise, since his tennis days were over. But these were trivialities, not to be compared with the enormity of their father's personal tragedy. Among the four it was Steve who had seemed to be most shaken. He had come home when he heard the news, not out of love, Iris knew; there had been too much bad blood between Theo and him for that; he had come home merely out of a basic, ordinary sense of decency, much as one attends a funeral even when one hasn't liked the deceased. He had had the least to say, and yet his had been the most visible recoil from the sight of Theo's mutilation.

I think . . . I feel . . . I don't know what I feel, she said to herself. It's as if somebody has thrown a cloak over my head. Her eyes were still on the street below, not seeing.

After a while she roused herself and went downstairs.

Here the furniture had all been crowded in. The blond Danish woods made a hopeless contrast to the mud-colored walls. Musty, Iris thought. The place is dingy and musty.

Pearl had supper on the dining-room table, fried chicken, a salad, and an apple pie. I shall have to do all the cooking, Iris told herself, and I'm not a very good cook, either. Laura is, she loves to, so she'll help. They all ate their meal in silence. Even Philip, who was normally lively, was subdued.

After dinner some neighbors came to introduce themselves. They were welcoming and friendly, free with advice about the best market and the dry cleaner who delivered. It was the kind of happening that would never be encountered in the old neighborhood, Iris knew, and felt the warmth of it. Yet after they had left the kitchen counters loaded with their gifts, cakes, a basket of strawberries, even homemade bread, she felt for a second a sharp stab of distaste. It felt like charity! Then she was terribly ashamed.

In the days that followed, it was Philip who accepted the change most easily. Twelve now, he had much of Jimmy's friendly nature and much of Steve's brilliance although, thank heaven, none of the restlessness that had been so apparent in Steve at the same age. He was satisfied with his little room and took a certain pride in having his mother teach at his school. In the evenings he sat down at the piano and played for his parents as willingly as he always had, and as though nothing were different.

His teacher had recently given him a book of Chopin's waltzes. Twilight music, Iris had privately called it, lovers' music to listen to or to dance to. But now it produced a shiver down her spine. The last time she had heard it, so beautifully played, had been that night at Carnegie Hall. The music stopped and Philip's waiting face was turned toward his parents in expectation of praise.

"Wonderful!" said Theo, looking up from the desk that he had managed to fit into one of the nooks, where he sat and studied.

It was Iris's turn to say something. "Your fingering is excellent. You have the right fingers for piano, anyway." And, shocked at the very sound of the word *fingers,* she stopped. But no one noticed, or if anyone had, no one gave indication. She supposed the word would never cease to pierce her through, although they never spoke about the accident anymore. All that could be said had certainly been said.

As it happened, they did not speak very much to each other about anything these days. Theo's desk was piled with books. It had been years since he had needed to memorize, and she supposed it must be a stupendous effort to get back into the habit. As for herself, she had papers to mark in the evenings and lessons to prepare for the next day. Fortunately, she had plenty of physical energy and was able to do all the things that were required of her in the household besides, not too skillfully it was true, but nevertheless they were accomplished. She did them by rote, mechanically, because they had to be done. Within her at the same time lay a deep mental tiredness, an absence of anything more than a wish to get through each day; she wondered, but did not ask, whether that could be true for Theo, too.

Sometimes it seemed that she saw him only in passing and said only things that had to be said, nothing abstract, no exchanges of ideas or emotion, merely talk of schedules and necessities. They were good to each other and considerate as they had always been, but—

How shall I put it? she asked herself. There is a nothingness; yes, that's the best word, not a very good one, but that's it, a nothingness. Or maybe a little more than that, a sorrow over not feeling anymore the things I used to feel, even the jealousy and the torments that used to interrupt the sweetness.

So the atmosphere in the little house was chastened, for although crisis had passed and peace reigned, there was still a heavy cloud over Iris, and she knew it, and knew that inevitably it had spread over the house as well.

One day when she stopped at her mother's house, she saw a man getting into an old foreign car and driving away. As her car moved slowly up toward the door, she had a clear look at him: a very tall man and slender, with pepper-and-salt hair. There was something about him that she thought she recognized, for she had always had a remarkable memory for people, so that Theo had used to joke that she would have made a good politician.

Anna was in her little yellow study wearing a silk dress.

"You look as if you're about to go someplace," Iris said. "Am I interrupting?"

"You're not, and I'm not going anywhere," Anna replied.

Did she seem to be perhaps a little bit agitated?

"You had company, I see."

"Yes," Anna said.

"That was quite a fancy car."

"Was it? I didn't notice."

And Iris kept on, aware as she spoke that it was nasty to pry this way, "I thought I recognized him."

"Your curiosity seems to be getting the better of you," Anna observed rather sharply.

At that Iris shrugged, affecting indifference. "Not really."

"All right, since you're obviously dying to know. It was Paul Werner."

"Oh, he! The strangest man! He always seems to turn up at the oddest places."

"Odd? What's odd about coming to visit an old friend?"

The rebuke was so unlike her mother. "I guess I didn't know he was such an old friend," she said uncomfortably.

"I knew him years ago, you know that. He's leaving for a long stay in Europe, and so he's been going about to say good-bye to people. He happened to be visiting in Westchester this afternoon, that's all."

After the first strange one-syllable replies this detailed explanation seemed equally suspicious. And Anna's cheeks were definitely heated. Then Iris embarrassed herself with her own ugly suspicion. It was absurd. A woman of Mama's age! So soon after her husband's death too, the husband to whom she had been so devoted. Absurd. Nevertheless, that evening she mentioned the occurrence to Theo.

"It just seems strange. The man turns up in such unexpected ways, coming to you for surgery, for instance. When I was a child, as I've told you, we seemed to meet him always by accident, by coincidence. I remember two or three times quite distinctly, so something must have made an impression on me," she mused vaguely.

Theo looked up from the notebook, holding the pen in the air. It was remarkable that he had learned to hold it quite nicely.

"Why should it upset you?" he asked mildly.

"I don't know. It doesn't exactly upset me, it annoys me. I always remember feeling that he looked too hard at Mama and that she was aware of it."

"Imagination," Theo said.

"Well, all the same, I don't like him. I simply don't."

"Aren't you making a mountain out of a molehill?"

"I suppose so. But I simply don't like him," she repeated,

and refrained from adding, since it would have seemed too exaggerated, He gives me queer thoughts.

"Well, it's unimportant," Theo said, kindly enough. He returned to his notebook. "We have far more important things to think about, you and I."

13

"So you are back to normal,"
Paul remarked.

"Whatever normal means," Theo answered.

The man is an enigma, Paul thought. There had been moments when he had been so completely forthcoming that Paul had retreated, almost embarrassed at being told too much, and then other moments when, after asking what he thought was an acceptable question, he felt a door being closed in his face. Nevertheless, Paul was glad to be with him. It had been almost a year since that extraordinary day in Theo's moribund office, and now they were sitting among a noontime crowd having lunch in a midtown restaurant. The meeting had been arranged at Theo's behest, for Paul, having effected his "rescue," had felt it a matter of tact to stay away until asked for.

"Are things going well for you in the money department?"

"It's working out, it's a new regime. I sound sheepish, do I? Well, I am, a bit. It's surprising how many things one learns one hasn't really needed and can get along well without. Iris and Philip share the cooking, now that Laura's gone off to college. Whoever gets home first from school sets the table. Philip and I help clean up afterward. Then we all three get to our various books."

"You must have a load of books in your new specialty."

"I'm working under a marvelous mentor, one of the best in the field. I haven't learned so many new facts in years. It stretches the mental muscles. You rescued me, Paul, and not only financially. You restored my spirit."

Very much moved, Paul made no answer, but raised the coffee cup to his lips and hid behind it.

"Iris plans to go for a master's degree next semester. Night classes. It'll be a heavy load with the house and all. But amazingly, her mother"—Theo hesitated over the name—"Anna, is encouraging her. It was she, you know, who really brought Iris around when she came back unexpectedly from the country that time. She said she had just had a feeling, something told her she was needed, and so she simply got in the car and came back."

Now it was Theo's turn to raise the cup and linger over it; above the rim Paul saw a pair of thoughtful eyes cast downward.

When he put the cup back, Theo said, "I understand you've seen her."

Paul started. "What?" Surely Anna hadn't told—

"Iris saw you leaving the house."

"Oh! Well, yes." Paul felt the flush rise up his neck.

A curving driveway; a car had entered the far end of the semicircle just as he had come out of the house.

"I haven't told you, have I? No, of course I haven't. Well, I shall be going to Italy for a while. I'm renting a house on Lake Maggiore. I had an idea, a crazy one after all these years, that since she was free now—that maybe she might consider going with me."

"And she wouldn't."

"Not a chance. I should damn well have known better."

Yes, he should. It had been a wild, aberrant idea. He wasn't even sure, now that he thought about it, that he wouldn't have been somewhat dismayed if it had worked out. Anna was right a thousand times over: the complications were too horrendous even to consider.

And still Paul knew, as his eyes met those of the man sitting opposite, that this man would understand. They had an affinity, Theo and he. Who would have believed it?

He said abruptly, "This is something I've always wanted to do. I always think the Italian lakes are the most beautiful places on earth."

"I know. I used to go there, a couple of thousand years ago."

Memories. Theo would live with his, as we all do. And Paul said, "I've been feeling rather tired lately. I need to get away. If not now, when?"

"Of course. How long will you be gone?"

"I took a lease for a year. I might stay longer, I can't be sure. But your check will arrive on the first of every month, and you will have my address."

The other responded quickly, "I didn't mean that."

"I know you didn't. I meant, I should like to hear from you, to know what's happening. About your son, for instance."

"Steve? He's left college. There was a tragedy on the campus. You may have read about that professor who lost his legs when a bomb went off."

"I read it. A horror."

"Steve had nothing to do with it. But it shook him. Apparently he knew some people in the group that was probably responsible. So he left. Threw his education out of the window just before commencement and left. We never hear from him. His brother does now and then, just a card that says nothing except that he's alive on a commune somewhere in California. Making moccasins or God knows what. Oh," Theo cried with passion, "the waste! The waste. He was an A student. I blame it on the professors, Powers and his ilk, all of them roaming around the country dragging these young fools behind them."

Paul was thinking, He won't have to do any dragging, Timothy won't. Quite clearly he could recall Timothy's bright face and his candid way. They would follow him gladly, these young who were only waiting for someone to follow. He thought with a quick thrust of pain that his grandson, the unknown whom he had never seen and almost surely never would see, was among them. And resentment of Timothy was bitter in his mouth.

"Was Powers involved in that affair?" he asked.

"No, Powers keeps his nose clean. He's just an orator, Jimmy says. Steve's still in touch with him, though. Powers approves of what Steve's doing, taking a rest. Ah, God only knows what it will all come to."

Delicately, Paul broached a delicate subject. "And Iris? Have the two of you come to agreement about the boy?"

"We don't talk about him. To tell you the truth, we don't talk much at all." And as Paul said nothing, Theo continued, "There's an aftermath to the truthfulness that you recommended—if you remember that you did."

"I remember."

"Things are said, things one never knew about each other, never suspected had happened or could happen. One sees the other through changed eyes, so that we're not back exactly where we were before. I don't know whether I make myself clear."

"Perfectly."

So Iris must have told him about that man. And the unpleasant image of Jordaine, remarkably vivid when one considered that he had only seen the man once, rose up before Paul.

"It's all peaceful, but Iris is depressed. Although she denies it, I see it plainly. There's a rift, a space between us, an abyss that wasn't there before all this happened." Theo paused, frowning and reflecting. "And yet it probably was there, covered over so that we didn't recognize it."

"You'll cross the abyss one day," Paul said, glancing at Theo's hand, in which a fork was held between a thumb and two stiff fingers. The man had guts. Not easy to lose everything, start over, and keep that dignity, the head high, striped tie, the pocket handkerchief in place. . . . And he continued, "It's a funny thing about truths. Bad as they can be, I've always found that they clear things up in the end."

Theo raised his eyebrows. "Surely not every truth?"

"My God no! Not *every* one." Paul sighed. "Sometimes I feel absurd talking to you like this, as though I were an advice columnist. I've hardly done so well with truths in my own life." And he amended quickly, not liking the pathetic sound of the latter phrase, "In one respect, I mean. Just that one."

"You've made generous amends, if that's the right word, though I don't think it is."

The restaurant was becoming noisier with the sounds of departure, chairs scraped back and voices raised in good-byes. Lunchtime was over, and Theo looked at his watch, explaining, "I'm due back."

"Of course. You will write to me, then? But I won't answer. Letters have a way of falling into the wrong hands, no matter how careful one is."

"I'll write to you, Paul."

"Yes, I should like to know how you are, now that I know you a little."

"Paul? I understand more than you think I do. And I will write to you often about everyone. Everyone."

And the two men stood, shook hands, and walked away in opposite directions.

Paul had wrapped things up as neatly as he was able; there was no one who needed him now—more's the pity—so he was quite free, and his mind was already bound for Italy.

Old friends, warm friends, a Roman lawyer and his wife, had found a house for him, assuring him that it was not too large; it had been a stroke of luck to find it, since, as he must know, most of the villas along the lakes were enormous. This one lay between an olive grove (smooth, ancient, silver trunks) and the lake (still as a pool in the starlight). A cook came with it (pastas, and salads fragrant with basil) and a wonderful garden (purple velvet pansies around the base of a little fountain, spouting water from a marble cherub's mouth). The house was named Villa Jessica.

Why, Ilse had written, why Italy? Couldn't he spend a wonderful year in Israel with her instead? He supposed he could, and in a way he was tempted. But Israel was a strenuous place, and besides, Ilse would be working; he knew her schedules, and what was he to do, sit around until evening waiting for her? No, rest was what he craved now, under the Italian sun. Lately his breath had begun to come short, especially on stairs; he didn't like to think about that.

So Ilse was going to come to him instead. But not right away, she wrote, to his disappointment. She had opened a clinic in a poor neighborhood for mothers and babies; it was just starting to function; she was still short of good nurses and couldn't leave it just yet.

He understood, or rather, he made himself understand. He only hoped she wouldn't keep him waiting too long. A man didn't want to eat his dinner alone on the terrace with candles and flowers. A man needed . . .

Oh, the last of the romantics, I am! The body gets old while you still feel young, with all the craving for love and beauty still intact. Young people think you're a fool, but they don't know; wait till they get there.

All this he had poured out to Leah when he went to say good-bye. He had poured out much else too, and she had been horrified.

"I can't believe you told Theo!" she had cried. "I simply can't!"

"Well, I told you, didn't I? I told Ilse."

"That's rather different. You trusted us. You knew we'd die rather than talk."

"I trust him too. He'd never do harm to Iris. Never."

Leah said thoughtfully, "I take it, from what you say, that that Jordaine business didn't come to anything."

"Apparently not."

"I'm glad. She seems to be such a gentle creature. It didn't make any sense. By the way, she hasn't bought anything since."

Paul smiled. "They can't afford your prices, my dear." More seriously he added, "They've got real trouble with that son, the one who runs about with Tim Powers."

"Ironic, isn't it? They're cousins and don't know it."

"Second cousins once removed."

"You should be a genealogist. Anyhow, Meg is absolutely sick over Tim. He's always one step ahead of arrest. Have you said good-bye to her yet?"

"I'm going down this afternoon."

And so he had said his good-byes to Leah, who gave half a promise to come with Bill for a visit, had gotten into his car, and driven down to Meg's.

At the far end of the long country living room, Meg sat at the same tea table that her mother had set out every afternoon of her life. As he approached, Paul recognized the tray, the pink lustre cups and the repoussé silver basket of muffins. Also, to his vexation, he recognized Tim and a man who, on turning his well-tailored back, revealed the alert and skeptical face of Victor Jordaine.

Tim extended a hand which Paul had to take, crying, "Well, this is an unexpected pleasure! I never see you anymore." And as Paul leaned down to kiss Meg's cheek, he continued to effervesce, "I hear you're off to Italy."

"Yes, Friday," Paul answered briefly, wishing he might tell Tim to stop putting on the act for Meg's benefit.

"Tim's just back from there," Meg said and, turning to Jordaine, "You remember each other, don't you?"

Jordaine inclined his head formally. "I had the pleasure at one of your Christmas parties."

"Tim was Mr. Jordaine's guest in Italy during the semester break. Do have a muffin while they're hot, Paul."

Jordaine seemed to be waiting for some comment or question from Paul and, when none came, reported with an obvious attempt at a casual effect, "I have a nice little place on Lake Garda. Don't have time to be there much as I'd like, unfortunately."

Paul became aware that he was gritting his teeth. A *game*, Leah had said. *An innocent.* That makes it more *piquant.* He wanted to kick Jordaine's face in, that smooth, clever face. Instead he took a muffin and tried to swallow some tea.

"I hear the climate is lovely there all year," Meg remarked, being a proper hostess.

"Rather different from where I am in the Midwest," Tim said.

Paul could not resist a comment. "From what I read in the papers, you're hardly confined to the Midwest. You seem to be all over the place."

"Oh, I keep busy," Tim agreed pleasantly.

The pulses began beating in Paul's head. He hadn't expected this confrontation, for that is what it was, and a double one at that. The queer juxtaposition of Jordaine and Timothy was too much for him in his "getaway" mood of wanting to be rid of puzzles and problems.

So he turned to Meg to inquire, "Where's Bill?"

"Out taking care of a mare in foal. An emergency. Did you know—of course you didn't—he got kicked in the knee last month? There's this stable, you see . . ." And she launched into a long, not very interesting, story.

Paul, half listening, was acutely conscious of the two men. Tim, in his best boyish fashion, was displaying his appetite, sprawled in the chair, happily spilling crumbs and totally out of place in this traditional, old-fashioned setting. Jordaine, bored with Meg, was restless; his eyes, when he was intent on his own thoughts, were dead black. Terrible eyes, cold as marbles, Paul thought, and wondered what the thoughts were that passed now behind that strong, square forehead.

Presently, when Meg's tale ended, the two men rose.

"I'll be going into the city," Tim said. "Victor's giving me a lift to the station."

Each nodded to Paul, Tim saying, "Good seeing you."

"Likewise, Mr. Werner," said Jordaine.

When they had gone, Meg asked, "Did you notice the car?"

"Can't say I did."

"It was parked round the back. A Rolls convertible. He keeps it here in the country."

"Who the hell is he, anyway?" asked Paul.

Meg looked surprised. "My, you sound angry. The fact is I never can figure him out myself. That remark about the 'nice little place on Lake Garda'—don't you believe it. Tim said it's palatial, acres of gardens and a lake with swans, all kinds of rare swans. It even has a gatehouse. You have to be approved to get in."

"That's interesting."

"Tim says he's an international banker or investor or something."

"According to Tim's speeches capitalists like him deserve to be wiped out."

Meg sighed. "I know. I don't see Tim with Jordaine at all. I've said it a million times, and I've asked Tim about it, but all I get is his usual turnoff, that beautiful smile and a vague answer. So I've given up. I've got too much on my mind, anyway. I'm worried to death about Tom in Vietnam. That's enough to worry about. It's too much."

So after a while Paul had taken leave of Meg, with promises to write and admonitions to keep well, and had gone home.

The apartment was already shrouded in sheets, with valuables put away. Katie was to stay on there while he was gone, to guard his home for him and also because she loved the place and it was her home.

"There's a package from a florist for you, Mr. Werner," she said when he came in.

It was a bonsai tree in a porcelain dish. Tiny, strong, and gnarled, it bent like a tree on a windy coast. It looked brave and was very, very old. With it came a card without a signature. But the script was familiar and unmistakable, Anna's pointed European script.

Strong until death, he read.

It was her way, he knew, of saying she was sorry about not going with him. Sorry, too, about not having gone with him years before. A man could break his heart over it, and almost had! Well, so be it. He put the card carefully in an envelope and slipped it into his wallet.

He was to leave on the S.S. *United States* on its final voyage. It was 1969, and the jet plane had completely taken over. This was to be the great, swift ship's last race through the Atlantic, and possibly his own last voyage too. But who knew? As long as one was alive, each new day was a gift, and could be a surprise.

14

Theo looked down at the page. His handwriting was not exactly what it had been, yet it was respectably legible. Allowing his hand to relax for a few minutes, he drank some tea from the cup that Iris had put on his desk before going out to Parents' Night at school. She would be gone until at least ten o'clock, which gave him ample opportunity to write his monthly letter to Paul.

These, as time went on, were becoming more difficult to do. Bound to each other as the two men were in tight and secret fashion, they had yet neither a past nor an ongoing life in common, and so Theo often had to wrack his brains for something to tell. What Paul wanted, he knew, was news about Iris. He did his best to provide it.

"—wonderful success at teaching," he resumed. "She really seems to *study* each child. There was a pathetic girl in her class, terribly overweight and unpopular; Iris called the parents in and got them to do something about the child's weight, and the result has been a triumph—"

A gust of wintry wind shook the windows. It was raining hard, which should have made the house seem warm and snug in contrast, but it only seemed small and stuffy. Try as he would not to feel it and certainly not to show it, Theo, remembering glass walls and snowscapes, felt shut in.

They had been almost a year in this house. It had been a year and a half since the accident. Sometimes it seemed an eternity since that other life: the operating room, the crowded office, the spacious house, the wallet thick with bills— And, shaking himself, he returned to the letter.

"It's hard to believe that in only two more years Jimmy will be in medical school. We wish he weren't already attached to just one girl at his young age, but at least she is a fine girl, a hard worker. They are both solid people.

"And so is Laura. You might not get that impression because she's such a clotheshorse"—he started to write "encouraged by Anna" but checked himself. It would be unforgivably tactless to speak of Anna, or the fact that Laura was her lovely double. "She's surrounded by young men, most of them nice enough as far as one can see. But there are far too many of them. With a face like hers I suppose there's no help for it. But she has grown in many ways. She wants to work actively in conservation and has become a real outdoors person. The collie puppy that she found abandoned in the woods is already twice the size of our old poodle and takes up half of this kitchen, but neither Iris nor I had the heart to refuse him a home."

Theo's pen paused in midair. He had, for an instant, a vision of Paul reading this letter. Shut out from this family that was his, he would want to know everything there was to know, the

not-so-good along with the good. Resolutely, then, he continued.

"Steve is always in our minds. We haven't heard from him in
several months, although Jimmy gets a card now and then. All
we glean is that the country is beautiful, the commune is self-
sufficient, and Steve is in charge of the apple orchard. Iris says
that sounds peaceful enough, yet something tells me it is not
peaceful, but ominous, only a calm before the outbreak of a
new storm. I am more troubled about him now than I was even
on that awful day when he was arrested in Chicago."

That awful day. It was as if they had all, Iris and he and all of
them, been riding in a car, over smooth stretches and expected
bumps in turn, when without warning the brakes had failed and
the car gone careening down the mountainside. Then it had
landed, slammed to a stop, and they had all climbed out, miraculously still alive and in one piece. Alive but shaken, not what
they had been.

The dog came in, Laura's big, bumbling waif, and laid its
head on Theo's knee. He bent to stroke its head.

"Lonesome, old boy? Want somebody to love you, is that it?"

The animal's soft eyes seemed to comprehend, and the two
pairs of eyes, the man's equally soft and sad, looked into each
other. Yes, Theo thought, I know the feeling.

We're here under one roof, working together and holding
together, Iris and I. Friendly and civilized, we speak gently and
are kind. Considerately, she remembers to bring the evening
cup of tea to my desk. I answer the telephone and keep the
house quiet when she has papers to correct. We have trust. We
have—

And he wanted to write, to put on paper all his longing for
the passion and the beauty they had once known, he longed to
cry out: There is a wall between us, and will it ever come down?
Tell me, will it ever?

He wrote instead, "That's all the news for now, except to say
as always how grateful I am for your amazing goodness. . . ."

Then he wished for Paul's good health and a pleasant vacation, and signed his name.

In the lofty dining room Paul was enjoying a second cup of coffee and a panettone. The steady wind from over the lake stirred the red silk draperies and brought a strong fragrance with it. Camellias or roses? he wondered.

He returned to the mail; having just finished reading a letter from Theo, he now turned it over to read it again from the beginning, making sure to miss nothing. Theo expressed himself well in the clear, precise English he had learned and often spoke more correctly than did many a native speaker of the language. In addition, he seemed to understand exactly what Paul might want to be told—except that he still hadn't said that everything was perfect between himself and Iris, which was the thing Paul most wanted to hear. But that's foolish of me, he said to himself now, for what on this earth is ever perfect?

The delineations of the children, though, were so minute, so definite, that it could seem to Paul sometimes that he actually knew them. Jimmy was one of life's fortunates, dependable, steady, and sure to be admitted to one of the country's best medical schools. Philip was still their sunny little boy, while Steve—Paul returned to the letter to scan it again.

"We haven't heard from him . . . only a calm before the outbreak of a new storm. . . . I am more troubled about him now than I was even on that awful day when . . ."

Troubled too, Paul put the letter down. It wasn't easy to be a parent these days. But then perhaps it never had been. He wouldn't know.

And he turned to happier words about Laura, "surrounded by young men . . . far too many of them. . . . With a face like hers I suppose there's no help for it."

At that Paul had to smile. It was almost as if he were seeing before him Theo's humorous, mock-mournful expression. It seemed remarkable that after such slight contact with the man,

he could feel that he knew him well, as if there had been a
relationship between them. But of course, there was a relationship now. . . .

And putting the letter down, he sat back to consider his
surroundings. Morning light struck the mirror over the mantel
and showered sparks on its silver gilt frame. With its flowered
floor tiles, its massive silver ornaments, and carved Renaissance chests, the room could most certainly be described as
"elegant," and yet it would be no contradiction to say that it
was also simple. For there was no clutter and no excess; everything it contained was used and necessary. Except perhaps the
paintings, he reflected, although some people, and he was one
of them, would say that art ranked very close behind necessity.
Indeed, he would rather have done without a rug, would perhaps gladly have sat on the floor, rather than be deprived of art
in some form. Just as books of poetry that you have known as a
child in their worn, familiar bindings were friends, so, too,
pictures were friends. He had no compunction about spending
for them. He was enabling artists to live and he would enhance
the museums to which he would bequeath them on his death.

He stood up and walked through another lofty room toward
the terrace. In a previous letter Theo had sent a snapshot of the
family in what Paul supposed was the backyard of the new
house. It must be a very small place, humble in contrast to what
they had left behind. The corner of the neighboring house was
just visible along the edge of the picture. He had had it enlarged, and now it stood on the console table along with a pile
of books and other family photographs, there being no reason,
in a foreign country where none but strangers ever came to
visit, why he should not display anything he wished. He had no
need to study Iris's face; he knew it now by heart. The sight of it
had troubled him of late, and at the keen recall of Theo's words
he felt a dart of sorrow. *She didn't like him. He made her feel "queer."*
And he turned away from her dark, brooding gaze.

Two of the sons were in the picture. The medical student

resembled his father's description of him. *Nice* and *typically American* were some of the adjectives that came at once to mind. The little fellow holding a bat and mitt looked appealing. And the girl—it was no exaggeration, the girl was a beauty.

From her Paul's eyes went to that first, other beauty, so like her. That dog-eared snapshot, now enlarged, had been taken one day with her own Brownie box camera, many ages ago in front of the obelisk in the park behind the museum. He had put Ilse beside her. The contrast! The one so soft and flowery with her wealth of hair let loose and her dreaming, almost golden eyes; the other crisp and purposeful, with her frank, straight gaze, her sleek black hair, and the touch of humor on her lips. She had had the picture made in Israel and sent to him.

Two loves, he reflected during the minute or two he stood there, the one warm, hearty, and stubborn, whom he knew so well, and the other whom he knew—how? In vanished, fleeting recollections, longings, and fantasies. . . .

Well, there was no reason why a man couldn't love two women, even in some sort of muddled overlap, was there? Yes, and he could be a little bit resentful of both of them, too, at the same time. A pity it was that neither one was here with him on this perfect morning.

Then he straightened himself and looked into the mirror that hung over the console. Tall and thin, with not even a trace of baldness, he was still able to find a pretty woman to escort to dinner, still able to enjoy life and, God willing, would continue so to the end. God willing.

Out on the terrace he sat down with the *Herald Tribune* and *Il Messaggero.* He was doing well with the language. It was good to keep your brain young with the effort of learning something new; Italian grammar was not the easiest to master. Also he had begun to take cello lessons again. Years ago he had played, had never been really good at it, but had loved its plangent tones. Even a single chord sent a wave of sweetness into the air, and he was determined to do better with the instrument, just as he was determined to fit himself into Italian life as long as he was here. Otherwise, there would have been no point in coming to Italy in the first place; there were plenty of lovely, warm places at home where one might sit on a terrace and look out at water.

Today he was going to a wedding. The niece of his Roman friends was to be married in the village church with a reception afterward in a grand old Edwardian hotel, between banks of flowers, under crystal chandeliers and carved ceilings. Out-doors, the gravel would be raked fine in the gardens, and pastel parasols would shade all the little iron tables and skinny iron chairs. Tiny boys and girls in their bright little suits and dresses would go tearing down the paths. It would be a family affair, for all these Italian parties included everyone of every age. Paul liked that. There'd be music, he would dance and be grateful that he had been invited.

Beneath the stone balustrade now, the gardener's young daughter had been picking roses on the slope. She came up the steps with an armful held against her young white breasts, between which hung a gold cross on a thin gold chain. In another year she would be honey-ripe and the young men would flock like bees. Unless the city should lure her away, she would quickly marry one of them, breed one perfect baby after the other, and soon would become as fat as her mother.

Accident! All—well, not entirely all—but a great deal of it anyway, was accident, where you were born and to whom. If your ancestors were stronger or smarter or simply luckier than most, you would likely be in a position different from those whose ancestors had not been. Thrown dice, he thought. I have been fortunate, fortunate to be enjoying the pleasure of this breeze, and the girl walking away with the heap of roses, and the lake below as deeply blue as stained glass.

His brown-and-white spaniel came bounding around the house, jumped up on him, and licked his hand. For years, ever since childhood, he had missed having a dog because he—and most emphatically, Marian—had thought it wrong to keep one in an apartment. But that had been foolish. The apartment was across from the park, where a dog might have plenty of exercise, and so he would take this one home with him when he went. But when? Whenever he should get tired of being here. That was the answer. He had set himself no time limit. He had earned this rest, he thought defensively, at the same time asking himself what puritan conscience made him feel that he needed defending.

It was good just to be in the sun, here in this peace where, if he did not want to trouble himself about it, he could pretend that there was neither Cuban nor Libyan terror, that there was no Israel, still wary and insecure even after its victory in the sixty-seven war, that there was no Vietnam, and that his own country wasn't being torn to pieces because of it. . . .

The dog had gone racing down toward the shore and now came back to stand at Paul's knees, barking and wagging in some private, ecstatic joy.

"Oh, all right," Paul said, "I understand. You want a walk, and you want me to come too."

So he stood up and strode off down the hill to where the lake lay rippling in the wind.

15

You come to the land by cross-
ing the Golden Gate Bridge in the morning, with the wrinkled
silver ocean on your left. You pass through Sausalito and on to
where the green shoulder of Mt. Tamalpais bulks in the west,
then go up by the Muir Woods, where the great trees are older
than the United States, were already old when William the
Conqueror crossed the Channel, and already old when the
Saracens fought the Crusaders. In Marin County smart new
houses arranged themselves on the cliffs like glass boxes on
shelves. Farther still, in the wine country, in Sonoma, lie the
vineyards where the tended grapes lie evenly on the earth like
ruled lines on a light brown pad; the sun is blinding.

Early in the afternoon as you climb gradually into the easy

roll of hills and slanted fields, the land greens into pastures and meadows ringed by woods. You turn off the asphalt pavement onto a dirt road, bumping and swerving around boulders in your way, follow the road along a dry gulch for three miles, take a fork onto a lane just wide enough for the car, and come to a stop at a dead end in front of a large Victorian house at the edge of a spreading farm.

This is what Steve had seen when, for the first time, he had walked up the lane, carrying all he owned in his duffel bag. But now, from where he was standing on the hill above the house, he had an almost aerial view of Peace Farm, with its apple orchards, its sturdy, black Dutch Belted dairy cows with their wide white cummerbunds, and its human traffic, small, dark spots moving among the houses and the barns. Beyond all these lay a distant blur that might possibly be clouds or possibly the sea.

It was high noon and the heat lay heavily on his head. He had been working all morning on the rail fence that was going, eventually, to keep a flock of sheep from falling into the ravine. He was tired, but it was a good tiredness, the kind that comes when healthy muscles have been well used. The upper half of his body was brown; his hair was sun bleached and his spirit calm.

"You need a change and some quiet," Tim Powers had urged.

They had talked in Tim's office a few days after the campus bombing, in which a man had lost his legs.

"I saw him, I was passing on my way to the library when I saw the crowd. They were carrying him to the ambulance. . . . Tim, I haven't slept for two nights, I keep seeing those bloody stumps and hearing his screams. . . . God, Tim, those screams ringing in my ears. . . ."

Tim had come from behind his desk and laid two firm hands on Steve's shoulders.

"They will stop ringing. Believe me. Nothing lasts forever.

Time is merciful," he'd said kindly. "Besides, you had nothing to do with it, anyway."

In all the disorder and fury of the demonstrations in which Steve had taken part, even on that day of fear and trembling when they had invaded the Selective Service office, he had never been so shaken. But the mutilation of that one man, a man he had known, had shaken him most awfully.

And he had demanded of Tim, "But what if I had had anything to do with it?"

"You know perfectly well that it's our policy to do no harm to persons, but only to property, if we can help it. You do know that."

"Yes. I know."

Tim had dropped his hands and sat down again, while Steve stood, staring at some dust motes in a stream of sunlight over the desk.

"That's not to say," Tim said suddenly, "that a time may not come when we have to—to escalate. You know that too."

Steve nodded, feeling desolate.

"The man was a victim, but the struggle that made him a victim is a pure one all the same. It's the cause of peace and justice. Sometimes, in the most noble causes, mistakes are made. That's all there is to it. Don't you agree?"

"Of course I do. But still, Tim, my nerves . . . I surely never thought—I thought I was the last person ever to be talking about nerves."

Tim smiled. "Nobody's made of iron. What you need is a rest in the fresh air. One of those communes in California is the place. Nice warm climate, nothing on your mind. Stay until you feel ready and whole again, and then come back."

As always, Tim had understood him better than he understood himself, Steve thought now as he collected his tools and started the long walk downhill. For in the months he had been here this place had truly healed him, so much so that he had no thought of when he might ever want to leave it. This was *his* place and there were his new people, friendly and undemanding.

The forty-five or fifty men and women who were usually at the farm at any given time described themselves as "apolitical." Some of them had once been involved in public causes, but had given up. The political was irrelevant, they said. They neither listened to the radio nor read the newspaper, and there was not one television set on the place. The simple life of sharing was all. And this new way of life was the true revolution, they believed.

Everything was held in common: books, food, clothing, drugs, and lovers. Happy, independent, half-naked babies toddled about in the sunshine. Whoever happened to be nearest watched out for them and answered their calls. Any mother took care of any other mother's child, and the men did the same. Often enough, a man wasn't sure which child was his or whether any child was his; it didn't matter.

Well, there'd been plenty of free sex, although not babies, on the campus. So all this was nothing new to Steve. As to the sharing of drugs, that was all right too, although he himself had never been big on drugs. Clothing he had to share, and that was good. There was a free store in town that kept a bin for such as he; one reached in and took whatever was needed.

Very soon he learned to do things he had never done before, some carpentry to keep the houses in repair and some work in leather. One made one's own sandals here. He had learned how to milk a cow and deliver a calf. He now knew the difference between a Delicious and a Gravenstein apple. He tended goats and made "garbage runs" to town to pick up the vegetables and fruits that were discarded by the supermarkets.

A long way from Westchester, from the tennis courts and the pools, he thought now, and, for that matter, from the university too. And smiling a little, both with amusement at himself and with satisfaction, he entered the tool shed to put away the various hammers, saws, and planes that he had been using.

For some unknown reason, after these things were neatly stowed, he stretched out his hands, splaying the fingers, and regarded them. They were large, strong hands, the nails somewhat worn and the palms calloused. They were competent hands that knew how to make things. And he smiled again, only to be stopped so abruptly that the smile broke. This happened now and then, this sudden brutal stab of memory, of home. . . .

Sad, hurtful memories. His father's hand. He shuddered, and in his own fingers felt the bloody shock of the smashing door. My God, it was the man's whole life gone down the drain! Selfish and narrow as was that small, arrogant medical world, yet it had been the man's whole life! There was no denying the horror of it, or the pity, too, of his mother who had caused the wreckage.

He tried now to block out a vague, uncertain recollection of some words he thought he had overheard during that brief time when he had come home after the accident. The maid and the gardener had been whispering outside the kitchen door, and did he imagine they'd said something about his mother's trying to kill herself? He had never mentioned it to anyone, half disbelieving that he had heard it, wanting to disbelieve it. . . .

For a minute or two he stayed in the shed, leaning against the doorpost and looking out into the noonday quiet as if the sight of it would return to him the sense of well-being that had filled him up until now.

To the right of the cow barn, farther down the hill, stood a crudely fashioned wooden dome on pillars. It looked something like a bandstand on the central green of an old town, except that it was larger and contained benches in a circle. There in the evenings everybody met to meditate, joining hands and facing west toward the setting sun. In the warmth of this contact, warm palm against warm palm on either side, you could forget everything that troubled you, forget about the

ugliness and evil of the world, forget even that any world existed beyond these meadows and these hills.

Resolutely, Steve straightened his shoulders, as the tragic
mood ebbed. He became aware of hunger. Of course that was
why the place was deserted—everybody was in the big house,
eating.

"You're late," someone said. "So am I. Are you going to
lunch?"

He looked down—he had to look down, for she was quite
small—at a young girl. Then he corrected his thought: You
were supposed to say, even to think, "woman," not "girl." She
was carrying a kitten not much larger than a full-sized mouse. It
could not have been more than a week old, and it was desperately mewing.

"It's starving," the girl said. "The mother had too many, you
see, and this is the weak one. It gets shoved aside. Do you
suppose it can be saved?"

"Let's see. Give it here." Steve weighed the limp creature in
his hand. "I think it's dying," he told her.

"Poor little thing! It wants to live."

The genuine sorrow in her voice appealed to Steve and
piqued his interest. She was new at the farm, having arrived
only a week or two earlier. He had scarcely spoken to her, knew
only that her name was Susan and that, because there were
several other Susans on the place, she was called Susan B.

"Well," he said, "let's get something to eat ourselves and
then think about how to get some food into him—or is it her?"

"It's so little and frail, I haven't bothered to look."

You look sort of frail yourself, Steve was thinking while she
trotted along beside him. He wondered why he hadn't noticed
her that much before. She was—well, different; it was the best
word he could think of. Different. Rosy beige all over, from her
two fat braids to the cotton shift and the bare, narrow feet.
Only her eyes were very dark, and soft as flowers.

His thoughts flitted: She doesn't look like a person who's

cast off her bourgeois hang-ups. I don't see her doing free and easy sex. There's something about her that says she wouldn't. To begin with, she can't be more than fifteen, can she? Still, you never can tell for sure, not about age, or about sex either.

"I've asked around for a medicine dropper, but nobody has one," Susan said.

"When I go in to town this afternoon I'll get one," Steve offered.

"Oh, would you? When will that be?"

"Soon's I have lunch."

The dining room, the pantries, and the spacious kitchen, in which servants must once have prepared splendid dinners, were crowded now with people cooking, eating, and washing up. The food was cooked in huge battered pots and eaten on chipped plates. Things were spilled and nobody minded, babies cried and were nursed, children climbed on the tables and were never reprimanded.

Steve and Susan, with the kitten in her pocket, found places on a bench and helped themselves to stew from the communal bowl. Suddenly she began to laugh.

"What's funny?" he asked.

"I was just remembering things. Linen table mats, polished mahogany, and flowers, and it struck me funny. Maybe you don't know what I mean, though."

"I know exactly what you mean." And he, too, felt the humorous contrast of his home to this friendly, merry hubbub.

"This must have been a millionaire's place once. That grand staircase with the carved banisters, and the organ in the music room—the solarium—and look what's become of it!" Susan exclaimed.

"All to the good, don't you think so?"

"Oh, yes, I only meant that there must be a story in it."

"There is. It was once a summer home for a family with a mining fortune. But after the first couple of generations died off, the heirs weren't interested in coming here and the place went to seed, fell apart. Then a rich man's young son finally bought it, but he was supposed to be not responsible, not quite right in the head, I guess, but maybe he was very right, because he wanted to give all his money away to the needy. Anyway, they appointed a conservator to take charge of his affairs, although not before he had already given this property to the group that has it now. So that's the story."

"I think that's wonderful," Susan B. said earnestly. "Are you going to stay here always, Steve?"

"Maybe. Anyone's welcome to stay as long as he wants and as long as he's willing to share the work and whatever he owns or can earn."

"That's wonderful," she repeated.

The kitten mewed, its cry surprisingly loud for such a weak creature. Steve got up.

"I'll be going to town. Where shall I look for you when I get back?"

"Somewhere around the cow barn. I'm supposed to clean up there this afternoon."

While going about his errands in town, Steve's preoccupation with seeds, baling wire, light bulbs, and cattle feed was interrupted from time to time with a thought of Susan B., the kitten, and the medicine dropper. What a *child* she was! No, definitely, she did not fit at Peace Farm. Imagine walking up to her and saying: "How about it tonight?" Or even more impossibly, imagine her walking up to a man saying: "How about it tonight?" She was cut of the same cloth as his own sister, Laura, typically middle class, uptight, and he certainly couldn't imagine Laura here in this place. So whatever had made Susan B. come here?

He found her in the barn, sweeping up spilled grain, and gave her the medicine dropper.

"Where's the animal? Still alive?"

"Yes, but only just. I put it in a shoe box by itself so the others wouldn't trample it."

It turned out that the kitten accepted the medicine dropper. The feeding process was slow, taking almost an hour before it was satisfied and fell asleep in the shoe box. The dinner bell had sounded over the fields long before, but Steve and Susan B. had sat on under a eucalyptus tree unheeding, which was an odd thing for him to be doing, because he was usually hungry.

"I've got a couple of apples in my pocket," he offered.

"Maybe later."

The girl's delicate hands were locked around her knee, and her forehead rested on the same knee, so that he could look down at the nape of her neck where the center part ended and the hair on either side was tightened into the braids. Why is there always something touching about the back of a neck? he wondered.

It was quite still, except for the long chirp and hum of cicadas, which was so unbroken that it seemed almost like a stillness. And the graying twilight was so mysterious that there was sadness in it. He had to break the stillness.

"Have you come from far?" he asked abruptly.

When she looked up, he was surprised to see that her eyes were wet. But she smiled politely, answering, "From the Valley. That's Los Angeles, in case you didn't know."

"I've heard. I'm from Westchester. That's New York, in case you didn't know."

"I've heard."

Then he couldn't think of anything to say. His tongue was tied. A minute went by, and he knew he had to say something, so he said, "My sister likes animals too. Dogs, mostly."

"Is she nice, your sister?"

"Yes, but different from you."

"How old is she?"

"Nineteen. And you?"

"Seventeen."

"Oh."

Another minute went by. Then he asked whether she went to school.

"I have my high school diploma. I wanted to go to college, but I left home instead."

He knew that she wanted to talk, that she needed to, but was shy of unburdening, of blurting out to a stranger, perhaps fearing to embarrass or to bore him. So he spoke with particular gentleness.

"I'd like to hear about it, if you'd like to tell me."

"It's a disgusting story."

"That depends on who hears it. I might not think it is."

"Well, all right. My parents got divorced three years ago. My father went to Florida or someplace, I don't know. Anyway, we never hear from him. Not that my mother cares. She has plenty of money of her own."

"Do you care?"

"Why should I?"

"I suppose you shouldn't." Strange, he thought, her father just walking off like that while his father held everyone so tightly. Tight enough to strangle, almost. "But why did you leave?" he asked.

She looked away, out where gray was turning to black on the grass. "The house didn't seem—it wasn't mine. My mother had men—different ones all the time. A week with this one, and then another one." Her voice was a little hoarse, which oddly enough was pleasing to Steve's ears, a voice one would remember. "I could hear them all night, even with my door shut. I could hear everything through the walls. Sometimes there were two at a time. And there were women too. Parties." She turned back to Steve. "I hated it. Sex shouldn't be like that."

"You don't think it should be free? Like food and drink that one takes when one is hungry or thirsty?"

"No. There's got to be more to it than that," she said, in a kind of astonishment at his question.

Her face, turned up to his, was too thin and her eyes too

enormous to be called beautiful and yet it was a face one would remember. He sought words: wistful, delicate, intelligent, charming. . . .

And he saw that she was honest, no prig, no rigid moralizer from the bourgeois world, but merely an innocent who believed in what she was saying. He saw, too, that she was afraid. So he asked her how she had happened upon Peace Farm.

"There was an article in a magazine, something about places where you can work just for your keep, not for money, and it sounded so wonderful. Where I come from, there's always been so much money."

"I know what you mean. Money and things. Too many *things.*"

"Yes. I want to empty my mind of them. Of having to say or do or having to *have.* I want to clear my mind."

It was by now quite dark. With common intent they both stood up. The girl took the box with the sleeping kitten, the tiny dish of milk, and the medicine dropper.

"It will probably wake in the night and be hungry," she said.

When she moved, he thought he could smell her hair, or perhaps it was her skin. It smelled fresh and pure as hay.

"Susan B.," he heard himself say, "you're a lovely person."

The next afternoon he went looking for her in the barn. He could just say, he told himself, that he was curious about the kitten. Then he scoffed at himself for planning an excuse; this wasn't his usual way with women! Anyhow, she was just an interesting kid, a—a *type.*

"She's in the separator room," someone told him. "Jerry's put her to work there."

This room, in which stood a simple machine that skimmed the cream off the milk, was near the cow barns. There Steve found her, with head bent in attention and braids dangling, as Jerry explained the work.

He's standing too close to her, he's touching her. That was his first thought, followed at once by awareness that such thoughts were bizarre. It was no business of his where the man stood. A man was free to stand or to touch just as he liked. Everyone was free.

"You won't believe it, but the kitten's actually gotten lively overnight," said Susan. "I'll show you. Is it all right if I get it now?" she asked Jerry.

"Sure. We're finished here."

When she had left the room, Jerry said, "Pretty kid. Sort of bewildered. Scared of something." He laughed, winking at Steve. "Maybe she just needs a little loving."

Steve did not answer. An unaccountable sudden anger at Jerry rose in him, and he heard himself saying inwardly, Not from you. Not your red, hairy arms and chest, not your wet lips. It was strange because, as it happened, he liked Jerry.

The unwelcome image of that body persisted all the rest of the day, and in the evening he sought Susan to ask her something.

"Where are you sleeping, Susan B.?"

"In the big house, in what used to be the library."

He nodded. The whole first floor was used for the overflow from the bedrooms, for mothers and babies mostly, whose cradles and sleeping bags strewed the grand spaces, music rooms, a billiard room, and a wide wraparound veranda.

"But Jerry's offered me a place for myself. It's just a cubby on the third floor that used to be a maid's room, he said, but it's really nice, much quieter."

Jerry said that, did he? As fast as that? Oh, no!

"Susan B., have you got a warm outdoor sleeping bag? If you haven't, I'll get one for you."

"I have one. Why?"

"I think you should sleep on the front veranda in the corner. It'll be warm enough, and private enough, but not too private. It's not a good idea to be too private."

For a moment she was silent. Then, "What are you telling me? Are you telling me what I think you are?"

She was a kid, all right, but not naive, after all. How could she be, really, after what she had seen at home?

"Yes," he said simply.

"I see. Thank you for letting me know."

"It's a good place here, you mustn't think it isn't. It's just that we all share everything. Everything, you understand?"

"You too, Steve?"

He nodded. "On the theory that to possess any human being exclusively is wrong."

"Even if the person wants to be possessed?"

"Ah, Susan B.! Give me time to think of the answer to that one, will you?"

When he had seen her bring her sleeping bag down and prepare for the night, he left her. And all the way back up past the orchard to his own place, he was puzzled about himself. Since yesterday, he had known who was to be his partner for this night, and now all at once, he didn't want her. It had been so good with her too, easy and happy as it had once been with Lydia, whom he scarcely thought about, any more than he thought about a dozen others. Too bad, but he really had lost the mood tonight. The girl would just have to accept some excuse.

So it happened. Steve didn't recognize himself. He remembered innumerable conversations with Jimmy, and how absurd his brother had seemed with all his talk about "going steady" and being in love with his girl, Janet. It had seemed like an affectation, almost, something that people in this society had been reared to believe they ought to feel. It had been constricting, like being tied up and labeled. Now—now for the first time he wasn't sure.

But after a month or two he knew he had to believe what was happening to him. The days passed, the kitten thrived and grew to be indistinguishable from all its sibling tiger-stripes who ringed the milk pan in the barn. The grass beneath the eucalyptus tree was worn down where he and Susan B. talked the evenings away. He told her everything about himself, even, after a while, about the dangerous things he had done with Tim's group. Also, eventually he came to do the thing that had been strictly forbidden: He gave her Powers's name.

"Because I trust you," he said that night.

"You can," she answered.

"You understand me," he said. "You understand why I did what I did and why I am here now."

"I do," she answered.

And one night he told her he loved her.

She smiled. "I know that, Steve. And I loved you, I trusted you, from the very first day."

Strange, he was thinking as he took her in his arms, I hadn't planned to say that; the words came out by themselves. And he thought as he held her, so light, so warm, so fragrant, that his feelings, rising from hammering heart, to throat, to the joining of his mouth on hers, were all new, not anything he had ever known before.

Yet for almost a month he did no more than kiss her. She was not yet ready; slowly, slowly, he was moving toward the time when she would be ready for more. This was no "fun" affair, and it was not to be taken lightly. He did not reason these things out, he simply knew them and could not do otherwise, any more than, at this point, he could have agreed that possession of another human being is wrong. Now he knew that possession, full and forever, was the only way for himself and her.

At last he came to the sleeping bag on the veranda. It was deep night, pure black and soundless, but she was wide awake. When he found her face in the dark, he felt her smile beneath his fingertips. The wind from out of the hills was cold on his naked skin, yet within the soft bag her naked skin was burning hot. And when her arms opened, he knew that now, finally, she was ready.

·   ·   ·

Susan B. Lovable and lovely, trusting and good. Because of her Steve felt stronger than he had ever felt before. He had never known what it was to feel protective of anyone. But he was so fiercely protective of her that, to keep her safe, he would have killed in a moment anyone who would hurt her.

And the long, sweet months passed.

16

Gradually, life and the desire for life return. One morning the stomach that has for so long wanted no food feels greedy for it again, and the mouth waters at the sight of a warm cinnamon roll and the fragrance of coffee. One afternoon the eyes, which for a year or more have had no interest in shapes or colors, open wider to follow a woman going down the street, observing the cloth, the fit and cut of her dress. And suddenly you think: I would like to have that. It would look well on me.

With a mixture of pleasure, curiosity, and amazement, Iris looked around the vivid room. Here on one of the most fashionable streets of the Upper East Side, one expected to see celebrities of every kind among the lunchtime crowd; the astonishing thing to Iris was that they all looked like celebrities, even though they weren't, for they couldn't possibly all be famous.

The women were mostly blondes and smooth-haired. Their jewels—daytime jewels—were discreet, and their suits, she reflected, looked as though they had been bought at Chez Léa.

Anna, following Iris's glances, murmured, "It's a picture, isn't it?" And then, being Anna, added, "I wonder who does their flowers? Changed every day, I suppose."

In every wall niche stood flowers, fountains, plumes, and sprays, the oval cups of tulips and the silver, upturned faces of spring lilies.

"I could feed a family for three days, I guess, for the price of one bouquet," said Iris.

The remark was without bitterness or envy. Actually she was pleased with all this beauty. It had been a long time since she had been in such a place.

Anna, misunderstanding, reassured her. "It's your birthday, and it needs to be celebrated properly. We're going to have champagne and do it up right." She patted Iris's hand. "You're looking better than you've looked in a long time. Working really does agree with you."

"I love to teach, always did. I love feeling competent. You know, whenever there are problem kids they put them in my class. I have a reputation for setting them straight." Iris smiled. "Well, not all the time, but at least I make a pretty good stab at it. I'm finally starting on my master's too, did I tell you?"

"And then?"

"Doctorate. Oh, I know it'll take forever but I don't care. It's what I want and it doesn't matter how hard I'll have to work for it."

"I'm proud of you and glad for you," Anna said softly.

"Well, you're the one who really got me to do it. Remember when you came back from the Berkshires, and I was so absolutely hopeless, you said—"

"I remember, but let's not look back. Look at the menu instead."

She doesn't want to remember that time, Iris thought. She's still anxious about me—about us—ever since the accident. I know her quick glance, and the questions waiting to be asked, which she doesn't ask.

"And how is Theo these days?" Anna inquired now. "I don't see him as often as I'd like to."

"Well, he works almost day and night, it seems. It's not easy being a resident, a student, taking orders, when for years he was the one who gave the orders. But he has never once complained."

Yes, he was brave, very brave. And, observing a group of men at a nearby table, men whose faces, clothes, postures, and gestures all spoke security and power, Iris felt a wave of sadness.

"Status has always been so important to Theo. Whether it should have been or not . . ." She paused, and went on, "But in Europe a doctor is, or was when Theo lived there, anyway, a *personage*. And so this has been terribly painful for him in many ways. There are people, who used to invite us all the time and almost fawn on Theo, who've now dropped us."

"Good riddance, I say."

"True. But even the friends who've been wonderful, and there are plenty of them, even they must feel sorry for us when they visit."

"Your house isn't exactly a slum."

"No, but it must certainly be a big surprise, and I'm sure they have plenty to say about it in private, plenty of pity."

If I, who never cared much about that sort of thing—or so I thought—can feel it, Iris asked herself, how much more must he be feeling it?

But Mama had intended this day to be a celebration, so she said quickly, brightly, "At least we do manage without pressing worries now! With all Theo used to earn, we were always just on that worrisome edge, while now we have a regular amount every month to depend on. Of course, one day the bank will have to be paid back. I still don't understand how they could have made such a loan in the first place, without any collateral. . . ." And again Iris had to remind herself that this was a *celebration*, for heaven's sake, not the time for such a heavy subject.

"I suppose," Anna said, "they just had confidence in Theo's future earning power."

"That doesn't make any sense to me."

Anna merely shrugged. It occurred to Iris, as often before, that Anna might have signed a note for Theo and didn't want her to know for fear it might worry her, which it would. Mama had plenty, but she wasn't all *that* rich.

And she looked across the table at her mother's hand, on which the familiar, simple ring glittered, Papa's diamond legacy. He'd been a giver, her father had, and so was Mama; buying and giving were some of their ways of showing love.

Almost as though she could have been reading Iris's mind, Anna said now, "Steve still hasn't cashed the little check I sent him."

"Against his principles, I suppose." Iris could hear the wistfulness in her own voice. "We haven't heard from him in two months. My heart pounds when I read about another outburst or see one on television. Will I see his face, or get word that he's been beaten, clubbed, or jailed? I can't talk about it to Theo. He gets too angry. I suppose that's one way to cover grief."

Anna soothed, "Think of good things, like Jimmy's wedding."

At once Iris complied. "I have to marvel at Janet's ambition. Medical school ahead, and pregnant already!"

"You know, I guessed she was pregnant when I saw her at their little wedding. There was a roundness, a shine on her face that made me think so. I know it's an old wives' tale—what are you looking at?"

"Looking? I? Nothing. An old wives' tale, you said."

That man . . . oh, God! He was staring at her. Three tables away Jordaine sat, turned unmistakably in his chair to stare at Iris. *That man.* . . .

And for some crazy reason she had total recall of his naked body as he had stood in the doorway of that silken bedroom, passionate, expectant, and finally enraged. . . . She went hot and then cold.

"There was something very touching about their wedding in that little flat. The food spread on a card table in the hall and the aunts fixing platters in the kitchen."

Iris stiffened the trembling hand that held the salad fork. She wouldn't have thought it possible to tremble so.

"They could have had it in my house. Goodness knows it's big enough. I kept offering it," Anna was saying.

An answer was expected. "Janet's very independent. She would have been pretending to be somebody other than who she is, she said."

Jordaine was with a very young girl, probably no older than my Laura, she was thinking. A coarse-looking girl with a shrill, carrying voice. She had rhinestones on her sweater. While he talked to her, he kept coming back to Iris every few seconds. It was impossible to avoid his chilling eyes without bending over her plate.

"I kept thinking of your father and how pleased he would have been with the Orthodox ceremony."

"I don't believe he was ever really comfortable with Reform. He only went for our sakes," Iris answered automatically.

Her mind was racing: I am probably the only woman who ever rejected him. There's a lot of power in him, after all, in his worldly manners and in the treasures of his white-and-emerald eagle's nest. And to flee as I did from all that, and from the naked, eager man himself, is an insult he would not forget. Oh,

I hope never to be alone if we should meet again! Not, perhaps, that he would hurt me, but what he would say would be too terrible for me to hear.

Anna had a small, rueful smile. "But he surely would have been shocked to know that the bride was pregnant. . . . You seem so far away, Iris. I don't believe you're hearing a word I say."

"You said Papa would have been shocked." Think. Concentrate. Look straight at Mama. "Yes, he could be so soft about almost everything, and yet he would be absolutely unforgiving of that." *And of me in the Waldorf Towers with Jordaine.*

"True," Anna said. "He had no sympathy for transgression. Because he himself would never transgress, you see."

She must keep paying direct attention to Anna. She must seem to be deep in earnest conversation, as if she had not even seen Jordaine.

"Papa really kept the commandments," she said, and became aware that Jordaine knew what she was doing. Now he was laughing at her. His lips were drawn into a jeering laugh.

"Do you feel all right?" Anna asked.

"I'm fine. Why do you—"

"That man over there has been looking at you. Does he know you?"

"No. I mean, I don't think so."

"How odd! He certainly seems to. And he's with a girl, so I hardly think he's trying to pick you up."

I'm staying at the Waldorf. Why don't you come in and have a drink?

Oh, Mama, she cried silently, will you just stop talking and let's get out of here?

"Iris, you're bright red. What's wrong?"

"Nothing. I just—it's hot in here."

Say yes, and we'll leave . . . but we'd have to pass his table to reach the door . . . and besides, I'd be such a wimp to run away.

Iris clenched her fists on her lap. "I'm all right. I'm fine. Don't look so alarmed."

But Anna was frightened, very frightened. Although her voice was low and calm she said, "If you'll just let me help you—"

A sarcastic laugh sounded, then, over the hum of many voices from surrounding tables, so that people looked over in its direction. It was Jordaine's laugh, and it was shocking that Iris should be able to recognize it; after all, she hardly knew him. The shock must have been evident, because Anna lost her calmness.

"Iris! It's that man, it is! You know him. Who is he? You've got to tell me!"

This was unbearable. This horrible lunch. How long could it go on? Another hour, or more?

"I can't talk now," she whispered. "Not while he's here."

"Well, he's leaving now. Don't look that way. He wants to get your attention. Pick up the knife and cut the chicken, even if you don't want to eat it."

Mama was talking to her as if she were a child. No, not a child. Rather someone hurt in an accident, someone needing rescue. Obediently, she bent over the food, while out of the corner of her eye she watched Jordaine's dark tailored shoulders, along with the rear of the rhinestone sweater, disappear into the street. Then she laid down the fork and put her hands to her burning cheeks.

For a minute or two Anna did not speak. At last she said quietly, "I take it back. It's no business of mine, whatever it is, and you certainly don't have to tell me if you don't want to."

This familiar tact and kindness of her mother's had a curiously opposite effect; it produced a rush to reveal.

And she began, almost shyly, "I met him one day at Chez Léa. I was buying an evening dress for Theo's dinner party, when they were going to announce—" She had to stop. "I was angry at Theo. It was after the argument over Steve, and before

I slammed the car door." She stopped again, and for a moment had to close her eyes, where tears had begun to sting.

"This is too hard for you," Anna said gently. "Don't."

"No, I want to." And she might have added, I need to. Meeting Anna's attentive gaze, she steadied herself and continued. "We walked out of the shop at the same time, going in the same direction. He asked me to have a drink. He lives in the Waldorf Towers."

"You went to his apartment?" asked Anna, with no expression, no inflection.

"Not that time. He was very intelligent, traveled, interesting, polite. . . . Then a few days later I did go upstairs with him. I don't know whether I knew what I was doing, really. . . . I guess I must have. . . . Of course I must have."

Remembering, Iris shuddered now. For those few minutes she had felt real desire for that man.

"But nothing happened, because I couldn't do it, and he was furious, and I ran out. It was awful. That's why he wanted to taunt me just now."

"Who is he?" Anna asked.

"His name doesn't matter. He's very rich. An important man, that much I'm sure of."

"He looks important, somehow," Anna reflected. "Handsome too, in a cold sort of way."

"I thought he was handsome. But then suddenly he was revolting to me, and I was terrified."

"You weren't terrified of him, but of what *you* were about to do."

"I guess that was it."

Elegant, polished lady in her gray woolen dress with its fine lace collar, lady out of another generation, another world, how did she know? *She* could never have been "about to do"—

A long sigh rose in Iris's chest; it brought relief and unloaded a burden.

"There's so much about oneself that one doesn't under-stand," she told Anna, "and probably never will."

"Never mind. It's not likely that you'll ever see the man again. And if you do, why . . ." Anna shrugged, making light of the possibility.

"I know. I'm over it now. It's done me a lot of good to tell you." Iris picked at the food, for suddenly the food looked appetizing. "And I am so thankful that it turned out the way it did. Imagine having to keep a secret like that for the rest of your life! It would be like lead, like poison inside you."

"Yes, yes, I imagine it would." For an instant Anna's face looked thoughtful, almost sad. Then, deliberately, she bright-ened it. "Come, champagne!" And, touching Iris's goblet with her own, cried, "All's well that ends well. Happy birthday, darling!"

Iris finished her notes for Back to School night and leaned back on the English bench. The light of late afternoon lay warmly on the small square lawn and on the asters that Anna had planted and still often came to tend. The little yard was a friendly place now, vastly different from the way it had ap-peared on that dreary day, two years before, when they had moved here.

The whole neighborhood had a way of enfolding people, she reflected, that the old one surely had not had. It was not that anyone ever interfered; they were all too busy for that. But people did seem to be there for you when you needed them, as when she had the flu and the neighbors took turns inviting Theo and Philip to dinner all that week. Then there were events like the Halloween parade and the block party on the Fourth of July—

The back door opened and Theo came out.

"Well, you look comfortable," he said.

"I am. This is a nice spot to work in."

He picked a blue aster and put it in his buttonhole. "Look

like an usher, don't I?" He laughed. "You know, I would never have believed that I could grow to like this little house. It's come to feel like home, not just a stopping place on the way back up."

The way back up, Iris thought. In another year the big test has to be met, opening an office and starting anew. I hope he won't be disappointed. He's very tired. There are new lines around his eyes.

"We've done rather well, haven't we, all considered?" Theo remarked now.

"Yes, I'd say so," she replied, and was pleased that he had said "we." She remembered the time when, if she ever asked him about finances or something equally important, he would tell her nicely that it was his responsibility, not hers. Yes, they had come a long way.

Her reflective mood lingered through dinner. Philip and Theo had decided to spend one evening a week speaking only French to each other. Theo was fluent in the language, while Iris had only a vague smattering of it, left over from high school.

"Last year I was able to keep up with you two," she said, "but Philip's way ahead of me now."

It was a cheerful scene, the father and son enjoying the dinner she had cooked—and cooked quite well too!—in the pretty little dining room. Paint and paper had done wonders. Besides, Anna had been gradually bringing over a lot of things that Iris had stored in her attic, expecting never to use them. She had definitely not been in the mood for beautification when they moved here. But Anna was right; the copper pots in the kitchen, the silver candlesticks and tea service in the dining room, and the crystal lamps in the living room all added a lively, happy glitter.

"Well, men, take your time over dessert," she told them when she brought in the apple pudding. "I've got to get dressed to make a good impression on the parents."

She was standing indecisively at the clothes closet when Theo came upstairs.

"I'm still wondering what to wear," she said.

He reached into the closet and took out a garment that had been hanging far in the rear. It was Chez Léa's rose-beige cashmere suit, never worn.

"How about this?" he asked.

She did not answer. Only their eyes met. There was a small twitch of amusement at Theo's mouth while he waited.

And she said, faltering a little, "It's too expensive looking."

"Nonsense. You're not going to display the price tag. It's a tailored jacket and skirt, perfectly suitable." And as, with the memory of that day in Léa's shop still vivid, she hesitated, he admonished, "Iris . . . Iris . . . we need sometimes to see some humor in things. There's no survival otherwise. Put it on and walk in it happily."

He thrust the hanger toward her and she, reaching out, grasped his maimed hand instead. It was the first time since the accident that she had ever touched it and she was horrified.

"Oh, did I hurt you?" she cried.

"No. It never hurts anymore."

She had never thought she would be able to mention "it" like that, or to say "hurt." She would have expected the word to stick in her throat. And to touch that hand! The feeling it gave her was indescribable.

All evening the feeling remained, strange and also strangely intimate. Yet they—Theo and Iris—were not intimate! No, not at all. . . . And driving home through the mild night, she talked to herself.

Perhaps what I want is high poetry and not real life. I know that we loved each other once. We could not have sunk so low and come this far up again if we had not. Yet there is little desire for each other anymore; the fires are banked. Is it because we are both tired by the time the long day is over, so that we're satisfied with a murmured good night and a comfortable blanket in the comfortable bed? No, that's only an excuse. All around the globe people work harder than we do, and still they have the will toward passionate love.

The house was dark when she put the car back in the garage. Theo was already asleep.

We must have done more damage to ourselves than we realize, Iris thought. She felt deep loneliness. If being in love was only a kind of madness, as it was often said to be, then she could only hope to be a little bit mad again.

17

Steve was restless. He could not have pointed to any one moment when restlessness became resolve and propelled him into motion. As in any conversion or reconversion, insights flashed at odd times, were fought down, were reasoned away or absorbed by other business, until suddenly they returned a trifle stronger than before. And this was often repeated.

He was with Susan B. in a supermarket, buying the commune's weekly supply of staples. As they went out, two young men came in wearing the remnants of army fatigues. One of them had an empty sleeve, and the other had a healing wound that had destroyed one side of a handsome face.

At a filling station two middle-aged men pumping gas were talking to each other.

"Heard from your boy?" inquired one.

"Yeah. Got three months to go before his time's up. No telling whether he'll last the three months, though. We're getting the hell beaten out of us over there."

"You can't think that way. He'll make it. He's got to."

"Got to? My brother's kid didn't. Shot through the heart. Eighteen last winter, he was."

The second man, having no answer to that, put on a mournful expression and walked away.

Standing with Susan B., Steve watched a coffin draped with the American flag being carried out of a funeral home. A couple, farm people by their looks, he in his shabby suit and she in a cotton dress, followed the coffin down the front steps. The woman, barely able to stay on her feet, was helped into the lead car with her husband on one side and another man on the other. Then the little procession followed the hearse down the dusty street, leaving a desolate silence behind.

Steve broke it harshly. "It's a conspiracy. A conspiracy against youth. They'll kill off all the young before they're finished."

His vehemence made the girl anxious. "It seems so far away," she said. "I mean, so far away from our lives. I haven't actually thought about the war in ages."

Steve frowned. "Naturally. We never read the papers, do we?"

Now whenever he went to town, it seemed as if Vietnam had also come to town. Passing the newspaper office, he caught the headlines. In the market and on the main street he kept overhearing pieces of dialogue. Once a busload of men—boys—came down from an army camp on its way overseas, and Steve began to feel the rise of his long-buried anger.

"It won't affect you," said Susan B., "since you've got such a high draft number. And there's nothing you can do about it, anyway."

These words, for all their innocent intent, were stinging. And he answered shortly, "I used to do plenty. Have you forgotten everything I've told you about what I used to do? Think for a minute."

"I am thinking," she said, "and it scares me."

During an evening meal he got into an argument, started by his remark that Vietnam was spilling over onto the town.

"Let it spill," someone said. "Let the whole mess crash. Up in these hills we won't even hear the crash unless we want to."

"To begin with, that isn't true," Steve said. "You'll hear it, all right, and feel it too. There are no hiding places." And then, with the vision of the soldier in the supermarket, of the taut red grafted skin—there must have been blood; oh, terrible, bloodied face!—he felt a hot spurt of anger. " 'Let the whole mess crash'? As long as you're comfortable living the noble, simpler life, you'd turn your back on a burning world?"

His opponent shrugged. "Man, you're in a bad way. You need to meditate."

"Take some grass," he was advised. "Get loose."

There was no response to his anger, no comprehension. And he complained that night to Susan B.

"How is it possible not to care? Can you believe that these people just don't care?"

"You haven't, either, for a long time, have you?" she responded.

She was, of course, quite right, and he was ashamed. Yet he could not bring himself to leave, not this place that had become his home, and surely not to leave Susan B. So, always with the sense that he would not continue this way very much longer, he still did nothing.

Then one day a letter arrived from Tim, the first in many months.

"You've rested, hibernated, long enough. You're needed,

Steve. The revolution needs every soul it can muster, but you especially, with your intelligence, are needed. You've been temporarily derailed. Now get back on track."

The letter ended with an address in San Francisco to which he should come. Susan B., who had been reading it over Steve's shoulder, asked whether Powers was the writer.

"Of course. I told you he never signs his name."

And suddenly he felt a wave of the familiar old excitement. He was in command or obeying commands, no matter which. Gone was the indolence of sunny days, the cheerful routine of plodding between fields and barns. He was on the move. That day when they had destroyed the draft records, through all the dry-mouthed fear and the sly escape, what a feeling of achievement that had been! They had maybe saved a few poor devils from coming home with half a face or coming home in a box. And more important, they'd beaten a part of the system.

Already he could feel the adrenaline pour. It was marvelous.

"Are you going?" asked Susan B.

"I am. And you're going with me."

"I? I don't know anything about it except what you've told me."

She was so young, so little, and so tender. He held her tightly and soothed.

"I've told you plenty that I know you've understood perfectly. And you'll learn more from some wonderful people I know. It's time you grew up, Susan B. Tim's right. I've been hibernating. You have too."

"I'll go with you," she said, "because you're all I have in the world."

"And I'll take care of you always and wherever. Only trust me."

A few days later they got up early, before dawn, and left before anyone had stirred.

We're going away. Good luck. We love you all, Steve wrote, and stuck the note in the front door of the big house.

"That's a good idea. It's too sad to have to say good-bye," said Susan B.

"Not only that. We don't want to answer any questions. People might come looking for us someday, and if these people here don't know anything, they can't say the wrong thing."

Timothy was there. He had shaved off his beard, darkened his bright hair, and dimmed his bright eyes behind gray-tinted glasses with heavy black rims that gave him the sober look of an accountant or a banker.

"Just window glass," he said, laughing as he removed them. He caught Steve in a rough hug.

"Hey! It's good to see you. So damn good!" And holding Steve apart to get a better view of him, he cried, still heartily, "What have you been doing to yourself? You look lean and hard. You look great."

"Farm work. Real proletarian labor," Steve said, reddening with pleasure over the welcome and the praise.

"Well, you've been missed. A lot's been going on. It's almost incredible that you've been out of it, that you don't even know about it. But we'll fill you in right now. And who's this?"

For Susan, still standing near the door, was almost hidden behind a wide male shoulder.

"Susan. She came with me." Steve, speaking straight to Timothy's eyes, said solemnly, "She knows everything. We've had long talks, and she understands everything. She's all right, Tim, believe me."

"If you say she's all right, then she is," Tim replied with equal solemnity. "Come over, Susan. Join us." He took her hand between both of his. "This is a serious business that we're undertaking, Susan. There's a lot of risk in it. You do know that, I hope? And a lot of trust too. Total trust."

She nodded. "I know. And I know it's worth it." She added proudly, "I've learned so much since I met Steve. Where I came from—you would have to know where I came from to understand what I—"

Steve knew her emotional tender spots as well as he knew every intimacy of her body, and he said quickly, "You'll have a chance to tell about that when we all introduce ourselves." And addressing Tim, he questioned, "I assume that's still the procedure?"

Tim took over. "Oh, yes. Sit, everyone, so we can get started."

The small square room, which had once been a second-floor bedroom when the house was a single-family home and was now the front room of some anonymous apartment, held a rump-sprung green sofa, two soiled green upholstered chairs, and a card table with a single chair on which Tim now sat down to preside over the meeting. Since there were eight people present, two had to sit on the floor, Susan and Steve being the two.

"Hi, George, hi, Sam." The men gripped hands.

"Hi, Lydia. Susan, this is the Lydia I've talked so much about."

Her bravery and resourcefulness he had talked about, but he had never said that he'd slept with her, and he was glad of that, because Susan B. would have to be looking at her differently now if she knew.

He himself, as he looked at Lydia, was now totally dispassionate; like everyone else, female or male, she was a partner in the cadre and no more. He put his hand, tight with reassurance, over Susan's.

There were two new people, Ted and Shelly. Ted, who looked thirty but turned out to be twenty-two, had long, thin blond hair and a worried, ascetic face. Shelly had a pixie haircut and a finishing-school accent.

"I'm twenty-five," she began when Timothy called on her to describe herself. "I've been a radical all my life, ever since I was old enough to look around and really see where I was. Where was I? In a Massachusetts suburb. Horse shows, debutante dances, good families. That sort of thing, you know." She glanced at the strange assortment in the room, two middle-class eastern Jews, one midwesterner from a Catholic parochial school, and the son of a Pittsburgh coal miner among them. "Or maybe you don't know. All I felt was that this wasn't for me. I finally got away when I went to college, where I majored in political science and got into politics. SDS, of course. After graduation I went to Washington, lived in a commune, and have been pretty much based there since, although I do move around some."

There was a laugh, and Tim said, "Most of us are aware of your moving around, Shelly, as you can see. But for Susan's benefit, I'll just say that Shelly has been one of the most active campus organizers we've ever had. Tireless. She's been arrested half a dozen times or more, starting with stink bombs at the Chicago convention in sixty-eight and going on to high school demonstrations and the women's militia—well, you go on, Shelly."

The crisp voice continued. "I joined the Weathermen. There's no point in giving you long lists and dates. You probably know about them, anyway. And I'm sure I don't need to tell you that while stopping the war is an obvious goal, the main position, or what we're really aiming for, is to change the political system, to give power to the people who have none. And that means ninety-nine percent of the people. So, that's enough about me, isn't it?" she concluded.

Timothy said quietly, "She hasn't told you that she threatened a policeman with a club or that she's out on bail now, or that she plans to jump bail."

To Steve's surprise Susan B. spoke up. "What can happen then?"

"Nothing, we hope," Timothy replied. "Actually, we're fairly sure nothing will. We have our reliable network, safe houses like the one we're in right now. Ted, your turn."

Ted had a southern drawl that in no way impeded the force of his speech; this forcefulness, however, contradicted the general limpness, not only of his hair and wisp of beard, but of his very torso, which seemed to struggle its way up from the tangle of his crossed, lanky legs.

"I've had what you might call a checkered life," he began with an ironic smile. "Brought up by my Baptist grandmother, went to college, lost my religion; made a friend named Ben Weinberg who'd lost his religion, then, when we both dropped out, started real life, you might say. Joined the Weathermen and went to Chicago, where we lived in a large commune. There were about thirty of us. Communes are a good thing"— this with a nod toward Susan and Steve—"in that you get rid of hang-ups about privacy and private property. But they have drawbacks too, especially if they're escapist sanctuaries out in the boondocks. The main problem, though, is size. It's unwieldy to have thirty people when you need rapid movement and utmost secrecy, as when you go underground. So I left for New York with five others." Again he gave the ironic smile. "I must say we accomplished a few things: a bomb on the United Fruit Company pier, the Marine Midland Grace Trust Company, the federal office building, the army induction center, the criminal court building, the General Motors Building—"

Tim held up his hand. "Thanks, Ted. We've got the picture, and it's impressive. Now it's Susan's turn."

She stood up, looking more like a child than ever, Steve thought, with those braids dangling over the little shoulder blades exposed by her tank top. But her manner was assured.

"I have nothing like all that to tell you. I'm not quite eighteen, and I've never seen much outside of my home, which I despise just as Shelly hated hers, except for different reasons. Yet, maybe not so different. Mine wasn't a social-register family like hers, but it was materialistic; they were gimme-gimme people. Never cared much about anybody but themselves. I never connected that with the idea of revolution, I only hated it. Now

I'm learning. I'm coming late to knowledge, but I'm getting there." She looked around. "So that's it. That's me. I really don't know what else to tell you."

There was a little patter of applause as Susan sat down. Steve was proud of her. She had come a good way from the day she had walked up to him carrying the kitten.

"Well, now we all know who we are." Timothy's cheerful voice moved to its tone of command. "This is the working group, the affinity, no more, no less. No one enters it and no one leaves it except under further orders. Lydia will be in charge. She will know where I am at all times. No one else will, not because of any lack of confidence, as you well understand, but for the simple reason that information one doesn't have can't be gotten out of one either by an accidental slip or under threat or duress.

"Now as to what comes next. Our plans are simply a continuation of the same here in the West. We're going to move up and down the Pacific coast from one university to another and blow up the ROTC buildings. Also bear in mind that these are the ports from which troops leave. That means other possibilities for us: army barracks, trucks, the very buses leaving for the ports."

Tim looked at his watch, frowned, and stood up quickly. "I'll be late. Steve and Susan, leave with me. Here's a slip of paper with an address where you'll be staying. Memorize it and tear it up. Be there at all times so Lydia can reach you. You may, and probably will, be moved. She'll tell you. Ted, you stay here for an hour or so after everyone else has left.

"Ted's being watched," he explained, as Steve and Susan followed him down the stairs and out into the summer night. He gave Steve a piece of paper no larger than a postage stamp and pointed a direction. "That way. I go the other way."

"Shall we see you again?" asked Steve.

Tim smiled. "Eventually. By the way, you probably need money, don't you?"

"We've got ten dollars."

"Take twenty more till Lydia gets to you. Good luck."

They watched him replace the eyeglasses, go swinging rapidly down the street, around the corner, and out of sight.

"Well, what do you think of them?" Steve asked, feeling proprietary and then, not waiting for an answer, declared enthusiastically, "They're wonderful, all of them. I never got to meet Ted, but naturally I knew everything about him. He's traveled abroad a lot to student meetings. He even went to Cuba to meet Viet Cong leaders. I wanted to do that, but something always seemed to get in the way at the wrong time."

They were toiling up a street that was angled almost like a propped ladder. On either side were wooden houses built in the postearthquake style of the early 1900s, with gables, stoops, and little turrets. Some were painted in a pastel, lemon yellow or leaf green, and had geraniums in window boxes.

"I wouldn't mind having one of these," remarked Susan.

"In a fairer world, everybody'll be able to have one." Steve studied the address on the slip of paper. "It's near the Haight, I think. Matter of fact, from what I remember, it's right in the Haight."

"You've been here before? You never told me."

"Really? You'd think I'd have told you everything by now. Yes, I was here in the summer of sixty-six. I was just sort of passing through. I'd wanted to see it. And it was beautiful, the music, the art, everything new and free. They had good values, you know, like the Peace Farm people's. But then they went too far with drugs. Sure, they were against the war and against all the bad stuff, but they were too stoned to do anything about them except talk. Hippies, not New Left at all. I came back here in sixty-eight. After I got arrested in Chicago, I thought I'd go here for a while to cool off. But it was all changed, overcrowded, and gotten ugly besides with drug dealers killing each other on the streets. People were fleeing, going to places like Peace Farm." He grinned. "So I left again."

They had reached the top of the hill and now stood still, panting a little from the climb and the weight of their duffel bags. They had arrived abruptly at the very edge of the continent. Below and behind them stretched the city, tied together with the brilliant ribbons of its avenues and highways. Ahead lay the bay and the fabled bridge beyond which gleamed the vast Pacific, and beyond that Asia, while above it all, the restless city, the dazzling bridge, and the moving water, hung a dome of stars.

"How beautiful it is," Susan murmured. "So far away from what we talked about in that room awhile ago."

"Yes. The night hides all the world's dirt until the sun comes up."

"That sounds so sad."

"Not sad. True. And not sad, either, when you consider all the people who are cleaning up the world's dirt. Men like Tim, for instance."

She was quiet for a minute before asking, "Who makes the bombs?"

"We do. It's not hard. You need dynamite, blasting caps, there's a regular kit—it's not hard," he repeated positively.

"Have you ever done it?"

"Not exactly. Lydia once showed me some of the stuff, though."

"You admire her, don't you?"

"Of course. She's committed. And fearless! She even knows how to use a hand grenade and a submachine gun."

"Has she ever used them?"

"Not yet. But she would if she had to. . . . You look so scared, Susan. Are you?"

"More thoughtful than scared, though I am scared some."

Steve looked down into the girl's upturned eyes, dark flowers. "Nobody expects you to handle a gun. There are plenty of other things for you to do. Besides, Lydia's been doing this for years," he said gently, "and nothing's happened. And she's only one person out of many."

"I understand."

"We have to be smart and we have to be strong, strong in a good cause. But if you don't want to go along, my Susan, you don't have to."

"Oh, but I'm with you, Steve. Wherever you go, I'm going. Besides, I see the right of all this. I really do. You've convinced me."

Taking her face between his hands, he kissed it, forehead, cheeks, eyes, and lips. I'll take care of her, he thought, from here to the end of the earth and back. Nothing will touch her while I'm alive, so help me. We're in this struggle together, and we'll win.

"The house is just down the street," he said. "Shall we go?"

It was another narrow, clapboard late Victorian, neglected and shabby, with a gate and low railing at the top of the steps. Somebody had apparently started to paint the drab railing an electric blue and had, after doing half of it, given up for lack of paint or money or desire. But lively music was coming out of an open window. Bob Dylan was singing "Subterranean Home-sick Blues."

And to Steve came a charge of excitement as intense almost as the sexual. He was bursting out of a chrysalis, he was taking flight into life again, he was on the wing, he had his own woman, and he was a man.

18

"Such a pretty wedding in a perfect setting," Iris said to Theo.

A week had passed since Laura and Robbie McAllister had been married at Anna's house, and Iris was still talking about the garden, the marvelous food, visiting cousins, and Jimmy's brand-new baby girl.

"Imagine, Mama's a great-grandmother! You'd never think it, she seems so young and well."

They were having a slow Sunday-morning breakfast in a quiet house, Philip having gone to soccer practice.

Theo looked over the top of the *Times*. "Speaking of youth," he said, "Laura's too young to be married."

"You're just shocked because it's happened so soon after Jimmy's wedding."

"Maybe." Theo smiled. "And you don't have to tell me, because I'm well aware, that no father ever thinks anybody's good enough for his daughter." Becoming sober, he added, "I hope they never have a problem with the religious difference. There are enough other difficulties, God knows."

Yes, Iris thought. I tried to point them out to her. We sat talking for an hour in her room, but her only answer was that people make too much of a "big deal" about marriage; as long as you love each other, what can be so hard about it? You and Dad, she said, don't seem to have had such awful problems. . . . Oh, poor darling Laura!

Now Theo put the newspaper away and, still darkly sober, said, "I'll tell you what almost ruined the day for me! Steve's not coming to either wedding, that's what."

Iris sought to pacify. "He didn't forget, though. He did send those lovely white moccasins that he'd made himself. I thought that was rather sweet."

"Sweet! Is that what he's to be, a maker of moccasins, all his life?"

"Well, at least he's still on the commune," she said softly. "He's not in jail or on the way to it, or blown up in an explosion like that one in Colorado last month when the ROTC building was bombed."

"Thank God for small favors, I suppose," Theo muttered angrily. And she knew that he was not so much furious as furiously hurt.

"Besides, who knows what's coming next with him? Do you? Can you say what's coming next week?"

"No, and I'm not going to let myself think about it. You shouldn't either, Theo."

She was determined to keep alive, as long as possible, the glow of the wedding. They were a beautiful pair. Might they always feel as they so obviously had felt, standing with joined hands among flowers, friends, and birdsong! And she thought: I remembered, as I watched them, how it had been on my own day. I wish I could feel exactly like that again. But I suppose too much has happened.

She rose and began to clear the table.

"I think I'll call Mama. Maybe she'd like to go to an early movie tonight."

"Good idea. Go ahead."

The telephone rang in the kitchen. Agitated sounds came out of it when Iris picked up the receiver.

"Who? What? You went upstairs and—I can't understand you! What? Yes, I'm coming right over. Five minutes—yes." She called to Theo in the dining room. "It's Mama's new housekeeper. I couldn't make any sense of her, whether the house is on fire or Mama's sick or—hurry, hurry!"

Theo had already taken the car keys from the drawer and was on the way to the garage.

"Steady, steady," he said when they were in the car. "Let's not jump to conclusions. The woman may be overreacting to something that's not so terrible. We'll be there in a second."

Iris ran up the steps toward the open front door, crying, "What happened here? What is it?"

"I went upstairs. Missus always gets up early for breakfast, and it was late so I went upstairs, I went—" Lula wrung her hands.

Theo was already halfway up. "Iris, stay down there. Wait."

But she was just behind him. It flashed through her mind that her mother had had a stroke and Theo didn't want her to see. And she followed him into the familiar room.

Anna lay in the center of the bed under a white summer blanket. Her hair was softly spread on the pillow and the one arm that was exposed was covered with a lace sleeve. Theo, bending down, passed a hand lightly across her eyelids.

"Is it—is it a stroke, Theo?"

"No, dear. No stroke. Just quick and without pain. Just quietly slipped away." And putting his arm around Iris's shoulders, he led her to a chair.

It was so queer and sudden. A few minutes ago they had been reading the paper and eating French toast. Now they were here and Theo was saying—what was he saying? Her question came out in a high, harsh voice.

"Is she dead, Theo? Is that what you meant?"

He nodded. His eyes were filled with tears. In the background Lula was sobbing. Morning light came through the fine curtains. A strong fragrance came from the bowl of phlox, rose and cream, Mama's beloved flowers. Or was the fragrance from her powder, her perfume? She was always fragrant.

"I talked to her yesterday," Iris said. "She had a postcard from Laura. She was thinking about trading her car in. She had made arrangements for the concerts at Tanglewood. Yesterday."

"It was painless," Theo repeated. He wiped his tears. "It's the way anyone would want to die."

"Yes." Anna would want, too, to die without disruption or ugliness. Even in death she was elegant. The blanket was smooth and straight.

"We had no warning," Iris said, uncomprehendingly.

"It happens."

She stood up on shaky legs and, with Theo's arm around her again, went over to the bed.

"I need to look at her," she said.

Anna, my mother, lying in the bed where she had lain for so many years with the only man she ever loved. They were lucky, my parents. God rest them both. . . .

For a while they stood there together, until Theo led Iris from the room.

"There are things to be done," he said gently. "You go downstairs with Lula while I use the phone."

·　　·　　·

It was a few days after the funeral—murmuring voices, flowers, tears—before they had to deal with the painful, practical aftermath of death, a paper aftermath, addresses and documents wanted by the tax authorities, the accountants, and the lawyers.

"There are fifty years of life in this desk, maybe more," Iris said.

"This is the room where I proposed to you. Now it's filled with pictures of our children."

They were in Anna's downstairs sitting room. As far back as Iris could recall it had been painted and upholstered in white and yellow. Here Anna paid bills, knitted, and read. A book of poems lay on a table now, along with a pair of reading glasses. Directly across from the desk, on the opposite wall where she would have had to see it whenever she looked up, hung a photograph of Papa.

"That photo must have been a comfort to her after he died," Iris said. "It's so real, as if he were about to speak."

"Is this too hard for you? I wish I could do it for you, this whole business of dismantling the house."

"It's all right. But thank you, Theo. I'll get through it."

"You've been very brave."

There were cabinets and shelves, albums and boxes of old letters. It would take weeks to go through them all. This wasn't dismantling a house, Iris thought, it was the uncovering of a life, of many lives.

And she asked herself as she worked: Why am I not weeping in utter desolation as I did when Papa died? I don't know. Perhaps Theo is surprised that I am not. Oh, I loved them both, my parents, but I loved Papa more, that's all. Maybe that was because he really was a special person to me, or can it be because I do not feel abandoned by her death as I did by his, because at last and very late, I have grown up? If that is true, I owe so much of it to her.

Anna, my mother.

· · ·

One evening Theo went out for a walk with Laura's collie and the old, waddling poodle. It was the supper hour, and now in early fall, lights were being turned on. He could see families in their dining rooms and others cooking on barbecue grills in the backyards, having the last outdoor meals of the season. He himself had eaten alone, for this was Iris's late night at classes in the city. And as he strolled, he thought about her drive and determination. Years ago he would not have believed she had them in her. Well, he had been wrong.

Ever since Paul Werner's astonishing disclosure, he had been seeing his wife through more curious eyes. And Anna, too, he had observed with renewed curiosity. To think of that Old World lady, for he still saw her as such despite her having been in America since she was sixteen, so devoted to and careful of her husband's wishes, to think of her so, when all the time she had had another hidden life! And he could only respect her for having had the courage to carry such a heavy, hidden burden.

He hadn't had the heart to let Paul know she was dead. Those letters to Paul were growing more difficult to write, as it was. Knowing that the man was hungry for details of the family, he tried to supply them, but it was hard to avoid repetition, and now that everyone except Philip was away from home, two married and Steve doing heaven knew what, he hadn't very much to tell, nor had he very much to tell about Iris, either, except that she was busy and well.

After a long mile he turned about toward home. As he entered his street, he could see ahead to the living-room window, from which a gold light now flared. Iris had come home, then. He began to walk faster. Without her, even when Philip was upstairs doing homework, the house, small as it was, seemed to hold empty spaces in which his footsteps were too loud.

And yet . . . and yet much was still missing. The truth of it was that they were friends, yes, friends, absolutely loyal, absolutely dependable, with some occasional, perfunctory "lovemaking" thrown in, if you could call it lovemaking; it was little more than an appetite quickly satisfied. He sighed as he walked and now, no longer in a hurry, reined in the dogs to slow his pace. It had surely not used to be this way! Where had the joy and the longing gone?

Oh, he—he was surely ready to resume them. It was Iris in whom they had been quenched. Yet it was no fault of hers, he understood that. One couldn't simply command the return of passionate joy. It existed or it did not.

He walked through the house, hung up the dogs' leashes, and saw that the outside light was on in the yard. The little space enclosed by the arborvitae hedge that Anna had given them was warm and still in the mild evening, and Iris was sitting on the English bench under a light.

"May I?" he asked.

She looked up. "May you? So formal, Theo?"

He sat down next to her. "Sometimes I feel as if I have to be formal with you."

"That's not true," she said quickly, defensively.

"If I feel it, then it's true for me."

"Then I'm sorry, Theo."

"Well. That's a lovely dress. Have I seen it before?"

"No. My mother gave it to me the week before she died. I haven't been able to wear it until today."

The angle at which her head was bent and the graceful curve of her long neck reminded him for a moment of Anna and when, abruptly, she raised her head, he saw Paul's strong profile. And this living combination of the two shocked him into pity.

"Don't be sad," he said gently. "She would want you to wear it, you know."

"It's not that." The corners of her mouth were trembling.

"What is it, then?"

For answer she handed him a letter. "I found it yesterday

among her things. She knew I would find it when the time came."

Nothing extraordinary, he said to himself as he read through the first page, only some tender expressions of care for a daughter and grandchildren. But his attention was arrested at the end.

"Loving is all there is, Iris, when you look back and count up. Treasure it, for God's sake, because it's all there is. Everyone isn't lucky enough to take it when it's offered or to hold on to it when one has it. Things get in the way, circumstances that can't be helped or sometimes our pride and resentments, our absorption in self or a mistaken sense of duty. Dear Iris, don't let that happen. Remember how it was for you both when you began life together."

Theo put the page down. *"Circumstances that can't be helped."* Yes, Anna, you knew all about that.

"She wanted me," Iris said, "to have the life that she and Papa had, that's what it means. And if she hadn't brought you and me together that day, you would have gone away. I would have sent you away. Oh, God, Theo, do you hear? She's right. What is it all about? We work and we worry about children and jobs and money and houses . . ." And she said more quietly, "I covered up through all the cheerfulness and hope, I kept that frozen place inside where everything was stored, the ways I'd hurt you, the ways you'd hurt me, everything that had ever angered me, all lying there written in stone. And I forgot the beginning. What have we done? What have we broken, Theo?"

He felt a smile. It rose from his chest and spread.

"Nothing that can't be mended in our bed upstairs."

"What is it, Theo? Do you have to see death before you can know what life is?"

"Maybe so, my darling."

She was standing now, clasping him. And he kissed her, the cool, sweet forehead first, the eyelids and the still trembling,

warm, urgent mouth. So long it had been, so long. He could
have wept through his joy.

Then in a sudden recall he felt a chill and cried, "To think
that once I almost went away! And meant never to come back!
And I need you so, need you more than—" he was about to say
"my right hand."

And now she was picking up his hand, the right one, kissing
each finger. . . . So he turned off the light, and in the blue
darkness they went back to the house. They climbed the stairs,
went into their room, and locked the door.

19

The car moved out of the Milan airport, wound through noontime traffic, and turned north toward the lakes. Paul, in the driver's seat, looked over at Ilse beside him and shook his head in wonder. He had been staring at her like that ever since she had gotten off the plane, gone through customs, and claimed her luggage.

"When your letter arrived last week, I couldn't believe it. I had to read it through three times to get the simple idea that you were finally coming." He reached down and seized her thin, sun-darkened hand. "Why on earth did you take so long?" he demanded.

She turned a smiling face to him. "Ah, don't scold me. Here I am, and we have so much time to make up for!"

Despite the smile her eyebrows drew together in an expression of faintly sorrowful reproach. He had been about to ask further how long she intended to stay, but then, thinking better of it, did not ask and said instead, "You can't know how I've missed you."

Her hair had now turned to pepper and salt like his own, more salt than pepper. But it made a comely contrast to her tanned cheeks and black, shining eyes. She was wearing a dark blue travel suit that was typical of her and with it a fine white blouse cut rather low, so that the gold pendant lying on her bare neck was prominent.

He pointed to it. "Ah, so you actually wear it! I always imagine it stuck in its velvet box in that upper right-hand drawer where you keep gloves and handkerchiefs."

"I wear it all the time," she answered seriously. "Even when it doesn't show, it's under my clothes."

"God, how I've missed you," he said again.

It might not be the most romantic concept, but it was enduring—and wasn't endurance romantic when you came to think of it?—that the one person in the world to whom he could say anything was sitting next to him. She it was who would listen wholly, both with mind and heart, never agreeing just to please him, but giving to him her complete attention. Goodness knew, he had surely not always agreed with her either! But their minds had always listened to each other.

"I've made a reservation for lunch at the Villa d'Este," he said now, "a long, leisurely Italian lunch. You haven't had food like it since you went to Israel."

"No, long, leisurely lunches aren't the way we can afford to live these days."

He wanted to keep the atmosphere light, and Israel was clearly not a subject to be taken lightly. One had only to pick up the newspaper almost any morning to be reminded that the little land was still being heavily besieged.

"This is a beautiful car. What kind?" asked Ilse, and he understood that she, too, wanted to be joyful.

"A Ferrari, worth a fortune, but not my fortune. It came with the house for a rental fee. It leaps like a lion on the *autostrada,* but we're not leaping today. We're just going to amble along so you can feast your eyes on the scenery."

"I'm already feasting on this wonderful soft air."

"Shall I put the top down?"

"Yes, do."

"The wind won't spoil your hair?"

She laughed. "Oh, you've forgotten me after all, haven't you? My hair!"

He had not forgotten, but had asked the question only out of automatic courtesy, having gotten in the habit. He knew quite well that Ilse would let her hair just blow.

"We're going to Lake Como. Do you know about the Villa d'Este? It was a cardinal's residence during the Renaissance. Splendid. Wait till you see."

"Oh, I've heard. The height of luxury."

"Yes. You deserve some," he answered simply.

Between a mild slope and the lake stood the great stone edifice in all its grandeur. Behind it and spread up the slope, among clipped formal hedges, white statuary, and urns of overflowing petunias, the gardens were in the full bloom of spring as it moved toward summer. Paul had reserved a table at the edge of the overhanging roof, where the windows had been rolled back to suit the season and a fresh breeze from the lake stirred the shrubbery. The lovely room was already filled by tourists and by Milanese businessmen with their fashionable women in white linens and pastel silks. And again Paul remarked to himself, as he had so often done through their years together, that it never occurred to Ilse to worry whether she was dressed well enough because, in the elegance of her simplicity, she always was.

A woman at the next table flicked her eyes for a bare second over the pendant on Ilse's chest. They were expert eyes, Paul thought with amusement; that woman knew what she was looking at.

Ilse asked him why he was smiling.

"Just feeling very, very good. Look down there." He pointed. "Right at the lake edge there's a spot where you can dance at night. It's a spectacle with the lights reflected in the lake and all the young people dancing. Such beautiful young people. We'll come over one night. You haven't forgotten how to dance, have you?"

"Of course I haven't."

"Well, then. I haven't, either, and the music's great."

"I take it you've been dancing here."

"A few times. I've made friends here, Ilse. This has been a good change for me. I'm glad I finally made it. Hey, what about food? You've got to have pasta. They have a wonderful carbonara. And wine. They have a white wine that I swear is like bottled sunshine. I sound like an ad, don't I?"

Silly with happiness, he heard himself prattling, couldn't stop, and didn't even want to stop.

Almost two hours later as they were finishing their espresso, Ilse leaned back in her chair and said, "Well, now, tell me all the news about everybody."

"I've kept you pretty much abreast of things in my letters. I did tell you, didn't I, that Theo's opened an office? He's making a good start, he says, and even sent me a check to begin repaying the loan. You know, I don't want it, but I have to accept it. Meg and Larry are confining their practice to small animals. Larry's getting too old to handle horses. Meg's fine, but awfully worried, naturally, with Tom in Vietnam. And then Tim—" He threw up his hands. "What's there to say about him?"

"Is he still so involved with that odd man?"

"Jordaine? As far as I know, he is. And odd it is, a real puzzle."

He had let Ilse know everything about Jordaine except for
the business about Iris. That was something he preferred to
forget and would therefore never mention, even to Ilse, just as
he would never mention Iris's attempt at suicide, if indeed it
had been one.

Ilse asked now, "Is Iris's son still joined up with him?"

"I don't know. Theo hasn't written anything lately. Queer,
isn't it? The whole business is queer. 'Don't trust anyone over
thirty.' Toss us and our experience onto the junk heap. For
God's sake, Tim's way over thirty himself. Theo did write one
thing that sticks in my head, though. He said that this young
generation seems to have some of the best people in it and also
some of the worst."

"Not necessarily the worst. Often just the most troubled,"
Ilse said soberly.

"Take his other son, Jimmy, for instance. He and his wife are
both in medical school, and they've just had a baby girl besides.
Young people like them are building. And then you get these
others who are tearing down. I know it's a terrible war in
Vietnam. I myself think it's useless. And yet, what good does it
do to bomb the hell out of our cities? A strange form for
idealism to take."

"It's not just idealism. Yes, for many it is. But the big question is, who's behind the terror? Idealists? I don't think so. I
think they're the people who're using these kids. It's like the
sixteen-year-old boys in Al Fatah, who are trained in Lebanon
to think they're following a noble cause when they blow up a
bus full of Israeli schoolchildren or old ladies going to market.
Do you remember?"

"Remember? Ilse, I still wake up sometimes with my heart
pounding after I've dreamed about it, the same as I sometimes
still dream about the war in France. After all these years."

Ilse was following her own train of thought. Suddenly here in
this sparkling room—sparkle of blue water, sparkle of fashion,
flowers, and crystal glasses—she was back in Israel.

"Think of it. Golda was over seventy when they made her prime minister. She didn't want it, but everyone wanted her because she was the one who knew best that we would never give up. Terror will not win over us."

At that they both fell silent. Voices from outside, with ominous distant roar, had abruptly drowned the pleasant ripple of conversation in this peaceful room. For several minutes with this roaring in their heads, neither Paul nor Ilse spoke again.

And then, fortuitously, there came a nearby ring of jovial laughter. A group of young people, rising from their table, were taking merry leave of one another, and this laughter of theirs scolded Paul, reminding him that this was a day and a place that they had come to for gaiety. May in Italy, after all!

"Come," he said, "let's take a little walk down to the shore. Then we'll start home. Wait till you see where I'm staying. It's a paradise."

Westward toward Lake Maggiore and toward the sun they drove. The car sped with the wind past old stone villages strung along the narrow roadway, up hills and around curves, past wrought-iron gates at which stone lions guarded the pink- and white- and lemon-colored villas that overlooked the water.

Ilse sighed with pleasure and said, "I feel as if I'd been away from home and work for weeks instead of only hours."

The sky was melting into stripes of mauve and pink above the Villa Jessica's tiled roof as they turned into the drive and up the easy incline between ranks of flowering bougainvillea. In the warm light the stucco walls of the house were also touched with the sun's last fading pink, and the windows gleamed like mirrors.

When the front door was opened, one looked straight through the hallway and through the door that opened onto the terrace at the rear.

"Come out here before we go upstairs," Paul said. "I just want you to look."

The vast lake lay still as a pool. The perfect lawn, now in

evening shade, was almost black and would be soft as fur to the touch. Lou, the spaniel, hearing Paul's voice, came bounding up past the rose beds.

"The roses!" exclaimed Ilse. "They're as big as cabbages."

"I have a thousand things to show you. Oh, Ilse, if you'll stay long enough, I'll show you all of Italy."

"You forget, I was here before."

"During the war? That doesn't count. Have you seen Florence, Venice, Capri? Have you ever taken a steamer ride around this lake?"

Smiling, she shook her head.

"Well, then. We have all that to do. Now come upstairs."

He had moved himself from the smaller room with the single bed into a larger one. Here stood an enormous old bed, carved, painted, gilded, and hung with a canopy and side curtains of silver-blue brocade. Elaborate ornament like this was not to Paul's taste; in a home of his own he surely would not have had it, but it belonged in this room, as did the marble fireplace, which they would not be needing unless they were to stay for the winter, something he would not let himself think about. There was a marquetry desk for letter writing. There were books and current magazines on a table, upon which the maid had also put an arrangement of those roses large as cabbages.

Tonight they would sleep together in that bed. He hadn't begun to realize how much he had missed her, hadn't truly realized it until this minute now when he could see her, hear her, and touch her, still strong, still slender, firm where she ought to be and soft where she ought to be, and so dearly to be desired.

"Unpack your things now. Get it over with," he said. "It'll be almost time for a little supper soon. Would you like to eat outdoors on the terrace or inside?" His thoughts and his tongue were whirling so, he could hardly keep up with either. "I hope you brought something to wear to a party. Some friends are giving one tomorrow. People I met through my Roman lawyer. They have a place across the lake. We'll go by boat, just a short ride, but beautiful at night coming back in moonlight."

"I know you well enough to come prepared," Ilse told him, as she unfolded clothes. "Where Paul is, there are always parties."

He stepped out to the balcony. The sun had fallen just a moment before, dropped out of sight behind the burly masses of the mountains whose tops now drew penciled lines across the gray sky. A sailboat moving slowly across the water left an unwavering streak behind it, black against lighter black, as on a Japanese print. Everything had been reduced to a minimum, light, sky, water, and the little boat growing smaller as it moved away.

Tomorrow, he thought, we shall take that steamer tour of the lake. Then we'll drive over to Venice, stopping at Verona and Padua on the way.

His head was filled with plans, and his heart was full.

If I had to go back over my life and pick out any space of three weeks, I wouldn't be able to find one in which I had been more content than I've been in these last three, Paul thought, as he sat in a kind of tropical trance watching Ilse plow through fifty laps in the pool.

They had followed most of his design, having seen the hill towns of Tuscany, explored Florence, ridden the Amalfi Drive, examined almost every corner of the Vatican Museum—quite a feat!—swum at the Lido, and even traveled down to Ravenna.

Now the morning shone. On the lower level of the lawn a whirling hose threw spray like a spangled streamer into the wind. Up here Ilse's arms rose and fell to the strong rhythm of the crawl. When she climbed out and sat on the edge, glittering drops fell about her. There wasn't a curve in her back. Her white suit clung like skin. A woman is blessed to have a body like that, Paul was thinking when she hailed him.

"Why don't you go in? What's wrong with you today?"

"Not a thing except laziness. And besides, the New York paper's just arrived, and I want to see it. You know I get it at least a week late, anyway."

"Well, I need a few more laps."

"Go ahead. I'll go up to read."

A small pile of newspapers and several magazines to which he subscribed lay ready for him on the table near the balustrade. Eager for home news and accustomed to rapid reading anyway, he was always able in rather few minutes to get the "feel" of events. He read: Firebombs at the University of Colorado; Explosions at the University of Michigan; Thirty incidents in Detroit this past year alone. *The New York Times* reported: "A seven-hundred-fifty-pound bomb exploded today during loading operations at Port Chicago's Navy Ammunition Shipping Base." An unexploded bomb had been found at the Oakland Army Base. After another series of bombings, a letter sent to United Press International contained a long complaint about racism, sexism, pollution, and imperialism: "In death-directed America there is only one way to a life of love and freedom." Paul's head was swimming as anger mounted. And he skimmed through the red-hot words. ". . . attack, attack and destroy . . . build a just society . . . revolution." Then he threw the paper on the floor.

All this was actually not new. It had rather become routine to read about the bombing of the ROTC, the invasion of the draft-board offices, and all the rest. That was the worst of it, just that it had become routine and there seemed no way to end it.

The color bled out of the day.

"Revolution," he said aloud. "Yes, as in the Soviet Union, as in Cuba or China. Oh, yes, a life of love and freedom. Stupid bastards."

"Who?" asked Ilse, wrapping a terry robe around herself as she appeared at the top of the stairs.

"Who? These. Read. I can't even talk about it, I get so mad. Oh, here's a letter from Leah. Oh, God, oh, no." He groaned.

"What is it? What's happened?"

"Tom. In Vietnam. His car was just behind one that hit a mine, and he's had a face wound, a bad one. They're bringing him back to the States for surgery. He's a handsome man too, handsome as Tim, but different, without the personality and the charm, for all that's worth." He read on. "Oh, poor Meg. As if she hadn't enough with Tim on her mind. God, this war. This war." And turning over the pile, he came upon an envelope addressed in Theo's precise script. "Here's something from Theo," he said, wondering how the man managed a pen as well as he did. When he had finished the letter, he read it again, so absorbed in what he had read that he was unaware of Ilse's expectancy.

"You look puzzled," she said.

"I'm thinking. Of course, there may be nothing to it. Listen to this: That professor, the one Steve—that's their son, the one who's always in trouble—admires so much, is being sought by the FBI. Apparently, he's been involved in some of these explosions. Another man in the group, an ex-priest, has been caught in a safe haven, some young lawyer's house in Rhode Island. A couple of students escaped from the house and are being sought too." Paul read on, frowning and muttering, "A mess. It seems that the other son, this kid's brother—I don't know why I should call him a kid when he's twenty-two—was in California and went to some commune where he'd been living for a year or more to see him. And he had disappeared. Been gone for several months. So putting two and two together, he may well be wherever Tim Powers is."

"Very farfetched," Ilse cautioned. "You can't put the numbers together when you don't even know what the numbers are."

"Well, still I can say it's awful. Awful. Theo writes that Iris is frantic."

"Paul, your pain is written on your face, and I don't like to see it. Oh, I don't mean to be hard on you, my dearest, I only want to remind you, as I used to do long ago, that she's an adult and no responsibility of yours. Even if you had a normal relationship, she wouldn't really be, but she certainly isn't now."

Although he heard Ilse clearly, Paul was again thinking of, and overwhelmed by, the clash and reunion of opposites. Donal and Timothy, father and son, the one who, loving money more than anything, supported the Nazis for their industry and the Arabs for their oil, the other who despises money and claims to support the cause of brotherhood, have come together full circle at last, in horror and blood.

Then, rousing himself to answer Ilse, he sighed. "You're right, of course, you're right."

"Look around you. That's what you keep telling me to do, isn't it? Don't let anything spoil one day for you, especially when it's something you can't do anything about."

"You're right," he repeated.

Something had happened in his head, nevertheless. A remarkable change of mood had abruptly swept him, and he found himself thinking that he'd been away a long, long time. This, if he were to stay here, would be the second summer. A dry, burning summer it would be. At home now, in the country at Meg's, tree frogs would be chirping in the evenings. Along Park Avenue tulips would tremble in the cool spring wind. Maybe this was some ancient tribal memory received from generations of dwellers in the north, a memory of a different kind of spring, a rejoicing at the end of the barren winter and the long cold. Whatever the cause, he was feeling at this moment a totally unexpected stab of longing for home.

Then he spoke reasonably to himself: You know very well that Theo's letter is the reason why you suddenly want to go home. . . . If only Ilse would go with him!

And the day that had been so smooth, so free of burden, only a few minutes before while he had been watching Ilse in the pool and before the mail had come, that day was now a tangle of contradictions. If only she would go with him!

Then he rebuked himself. Don't be a fool, Paul. Take what you have. Take what *is,* what's here right now, just as Ilse told you to do. And deliberately, he smiled, forcing the effort.

"Since we're going for a sail this afternoon, shall we have an early lunch here or shall we take a basket lunch to eat on the boat?"

And the halcyon days resumed.

One morning in June a man's scorched body was found on a highway outside of Milan. A bundle of dynamite sticks was still in his hand, and both of his legs were blown off. Apparently, he had intended to blow up the power station and had blown himself up instead. His clothing was that of a workman in poor straits, and the name found among his possessions in the rickety car parked nearby meant nothing to anyone. But the false passports did mean something, sending the authorities into frantic action. Police and army, Justice Department and investigators of every description, went scrambling and scouring through the land. The newspapers, as usual, kept reporting and repeating the same meager clues, all of which seemed to lead nowhere.

In the second week, however, there came stupendous news, shaking the country from end to end. Early in the morning, before breakfast, Paul was on the telephone talking to his friend in Rome, who had called in high excitement. When he hung up at last, he hurried to satisfy Ilse's curiosity.

"Can you imagine who the man was? Arturo Martillini, the millionaire. Billionaire! Blown himself up. Good lord, he owns —owned—just about everything you can think of, inherited acres, thousands of them, urban real estate, factories, a steel mill, you name it. The whole social crowd is in shock over this.

My friend tells me everyone has always known he's been way out Left, but only in the fashionable sense that we know at home. Radical chic, you know what I mean. But one doesn't conceive of such people going about with dynamite."

Ilse reflected. "People like me who suffered under fascism have generally thought of the far Right as the ultimate evil, and the Left somehow more idealistic, more virtuous, no matter what it does. And still terror is terror and dead is dead, isn't it, no matter who does it?"

"You wonder what in the man's life could have led him into something like that."

Ilse continued her reflections. "I've got some friends in Mossad—you know, they say the Israeli intelligence is one of the cleverest in the world—and I've heard bits and pieces about money coming from someone in Italy, someone with a bottomless pocketbook who finances the German Baader-Meinhof gang and the PLO training camp in South Yemen and a dozen other things. In South Yemen practically everybody's there, Swedes, Japanese, even the IRA. I've told you about it."

"And you think this is the man?"

"It's not impossible. In fact, it's very possible."

"This is like first-rate espionage fiction. Let's get hold of a newspaper right away."

A queer thing happened. The front page displayed a photograph of Martillini that startled Paul. It seemed to him that he must have seen that face somewhere before. He examined it with care, trying to remember. This was a posed photograph, so the mouth had an amiable smile, yet the eyes had none. The eyes were striking. Where had he seen such eyes?

"What are you studying?" asked Ilse, looking over Paul's shoulder.

"Nothing in particular. Just reading," he replied, not wanting to disclose the sudden thought that had come to him: Jordaine.

He looks like Jordaine, which is of course absurd. I saw the man only a couple of times at Meg's. How could I, why should I, remember him? Besides, it makes me sick even to think of him and his cynical "game" with Iris. . . .

During the next few days each issue of the paper brought more startling information about the dead man. He had gone all over the world, linking the Libyans to the Japanese and the Soviets and the Cubans; he bought arms, provided safe houses, financed terrorist training camps from Prague to Beirut to Cuba. He knew everyone from Habash to Guevara to Castro. He'd been in South America to learn from the Tupamaros, who incidentally, Ilse told Paul, were linked to the Palestinians.

"Did you know that?" she asked him.

"How would I know? It seems that a lot of other people who should have known didn't know either. Now it comes out that he was in Havana in 1966 at that big congress where the world-wide workers' movement and students' movement were united."

"Al Fatah was there too," said Ilse.

"And with all this the bastard was living the life of a billionaire."

The newspapers and weeklies were delighting in descriptions of Martillini's lavish, titillating wealth: an estate in Liechtenstein—a tax haven—a mountain lodge in Switzerland, a winter retreat in southern Spain, and a splendid villa on Lake Garda with a garageful of Rolls-Royces, a beach, a yacht, magnificent gardens, and on the property, a private lake stocked with swans. He had a special fondness for swans.

Paul put the magazine down.

He had a special fondness for swans. . . .

Somewhere, sometime, he had heard that. Where? Who could have had a special fondness for swans?

"It's a funny thing about memory," he said. "You know you know a thing and you know it's got to be in your head, because it comes to the tip of your tongue and then slides back up to wherever it's been hiding in your head."

"What is it you're not remembering?"

"Swans. What can it be that I want to remember about them?"

"I can't imagine, but it will come to you. It always does."

"Probably sometime in the middle of the night."

"Please don't wake me up when it does, will you?"

"I promise. Anyway, it's probably not important."

A few days later Paul had an urge. "How would you like to drive over to Lake Garda to have a look at Martillini's place?" he asked Ilse.

She was less than enthusiastic. "They'd never let you near it with all the investigation going on."

"Just to drive by would be enough. I'd like to have a look."

"That's silly curiosity."

"Okay, so it is. But it's a beautiful drive, anyway."

"Well, all right, I'll go. But I still think it's silly."

Shortly, then, they were on the road in the Ferrari heading eastward. In Brescia they stopped for lunch where Ilse, who hated to shop, decided it was time to get a few presents to take back to Israel. Paul followed her in and out of the fine shops, where foreign tourists and vacationing Italians were buying silk and leather and expensive trinkets. In her quick, decisive way, knowing precisely what she wanted, she collected scarves and gloves while he stood miserably behind her, with the question *When are you leaving?* unasked because he did not want to hear the answer.

They got back into the car and were soon off the main road and into the villa country.

"Have you any idea where you're going?" asked Ilse, when they had been wandering for half an hour past stone walls and curlicued iron gates.

He was aware of her impatience with this whim of his. Perhaps it was a foolish whim, and perhaps it wasn't. An unanswered question was still bothering him, so he replied with deliberate firmness, "I know very well where I'm going. The village was named in one of the newspapers."

They drove through more narrowing, more winding, hushed, and shaded avenues, through the fragrance of orange and lemon trees, past more walls and gates and glimpses of great houses far beyond the gates.

"This must be it," Paul said at last.

Four or five cars were parked along the road. People were clustered at the gate, on which an enormous padlock had been fastened, trying to peer up the driveway.

"Sightseers," Paul commented as he got out of the car.

"Like us," sniffed Ilse.

A man was arguing in broken Italian with another man, apparently the gatekeeper, who was shouting from the portico of a small stone house that stood just within the fence.

"No, no, nobody goes in, I tell you. You can argue all day. You don't go in."

"Come," said Paul, "we'll drive on."

Some yards farther down the road he stopped again and got out.

"Paul, this is really silly," Ilse complained.

He made no answer, because he had barely heard her. An idea had seized him with an explosion of white light in his head. He remembered now what he had wanted to remember. . . . And jumping again from the car, he walked over to the fence. It was built of narrow, graceful black iron posts an arm's width apart; eight feet high, it was tipped with gilded spearheads and lined on the inner side with a thick variegated shrubbery, scarlet hibiscus, old rhododendrons, long-needled pines, all to screen the property from the road.

Along this barrier he walked slowly, looking for a keyhole space to see through. Ilse followed. They went on for a hundred yards or more. The property was enormous and endless. Suddenly Paul turned around.

"Wait a minute. I'm just going back to the car for the umbrella."

"The umbrella!" The sun was blazing in the afternoon sky. "Paul, what on earth do you want with an umbrella?"

He knew. When he came back on the run with it, and still on fire with the idea that had seized him a few minutes before, he climbed up on a stone, making himself as tall as he could, and, poking the umbrella through the fence, managed to part a crevice in the foliage. It was enough to give him a glimpse of the grounds.

"Lawns," he muttered to himself. "You can't even see the house. Just lawns."

"Of course. What did you expect, a chicken farm?" Ilse demanded.

He didn't know what he expected, but he knew what he hoped. And he moved down along the fence for another few yards and then repeated the action. He kept trying. At the fourth attempt he drew in his breath. Here among the bushes were willows, young and supple, more easily pushed aside to afford a better view. So he stood and stared and then cried out.

"Yes, yes. This must be it. Come look, Ilse. Here, I'll hold the umbrella. Peek in."

"Oh, yes, it's lovely. Worth all the trouble," she admitted. "Beautiful creatures, aren't they? So proud, the way they hold their necks up. And the pond's like glass. Would you call it a small lake or a large pond? Blue glass. But is this what you were looking for?"

"Swans. It was at Meg's house. She said that Tim had gone with Jordaine to this place on Lake Garda that was famous for swans."

"What does that prove? Does it prove a connection? You don't suppose, do you, that this is the only estate that has a pond with some swans on it?"

"She said it was a hobby, that he had flocks of them," Paul argued stubbornly. "There must be fifty in there. I don't think many people would have that many. Three or four pairs, perhaps, that's all."

"Well, now that you've seen them," Ilse said doubtfully, "what next?"

"Nothing. But let me take one more look."

He had just climbed out when a young boy, no older than ten, came walking down the road along the ditch.

"Signor," he called, "you can't climb in there. It's not allowed."

"I was just looking at the swans. Isn't that all right?"

"You're not supposed to look. All the crowds should stay away, my father says."

"Oh? And who's your father?"

"The gatekeeper. That's where I live, in the house by the gate."

"So you must know everybody who comes to visit. Mr. Martillini's friends."

"Of course. He has important friends. From all over the world. Speak many languages. We know them all."

"Really? Do you know Mr."—and Paul sought a name out of the air—"Mr. Applegate from England?"

The child shook his head, and then, visibly remembering something, he sobered. "I'm not supposed to talk to strangers."

Paul was not going to let go. His heart was pounding. The swans. The face in the newspaper. The dark, sardonic face.

He took a coin from his pocket. "This is for candy, for you. Now tell me, do you know Mr. Powers? Tim? Timothy?"

"Oh, yes, Mr. Martillini's good friend, the one with yellow hair. He stays a long time, sometimes two weeks at Christmas. Last year he gave me a dog, a real hunting dog. He—" The boy stopped, clapping his hand over his mouth. His eyes went wide, appalled at what he had done. "Oh, oh, I told you a name!"

Paul laid a hand on his shoulder. "I hardly heard it. I've

forgotten already. Listen, go home and don't think about it a minute. Nobody will ever know."

They walked slowly back to the car. Paul's white explosion had settled now into gray ashes. His heart, quieted, lay like a stone.

He spoke grimly. "Well, Ilse, what do you think now?"

"I'm remembering that night at dinner in Jerusalem. Your young cousin has come a long way." It was as if the information they had just received were almost too heavy to carry. They rode some miles on the way back before Paul spoke again.

"I can understand the agitation at home about Vietnam. I can even *understand* how someone like Tim can be part of *that* violence. But this horror, I can't comprehend."

"Easy," said Ilse. "It's revolution. You disrupt whatever you can. Wherever there's a fire, as there is now in America over Vietnam, you pour gasoline on it. That's the idea, to destabilize governments, to weaken them until they topple. We in Israel have known that all along. The rest of the world has still to find it out. I hate to be a prophet of doom, but I predict that the seventies are going to show us all a thing or two about terrorism."

"All right, I see the picture. What gets me is, why Meg's son? Why Tim?"

Ilse shrugged. "Who knows? Why this spoiled son of wealth, this Martillini?"

"Also known as Jordaine and God knows how many other names. And the kids," Paul asked, "the kids who rioted all through Europe and the ones who are rioting at home now, what about them?"

"Some of them are just as cool and tough as Martillini. The rest—oh, some are pure, misguided idealists, and a lot are just unstable and unhappy, looking for some cause that will make life worthwhile."

"A dismal picture," Paul muttered.

Iris is frantic. We haven't heard from Steve.

"Not entirely. They're not going to break up American or European society. I give them ten years, maybe twenty. By the nineties, at least, I think the tide of world revolution will have played itself out. I hope."

"But it will get worse before it gets better, you think."

"Things usually do. When you look back at history, you see that." Ilse paused, then reached over and laid her hand over his hand that was on the wheel. "Paul, I'm going home now."

He looked straight ahead. "Yes, I know."

"I'm sorry, but I have to."

He swallowed hard. What they said about the proverbial lump in the throat was true. "I'm going home too. I've been away long enough."

When he looked over at her, he found that she couldn't face him, but was looking out in the other direction.

"When?" he asked.

"Next week." It was almost a question.

"Good enough, since you must." And he was thinking, It would have been better if I hadn't seen you again at all.

"Maybe there's some music on the radio," she said.

Obediently, he turned the dial, and an orchestra from Switzerland obliged with the overtures from *William Tell, The Merry Widow, Gaieté Parisienne,* and more bright, weightless music, as if the orchestra had known how much they needed a cover under which to hide their sadness.

They were both to leave from the airport in Milan on the same day. There was little packing to do except for the crating of the paintings that Paul had acquired while he was here. The servants had begun to crate them, but somebody had dropped one, breaking the frame, and Paul, to whom a painting was always more precious than the crown jewels, had decided to do the rest of them himself. It was while lifting a large oil—a seascape, or more accurately, a lakescape of a fishing boat in early-morning fog—that he felt a stab of the most excruciating pain in his chest. The young servant caught the painting as Paul, grasping his chest, sat down on the floor.

Ilse, who had been watching, ran to him, crying for brandy. She made Paul drink, got him onto a sofa, and made him lie down while she took his pulse. In a few minutes the pain had gone, and Paul sat up with a feeling of enormous relief and also of embarrassment. He'd "made a scene." He'd been "conspicuous."

"Now, what the hell could that have been?" he demanded. "Something I ate, I suppose."

"Not likely," Ilse said. She had a serious expression. "I want you to see a doctor."

"I am seeing a doctor. Right now, in front of me."

"Very funny. I'm taking you to Milan this afternoon to a doctor."

"Now, look here. I'm perfectly all right, as you can perfectly well see. It's all over and I feel fine."

"Yes, and you felt fine twenty minutes ago too, didn't you?"

"No, I admit, it was a wretched feeling, but it's gone, and there are these pictures to pack and—"

She interrupted him. "Giorgio will pack them. He'll be very careful not to drop them, while you and I go to Milan. Now, get up and don't argue with me."

In a way, embarrassing as it was, it felt good to be ordered around by someone who cared. That was one thing about the single life that he had been living so long; one forgot how it felt to be cared for.

So it was that they went to Milan and saw a doctor. How Ilse managed to get an appointment, he didn't ask and never found out.

He was examined, X-rayed, cardiographed, and lectured to. After the examination Ilse sat in the office with Paul and the doctor, who, after the very thorough examination, turned rather vague.

"One gets older. . . . The heart gets weaker, inevitably.

You fooled me. . . . You don't look your age at all, but still . . ."

"I strained myself lifting pictures," Paul explained.

"Ah, yes, well, one must accommodate time. Don't go doing strenuous things anymore. Really not. I'll give you some medicine, and when you get home, you will of course see your internist. Be sure to have regular checkups. But you know that, I'm sure."

"Oh, I know," said Paul, feeling the whole business to be unnecessary foolishness.

"I have longevity in my family," he assured Ilse on the ride back to the villa. "My grandmother, who went through the Civil War and lost everything, still managed to live until she was almost ninety."

"I'll bet she didn't lift crates, though."

Paul smiled to imagine the elegant Angelique, with her ruby-ringed fingers, lifting much of anything.

"I'll be good," he promised. "I'll see a doctor when I get back. I'll write and tell you all about it."

"You needn't write," Ilse said.

"What? What do you mean by that?"

"Because I'm going back with you."

"Traveling back with me? I don't need a nurse on the plane, for God's sake. I'm not sick, Ilse."

"All right, I'll make myself clear. It has nothing to do with what happened this afternoon. I've changed my mind, that's all. I'm going back with you to stay. You'd better buy a collar and leash for Lou, so I can walk with him in Central Park."

20

It was good to be home. If any-
one had ever told Paul that he, with all his need for quiet spaces
and long green vistas, would actually savor New York in the
summer, he would not have believed it. The city spread itself
now before his eyes as if he had never seen it before. There
were new office buildings throughout midtown, along with
pocket parks, pleasant innovations where people could sit outdoors on a bench to eat a noontime sandwich or read the
newspaper under a freshly planted ginkgo tree. The European
custom of sidewalk dining under an awning had taken hold too,
as if people had made up their minds at last to enjoy the city
even in a muggy July.

Katie, forewarned, had taken the dustcovers off the furniture, stocked the pantry, polished the beautiful old apartment, and decorated it with flowers. At the office Paul's room was as undisturbed as if he had never been away. The ficus in the corner had added inches, but the stern eyes in his grandfather's portrait still followed him around the room as they had done when he, a neophyte just out of college, had first come to work for the firm and uphold the family's name.

The younger partners came crowding in to greet him. "We knew you'd be coming back. You couldn't leave us," they told him. And Paul, pleased with the welcome, answered, "I guess you'd have to shoot me to keep me away."

He had, however, no intention of going back on the old schedule. The time for it had passed, and he recognized that. Besides, he wanted to spend time with Ilse, who, she said, was still trying to decide whether to retire completely or to reopen some sort of practice in New York. Two or three mornings in the office would be enough.

He was feeling fine. Naturally, he went to see his doctor, and would have done so even if Ilse had not insisted. He was, after all, no fool, he told her. The episode in Italy could not be entirely disregarded. After another cardiogram had been taken, it turned out that he had indeed had a heart attack, a very slight one, the doctor assured him, and added that people had been known to live for thirty years after one like it.

Well, he knew he wasn't going to have thirty more years, he said; could he possibly expect another ten, perhaps?

"Perfectly possible," the doctor told him. "Continue your medicine, live sensibly, and carry the nitroglycerin with you just in case."

"You see," Paul said to Ilse when they came out into an unexpectedly cool and breezy morning, "we'll have some good times yet."

"I never doubted it," she replied. She tucked her arm through his, and they walked on down Madison Avenue.

"There's a new gallery, I see. American primitives. Shall we take a look?"

Yes, it was good after all to be home.

Yet it was not a pure and simple good. . . . He had been back for three weeks; he knew what he should be doing and that he should have done it before now. It was a thing that he wanted to do and at the same time dreaded doing. Looking out of the library window one afternoon, he saw Ilse coming from the park with Lou on a leash. He saw a party of Japanese tourists in a long line, like schoolchildren following their leader to the Metropolitan Museum. He saw two young women in summer dresses pushing their high English perambulators. What had all these to do with the reason, the real, true reason, why he had come home in such a hurry?

"I must see Theo," he said abruptly when Ilse came in.

He expected a cogent argument from her as to why he should not, but she said only, "If it will ease your mind, do it."

He sat in Theo's office waiting for the last patient to leave. This office was light-years away from the one where he had first known Theo Stern. It was properly professional, functional, and sunny. The furnishings were of good quality, but nothing cried out: Money! The paintings that had adorned the previous reception room had been replaced by well-hung photographs taken with an artist's eye: sand dunes; goldenrod against a rail fence; a red-haired young girl sitting on the grass with her knees drawn up to her chin.

The receptionist had been following Paul's glances. "They're lovely, aren't they? The doctor's taken up photography. These are all his."

The girl with the flaming hair must be the daughter, Paul was thinking, when Theo appeared in the doorway.

"Admiring my work?" he asked as they shook hands.

"Yes, very much. And I'm admiring you too. You're looking great."

"So they tell me. Work always did agree with me, and I'm thankful to be getting plenty of it, though in my field it's too often a tragedy for the patient. And you? How are you?"

"Well, thank you."

"And is Italy as marvelous as ever?"

"Yes. But I came to hear about you. You have troubles, you wrote."

Now that he was here, Paul wanted not to prolong the friendly courtesies but to get to the point. A sense of urgency propelled him.

"Well, then, come inside."

The consulting room, too, had been changed. Gone were the Impressionists in their gilded frames and gone from underfoot was the precious Oriental. All that was left of the former splendor was the massive desk.

"Don't fend me off," Paul began. "I need to know."

"All right, here it is. Steve's still gone. There's not a trace of him. There's nothing. We're a house in mourning. Iris is— What can I tell you? Like any mother, she—" And Theo's voice broke.

Paul looked away, thinking, It's easier perhaps to know that someone is dead rather than lost. To be lost is to drop over the edge of the world. When the dog Lou strayed for two days last year, I couldn't sleep for thoughts of that soft, helpless thing crushed on the road or wandering somewhere in pain. And he's only a dog.

"What are you going to do?" he asked softly.

"What is there to do?" was the reply. "He must be somewhere with that man Powers. We think so, at least. Steve almost worshiped him. He was some sort of guru. But where do you look? The country is three thousand miles across. And he may not even be in the country at all."

Indeed. Paul's thought went back and back. Martillini. Jordaine.

"If I can help you," he said. "I will do anything I can."

The offer was inept, vague, and halfhearted, as when some-body says "Come visit us sometime" without saying definitely when. Yet it was the best he could do.

"It seems," Theo said, "that whenever you come, I have only troubles to tell you about. This has been a specially hard time for us." He hesitated, his eyes searching Paul's. "One thing after the other. All this so soon after Anna's death."

Paul started as if he had been struck. "Anna died?"

"Last summer. In her sleep. She hadn't been ill at all. They just—we just found her in the morning."

What he was feeling Paul could not have described, because pain is after all indescribable. This was a wounding such as doctors call an "insult," to the heart, or the lungs, or whatever. And out of these burst an accusation.

"Why didn't you let me know? You wrote about everything except the—" He was about to say "the most important thing" —and stopped.

"I'm sorry. I should have told you, but I kept putting it off. I suppose I wanted to spare you."

Paul did not answer.

"It was an easy death, a good death."

"Yes."

There was no sound in the room except the creaking of Theo's swivel chair. Presently, he spoke again.

"It's strange, Anna was always able to do more with Steve than anyone else could. I don't know why. Some chemistry, perhaps, although that's the same meaningless word we use to explain why people fall in love or don't fall in love. Chemistry is either good or it's bad. Meaningless."

"Yes."

"I think that Steve, even if we ever find him, will always be out of our reach. Iris, poor mother, can't accept that."

The words drifted off into the stillness: Iris, poor mother.

But Steve and Iris had fled away from Paul. Instead he was silently demanding of himself: What did you suppose? That she would go on living forever? Just always there, unreachable, untouchable, but always there? And he saw her vividly as he had seen her, standing in her yellow dress near the white snow-ball bush, with her arm raised to him in farewell.

He roused himself and stood up, saying abruptly, "It's late. I'd better leave. I'll call you."

Theo stood too. "I'm sorry, Paul. I've upset you. Drive carefully. I'll call you too."

He had almost reached the parkway when suddenly he swung the car around. For no sensible reason at all he wanted to see Anna's house. It was not more than half a mile's detour out of the way, but he would have gone long miles at that moment to see it again; he had seen it only once before, when he had been about to go to Italy. And he recalled his first shock of surprise that time, which had been immediately followed by a reaction: The house was quite suited to her, after all.

He stopped the car now and looked. There were not many who in these days would choose to live in an old wooden house out of the last century, a sturdy pile wrapped about with a porch meant for evenings when a family sat on it, waiting for passersby to come down the road and enliven the quiet. A thick wisteria encased the pillars of the porch and fringed its roof. An elm, taller than the house, cast one side of the front yard into a deep, cool shade. She would have treasured that elm. It came to him that of the little he had really known of her, he was able to remember how she loved trees.

And he sat on in the car, staring at the house. It was easy to plot its interior; the dining room to the left of the hall with the kitchen and pantry—a house like that had ample pantries—behind it; to the right, the double parlor, probably with sliding doors between them and a solarium in the rear. Above the porte cochere the large bay window would admit the sun to an ample room, the master bedroom very likely.

The master bedroom was the heart of the house, because the heart of the marriage was in the bedroom, always. Always.

"I want that," he said aloud after a while, "late as it is, absurdly late, I want it. A solid, publicly acknowledged marriage. I never had it. What we had, poor Marian and I, was publicly acknowledged, God knows, but never a marriage in spite of that. What Anna had in that room up there—how can I know? It might have been secret torture or she might have made her peace with it, or it might have been something in between. Anyway, whatever it was, it wasn't with me. And I want a try at the real thing even now, as old as I am."

He put the car into gear and drove home. Ilse was reading when he came in. The little dog lay at her feet, and a cup of coffee stood on the table beside the chair. The domestic scene was comforting. And he asked himself again: How many kinds of love can there be? The number may well be as large as the number of men and women in the world, added to the pattern that they make together, for the same man and two different women make two different patterns.

He kept standing in the doorway looking at her.

"What is it?" she asked.

"Nothing new. Just that I love you, Ilse, and I think we should be married."

"Married? That's new."

"No, it's not. Have you forgotten I asked you before you decided to stay in Israel?"

"Ah, yes, so you did!" At the corners of her jet-black eyes fine threadlike rays, called wrinkles, gave her face a touch of humor. "But why now? Isn't everything good the way it is?"

He came to her and laid a hand on her shoulder. "Not good enough. For far too long I've felt loose ends. Unfinished business. I want"—he sought the right words—"I want to tie things up, to make life orderly, as it's supposed to be."

"Tie things up? Like a birthday present, nice glossy paper and a bow on top."

"If you like. But why not? It will be a real birthday present. We'll go to the rabbi's study with two witnesses, whomever you like." His mind worked now in its best decisive rhythm. "Not Meg. She's on the Coast, seeing Tom in the hospital. But Leah and Bill? I don't really care who. Afterward we'll have lunch or dinner at some festive place, just the two of us—"

She interrupted merrily. "Not going to invite the two witnesses? How will that look, you proper gentleman?"

"It will look terrible. You are absolutely right. So the four of us will have dinner. Then you and I will come back here and kick everybody out except Katie."

"And Lou?" Ilse was laughing.

"Lou can stay too. Ilse, I want this!"

She got up, put her arms around him, and leaned her head on his shoulder. "Oh, my dearest, you shall have it. Anything you want, you shall have."

The witnesses were Bill and Leah, who were delighted with the whole thing.

"About time," Leah whispered in Paul's ear.

"No wedding presents, please," directed Ilse. "I mean it. This apartment has enough china, silver and knickknacks, very beautiful ones, I'll admit, to stock two shops."

"I mean it too," Paul echoed.

"I'll take you at your word," Leah agreed, "but you'll have to let me provide the bridal outfit, or we won't come. And that's that."

So, on the appointed day, Ilse set out in the most beautiful suit, she swore, that had ever been imagined. Of palest blue silk, it was lined and trimmed in jade silk. In the V neck of the blouse hung the pendant.

"That is a gorgeous piece!" said Leah, who knew by heart every jeweler from Tiffany to Van Cleef on Fifty-Seventh Street, down Fifth Avenue to Harry Winston and Cartier, along with others in between.

"From Vienna via Israel," was all Paul said.

The ceremony in the rabbi's study was brief and, as always,

very moving. After his blessing, the four went by taxi to lunch at the Tavern on the Green, Ilse's choice, because it was "too beautiful a summer day to be shut up indoors." Well into the afternoon they lingered over lobster and wine and a tiny wedding cake, ordered by Leah as a surprise.

"We go back a long way, we four," she said, regarding Paul and Ilse with affection and moist eyes, "and this is one of the best days we've ever had."

Ilse blew a kiss across the table. Then, in the glow of friendship, they all walked back through the park toward Fifth Avenue and home. Children were wheeling down the paths on roller skates, a long-haired youth was playing a guitar, and the day was mellow. Ilse kept stretching her hand out to look at the wedding ring. All of those things printed a picture in Paul's mind, these and the rim of the sky where blue merged into soft green; he had never been happier.

And he spoke it aloud: "I have never been happier."

21

An idea came to Paul after he and Ilse had gone to visit Meg. Here, too, as in Theo's office, the war had altered the very atmosphere. In burning grief Meg had wept over Tom's disfigured face, and wept in a grief that mingled itself with shame and anger over Timothy.

"I never thought," she had kept saying, "how could I have thought, that a son of mine would be on the FBI wanted list? Oh, I am thankful my parents aren't alive to know it!"

"Always we go back to our parents," Paul sighed on the way home. "It's the thread of pride that holds the family together or undoes it."

Ilse reflected. "Tim's a wild-eyed prophet, a hairy prophet

out of the desert. From such people comes good or else destruction.''

Paul let her talk, only half hearing her speculations. He himself had been in an introspective mood all that day, a mood that he liked to think was untypical of him, although Ilse said he was wrong about that, that it was only his upbringing and habit that had trained him to keep his emotions hidden, even to himself. Anyway, this day he was peculiarly aware of sharpened senses, of voice tones, colors and nuances, of flavors and the texture of the linen napkin. It was as if he was trembling inside.

But he said nothing more about it during the evening, and not until the next morning when, shortly after breakfast, he made his announcement. He had been thoughtfully watching Ilse comb her hair, observing the glint of light on the diamond wedding band as the hand moved back and forth and up and down. Then suddenly he said, "I'm going to try to find Iris's boy."

The brush fell, striking the edge of the glass-topped dressing table.

"Paul! What in heaven's name do you mean?"

Her tone, presaging as it did a stream of objections—and he knew they would be sensible ones—only tightened his determination.

He answered positively, "Exactly what I said."

"Oh," she cried, "do you know how crazy that is? I can give you ten dozen reasons why—"

He raised a warning hand. "I know them all. It's no business of mine. It's like looking for a needle in a haystack. And you're right, it is crazy. But I'm going to try anyway."

Now Ilse changed to the coaxing tone one would use to a rebellious child.

"You're not a young man anymore. You can't afford to go chasing off and exhausting yourself. I know the way you are when you get an idea—"

"I'm not going skydiving, Ilse, nor on a twenty-mile run."

"You keep interrupting me! What I mean is, the kind of emotional commitment that you always bring to a cause can be just as damaging as running. Oh, Paul!" Now the tone changed again into exasperation. "Will you please tell me what half-baked idea you have now? Where are you going to look? Number One Main Street, USA?"

"I have a few ideas. First I'm going to see Meg. I have a hunch she may have a hunch about Tim."

"Well, if she has, which I doubt, do you really think she's going to give it to you? Would you, if he were your son?" Ilse paused to look Paul up and down, from the ruddy tips of his polished shoes to the topmost wave of his hair. "Well, yes, you're different. You might well report your son to the authorities for the good of the nation. And for his own, you'd say. And I won't argue with that, God knows. But really, will you please, please, really stay out of this affair?"

He felt a wave of sadness. And suddenly wearied of the discussion, he brought it to a quiet end.

"Ilse, darling, do you remember—of course you do—that rainy night in Jerusalem when you said to me, weeping, you said to me, 'I have to stay. It's not I who am making the decision, it's making itself for me'? So now, this is the same for me. I must do it, Ilse. I can't even tell you why because I don't altogether know. I only know that I must."

After an hour's visit with Meg and her husband, Paul saw clearly that there was little or nothing to be advanced there. And yet, when he left them, he was not quite sure whether some seed had possibly been planted after all.

"I suppose," he asked bluntly, "there's nothing new about Tim?"

"If there were, wouldn't I tell you?" Meg responded.

Paul said only, "I hope you would."

"What is it you want of me?" she asked.

"Briefly, this," he answered. "There's a young man, a son of dear friends who are distraught because he's been missing. He was a student of Tim's. He venerated Tim. I want to find the young man without"—here he raised his voice and spoke somewhat sternly—"without harming Tim. I thought maybe you could . . . well, I'm not sure exactly what I thought you could do. It's only that I want so much to find the young man."

"I see. We none of us know anything, Paul. We, too, are distraught. Even Tom, in the army hospital, even he, a law-and-order man if ever there was one, and poles apart from his brother, is sick over this. And Agnes, who loved him so—you may remember how close those two were, Tim and Agnes, almost from the time they were babies?" Meg choked and stopped.

No, Paul decided, she knows nothing. As Ilse had said, there would be nothing to get from Meg.

But as he drove back to the city, these words kept repeating themselves: how close they were, those two.

He hadn't seen Agnes in years, and probably wouldn't see her in more years, unless someone's marriage or funeral should bring her here from the mountains of New Mexico.

And steering the car through traffic, through the Lincoln Tunnel back into Manhattan, a thought kept growing and growing larger. A wild goose chase. He could hear Ilse say it already. Just like the swan chase on Lake Garda. So he had found who Jordaine was, and what difference had it made? It had been merely another fact to join a thousand other useless facts in his head.

And still . . . and yet . . .

Well, let them all think he was a fool going on a fool's errand! Surely it was on their faces. It was in Theo's polite surprise when he asked for some photos of Steve with and without a beard, in Theo's guarded questions and cautions about Paul's health. My mental health, Paul thought ironically. He must think I'm senile or else have always been some sort of rich eccentric, like the ones you read of now and then who go about sprinkling money to the crowds as if it were confetti.

"May I ask what your thoughts are, how you're going to begin?" inquired Theo.

"You may ask, but I can't tell you," said Paul.

"I understand," said Theo, still very mildly and tactfully, as if to say "Heaven help us, he means well, poor man; he's trying to do this for his daughter. Yes, yes, one has to pity him."

They parted, with the photos in Paul's wallet.

"How long will you be gone?" asked Ilse.

"If I can't accomplish anything in a month, I'll come home."

"For God's sake, take care of yourself. Don't knock yourself out," she pleaded. And then with the humor that was so typical of her she admonished, "I've only just become a bride; don't make me a widow right away, please, will you?"

"Not to worry. I've never felt better in my life."

His plane, heading westward, crossed the Mississippi, the iron-gray river whipping and curving its way toward the Gulf; then it crossed Missouri, where the fields lay mottled green and brown like a tortoise's back; next it turned southward where the earth was red, the warm color of bricks. As it began descent, the mesas loomed stark and solitary over the expanse of the empty land. And the very loneliness of this land made another change in his vacillating moods.

"It will come to nothing." Common sense spoke out as if to armor him against inevitable failure. "It will come to nothing," he murmured aloud so that the man in the seat beside him turned with a startled look.

Nevertheless, when the plane touched the earth in Albuquerque, his adrenaline began to pour again. Excitement mounted as his plan unfolded: Rent a car, drive to Santa Fe, arriving at nightfall, and leave for Taos in the morning. There he would make the rounds of the art galleries. Surely some fellow artist would know Agnes Powers and where she lived.

He himself knew only that it was somewhere in the mountains beyond Taos. Something, he did not know what, had told him not to ask Meg for the address. Simply, he had had an instinctive feeling that it would be best to give no warning of his coming. Apparently, she had no telephone, which was not unexpected if you knew her, he remarked to himself, when in the hotel at Santa Fe he had tried and gotten nowhere with the telephone company.

But somehow he would find her. Perhaps if I hadn't inherited a banking business, he thought, laughing to himself, I might have made my way as a private investigator.

It was early when he left Santa Fe. Pueblo Indian women in front of the ancient Governor's Palace were just spreading their bright blankets on the walk and arranging their turquoise and silver wares. The air was pure and energizing, the sky was the deepest blue he had ever seen, and on his right as he drove northward, wherever clouds hovered on their peaks, the Sangre de Cristo Mountains blazed white.

The space! The enormous space! How did one ever begin to find anyone or anything in such enormity?

Yet . . . yet sometimes it happened.

Arriving in Taos, he set out through back lanes and courtyards where, so it seemed, every house contained an art gallery, to inquire about Agnes Powers.

"Why, yes," he was told, "she does bring her paintings in now and then." But she was a reclusive person, seen only rarely, and her house was hidden away some fifteen miles or so northwest of town. He would probably never be able to find it.

Nevertheless, with a rough sketch in hand he set out. To the north lay Colorado. On either side rose vermilion cliffs, tabletopped, among barren wastes covered in scrub and cactus. Sometimes, as the road sharply twisted, steep mountain slopes, richly covered with evergreens, stretched ahead. Now and then he got out of his car to stand at the side of the road and gaze at a stark, motionless immensity in which there was

not a sign of human life. He thought he had never heard such
total silence.

He came to a village, a cluster of gray adobe houses. There
he inquired of a man with an austere Indian face and was told
that yes, he knew the painter lady. She bought supplies at the
store.

Following the man's directions, he persisted. And so in
midafternoon he arrived at the top of a rutted lane cut between
great rocks, among which lay a little house colored and hewn
like the rocks. He opened a gate and entered a courtyard filled
with flowers. A double door of dark brown wood, most beautifully carved in Indian motifs, stood open.

One could live and die here, he thought before he knocked,
without anybody's knowing whether one was still alive or dead.
If anyone wanted to hide . . .

"Paul!" cried Agnes. "Paul! I don't believe it!"

Barefoot, she was in an Indian dress, a vivid blouse and skirt
held together by a turquoise-studded leather belt. Her hair,
dressed in a single braid, was almost entirely gray, although
she was still in her thirties.

He followed her into a large room whose adobe walls were
hung with blankets, baskets, and paintings. In a corner near the
small fireplace stood an easel at which she had apparently been
working.

"I don't believe it," she repeated when they sat down.
"Whatever brings you here?"

Not yet ready to state his errand, he answered only that he
hadn't been in the Southwest for years and had simply had a
wish to see it again.

"And how are you, Agnes? You must love it here."

"I do. To me it's the ultimate beauty. I work and I walk. And I
have a few friends in houses just like this one, hidden where
you'd never find them."

"That's what I've been hearing all day, that I'd never find
you." Paul's mind worked cautiously, feeling the way toward

his purpose. "I'd surely like to take a look at some of your work while I'm here," he said.

"Of course." She led him first around the room and then into a small back room in which more pictures were stacked against the wall. They were mostly southwestern pictures, naturally: red cliffs and coarse, brilliant sunflowers, redolent of heat.

"I know I'm no Georgia O'Keeffe," Agnes said honestly, "but I intend to keep working and I hope to grow. I feel sure I'll grow."

"They're well done," Paul told her with equal honesty, although he had no special interest in their subject. Then he spied a small watercolor propped on a paint-stained table. Quite different from all the rest of her work, it was a picture of goldfish and fronds of sea grass in a bowl, drawn from an odd perspective.

"I like that," he told her. "Is that for sale?"

"Not to you. To you it's a present."

"Not at all. The laborer is worth his hire." And he wrote out a check for an amount that brought a protest from her. "Ship it home for me, will you? And don't argue. I told you I like it. This is business."

"Well, then, you go sit down while I start some supper. I'm putting a chicken on to bake in the adobe oven. A long, slow bake. It's delicious."

He became anxious. "Agnes, I can't stay too late. I'd never find my way out of here in the dark."

"Who said anything about that? You'll stay for the night, or as many nights as you want, if you don't mind sleeping on the cot in that back room with my pictures. It's kind of messy, but I promise you, it's clean."

"All right. I'll stay till the morning, then."

During the little supper they touched on a variety of subjects from art to Italy and finally to the war in Vietnam, deplored by both of them.

"Tim sent me a quote once," Agnes said. " 'For war is hell, and those who institute it are criminals.' "

"The trouble is, it's usually hard to decide just who instituted it." And Paul added, "But no matter who did, there's no excuse for some of the violent things the antiwar movement is doing in this country."

"People like Tim?" she put in.

"Well, yes, if you want me to be truthful with you." When Agnes did not respond, he went on, "Your mother—your whole family, Tom and your sisters, are so concerned about him, having no idea what's happening, where he might possibly be or—"

"You want me to tell you what I know about him. That's why you came."

"It's not why I came," he lied. "But naturally I would like to know."

"The FBI would too, wouldn't it? You're asking me to betray my brother, Paul, aren't you? That's what you're doing."

So she did know something. . . .

"Not that I know anything about him," she amended quickly.

He gave his smile a twist of skepticism that would be unmistakable to her and said, "Actually, it's not Tim I'm seeking. There is a young man, one of Tim's followers, who happens to be the son of my oldest friends. They are, the mother especially is, in despair." He looked straight into Agnes's eyes. "It would mean a great deal to me, more than I can say, if you had any clue, any idea, nothing that would hurt Timothy, it goes without saying. It's only this young man, this boy. Trust me." He stopped.

"What makes you think I have anything to tell you?"

"I had a hunch. You were always close, two rebels in your differing ways. If he were to need help, it's you he would come to."

"Yes, he would come to me. He's the only one in the family, the immediate family, who ever really liked me."

That was quite true, Paul knew. A strange woman, reclusive, probably a lesbian, she would meet with little understanding from the rest of them. Meg, being kind, would pretend not to know; Lucy, in her smart clothes with her smart wit, would dismiss Agnes as a failure; Thomas would be solemnly disapproving; the Seattle sister, now happily pregnant for the fourth time, would shake her head in sorrow and wonder.

There was a long silence. It had grown dark, and the mountain wind had risen audibly, shaking the poplars. Agnes got up and lit a lamp.

She spoke abruptly. "I won't lie to you. He was here, but it was a while ago, and I have no idea where he is now. Not that I would tell you if I knew."

Harboring a fugitive, Paul thought. A very dangerous business, Agnes.

At Paul's look of regret Agnes continued, "The last time I heard he was in San Francisco, but that, too, was a long, long time ago, and he has left there. He may well be out of the country."

"I only care about the young man," Paul said again.

"I can't tell you any more. I shouldn't even have told you this much."

"Okay. I understand."

"Let me fix the cot for you. It's late, and you said you want to make an early start."

He did. It had been a stupid hunch after all, coming across the country for this. It served him right for departing from his normal way of conducting affairs; he had never acted on hunches, and had never been a gambler.

So he undressed and slept poorly. When he awoke it was only five o'clock, but light was already filling the room, and he was restless. Very quietly, not wanting to disturb Agnes, he got up and searched for something to read. On the battered desk lay a scattering of papers and a pile of outdated magazines. Agnes wasn't much of a housekeeper, that was plain. He had to move a little pile of papers to get at the magazines and, gingerly, in case there might be some reason to keep the papers in sequence, he tried to do so. There was an advertisement from a mail order house, then a grocery list and, on the side, an empty envelope, lying by itself, so that he could not help but see the writing, or rather the printing, on its torn backflap. There was no name, only an address in San Francisco. Turning it over, he saw that this letter had been sent to Agnes many months ago. He turned it back lest she should think he had been rummaging on her desk.

Then something occurred to him: It's lying conspicuously, on top. An empty envelope, months old: Why? For a minute or two he stood still, arguing with himself. It's sheer coincidence; messy habits; she might know a dozen people in that city. On the other hand, she might have wanted him to see it, while yet wanting to keep her conscience halfway clear by not actually giving him the address. Furthermore, since the letter was months old and her brother wasn't in the city anymore, no harm could come to him if Paul were to go there.

Such were Paul's conjectures, and any one of them, contradictory as they all were, might make sense—or no sense at all. Nevertheless, he made a note of the address.

At breakfast there was no mention of the previous night's conversation and none afterward until, as Paul got into the car to drive away, Agnes said, "I'm sorry I couldn't help you, Paul."

"That's all right, Agnes. You would if you could."

"I hope you can find the young man. I see that he means a lot to you."

He kissed her cheek. "You're a good soul, cousin. Take care of yourself." And as the car began to roll, he called through his open window, "I'm going to enjoy the fishbowl!"

All the way to Albuquerque he kept up an argument: Is this a fool's errand, or is it worth pursuing? His conclusion, reached

as the car approached the airport, was that the clue, if indeed it
had been a clue at all, was too slender to act upon.

*"Hello, I'm Paul Werner or John Doe, or the Man in the Moon, and
I'm looking for Steven Stern."*

"Oh, come right in, he'll be glad to see you."

Why, the whole thing was ridiculous, and only an old fool
playing Sherlock Holmes would have involved himself in it!

So he returned the rented car and bought a ticket back to
New York. There was a two-hour wait until the next flight out,
so he got a newspaper, went to the departure gate, and sat
down to read. The first thing he saw was a continuation of the
previous day's news that he had missed because the car's radio
hadn't been working. Rapidly, he scanned the lead item.

"Authorities sifting through ruins of the house in exclusive
suburban neighborhood north of San Francisco . . . basement filled with explosives . . . lead pipes packed with dynamite . . . woman's body found in basement workroom with
hands blown off and head badly damaged . . . quantities of
SDS literature . . . leaflets satirizing United States government."

A great weight seemed to fall upon him. Sighing, he put the
paper away and looked out unseeing at the tarmac and the
glittering sky. Young fools! Half cooked! Semieducated even
after four years of college; most of them probably knew little or
nothing of the ancient world or Asia or even of Europe, and so
could have no real understanding of what we have here in
America or of how hard it had been to get what we have.

Half an hour passed before he finally got up and returned to
the ticket counter. The same clerk was there and looked mildly
surprised at Paul's request.

"I've changed my mind. I need to go to San Francisco instead."

The taxi stopped in front of a wooden house trimmed, like all
the rest on the street, with carpenter's lace. It held a high porch

with a railing, which someone had started to paint a searing electric blue and had then, after a halfhearted spattering, abandoned.

Paul stood and looked through torrential rain down a street that was almost as steep as a ladder. It was an area of small neighborhood stores, of signs announcing various occult, mind-expanding services, tea-leaf readers, tie-dyed shirts, and handmade copper jewelry. Interspersed with these were high, narrow wooden dwellings left over, he guessed, from before the giant earthquake in 1906. A few years ago this had been "hippie country"; what it was now he had no way of knowing, but he had nevertheless "played safe" by leaving his suit at the hotel and wearing khakis with an open-necked shirt.

Now, at the foot of the porch steps, he paused. A sudden feeling of bafflement overcame him. The crowded city was as frustrating as Agnes's wilderness had been. He had come on a fool's errand. Still, having come this far across a continent with a purpose, no matter how foolish a one, would it not be even more foolish to turn around and go home without at least making a try?

And he tried to refresh his memory, rehearsing his opening, over which he had struggled and puzzled for more than a few hours. Because no other plausible way occurred to him, he simply decided to make a direct plunge.

"I've come from Tim," he would say.

If he were to draw a blank, the whole thing would have been an absurd mistake. That would be the worst that might happen. On the other hand, if Agnes's placement of this address had been deliberate, they might let him in. Then: Why had he come from Tim? Ah! Good question! Well, because . . . because . . . Tim had a message for Steve, Steve Stern. He would know by their faces or face whether they had ever heard of Steve Stern. If Steve had been blown up in that house, probably he would find that out too. If not, he would let them talk and possibly—barely possibly—he might find out where Steve was.

One unlikely possibility built on another, brick upon brick, or else only air upon air.

However, he was here. And with a still-pounding heart he climbed the rest of the steps. He rang the bell. The door was opened, and he went blinking out of glaring sunlight into a dim and dingy hall.

The boy—anyone under the age of forty seemed boyish to Paul—stood blocking him from walking any farther.

"What is it you want?"

Paul said quietly, "I've a message from Tim."

There was a pause during which the two examined each other; the one saw an elderly man, clean and simply dressed; the other saw a stereotype of the times: a young man dressed as Paul himself was except for having long hair and granny glasses.

"Tim? Who's he?"

For answer Paul's expression spoke alone, saying silently and emphatically, "As if you don't know perfectly well that I would never, that I am not authorized, that your question is the last thing I would or could answer if my life depended on it!"

There followed another pause, telling Paul that the other was suspicious and unsure of making a mistake, either by admitting him or by sending him away.

At that moment another man came down the stairs.

"Here's someone," the first one said to the newcomer, "who says he's got a message or something from somebody named Tim."

The newcomer had a keen, smart face. His manner was immediately assertive.

"You don't just walk in off the street and ask to see people. You might be an ax murderer for all we know," he said with a little mockery of a smile. "As for Tim, I personally am acquainted with three of them—no, four, counting my grandfather."

He did not ask Paul's name. In this business Paul understood that no one ever asked for names. This was a game, caution and wariness playing against each other. He caught the ball.

"All right. My Tim is tall, about six foot three, very blond and ruddy faced. He's a baseball freak, a Giants fan, he grew up in New Jersey, his mother's a veterinarian, his sister Agnes is an artist. . . ." Paul dug in his memory for facts that would not generally be known, most especially for facts that the "authorities" would probably not know. "He's a vegetarian, he spent the Christmas before last in Italy, he drinks wine but no hard liquor, and he's very interested in one of his former students, name of Steve Stern."

The two, who had moved together toward the foot of the stairs as if to block Paul from going up, were communicating by shifting glances at Paul and back again to one another.

Presently the second one asked, "What about Steve Stern?"

At this Paul's breath caught. For an instant of dread he awaited an attack of the pain that he had not had since that day in Italy. But nothing happened; his breathing regulated itself and he was able to speak.

"Tim asks whether he's all right, that's all. In the circumstances."

Again the two glanced at each other. It was almost as if Paul could see straight through their puzzled foreheads and into their baffled thoughts. Here was a man who was obviously well acquainted with Tim Powers. The "circumstances" must naturally refer to this week's disaster. All of this could make sense. Yet—could this man also be the enemy who had in some way gotten on their trail?

"I understand," Paul said next. "You need to talk. You may need to consult with others. And you're right to do it. So I'll step out onto the porch until you're ready." He moved back to the door, which was still open. "I can give you much more identification if you need it. For example, Tim has a brother, an establishment pig, in the State Department, the Foreign Service. His name is Tom. You see? Just ask me what you want to know."

He backed out through the door and, stepping into a puddle that had formed under a leak in the porch roof, soaked his sneakers. The rain, wind driven, teemed in sheets that were almost horizontal, soaking his clothes. His discomfort was great and his feelings mixed. Either he had stepped into a hornet's nest or he had struck it lucky.

It must have been ten minutes before the door opened again and he was called back inside. This time there were half a dozen people in the hall. A tall, brusque young woman spoke.

"We've decided to trust you. If it turns out that we're wrong, you'll be the one to regret it, not we."

Educated, Paul thought ironically. She had used "we," where the average person would have said "us." Educated and tough. An impression flitted across his mind: I wouldn't want to need her mercy. And looking her straight in the eye, that severe, penetrating eye, he smiled slightly.

"No one here will have anything to regret, I assure you. Now, what are you going to tell me about Steve Stern?"

"He's upstairs. Go up and see for yourself."

Paul trembled. His hands went wet. His mouth went dry.

One of the men said, "This way. I'll show you."

They climbed the stairs, one flight and then a second, past closed doors and open ones, with glimpses of unmade cots and strewn objects, cardboard cartons, books, and clothing. From the back of the house a radio blasted, and in one of the rooms somebody frying food on a hot plate wafted the smell of grease into the air. On the third floor Paul was directed to a door.

"He's in there, in bed."

"Hurt?"

"No, just sick. Maybe you can do something with him," the man added, and pushed the door open. "Here's someone to see you. He's come from Tim."

After this careless, unfeeling introduction Paul was left alone with the person who lay on the rumpled bed. The room was almost dark. A tattered green window shade was pulled down to the sill so that the faint light that entered was a morose green. In the small space between the shade and the sill, rain spattered, and the wind drove sharply over the bed. When Paul closed the window and raised the shade, a purer and more tender light came pouring out of the gray sky. Now he was able to see the man on the bed.

He moved closer, surprising himself by the sudden control that had taken hold of him. He had stopped trembling and, curiously, was having a sense of himself accepting this most extraordinary situation, taking hold of it, as in a dream one plays a heroic part in an improbable drama.

The man on the bed was dozing. His breath came whistling through his half-open, exhausted mouth. Wet hair clung to his forehead.

"He's burning up" was Paul's first thought, and the second one was, oddly enough, "He's not what I expected."

For Theo, through all his anxiety, had described only his son's intelligence, but never his beauty. Drawing up the only chair in the room that was not littered with dirty clothes, he sat down by the bed and studied the sleeper. The face was sculpted, strong yet sensitive; even the untended beard could not hide its symmetry. Not like his father, Paul said to himself, and then: not like me. For this man—this boy—was his! Of his flesh and blood!

For long minutes he considered this fact, the reality of the sordid room, and the path that had led such a boy to such a room.

Then he became aware that Steve's eyes were open and, glazed with fever, were staring at him.

"I'm cold," he murmured.

"Are you? Has anyone given you any medicine?"

"No."

"Well, then, I'm going to get some for you."

The commanding young woman was waiting in the front hall.

"He must have a very high fever," Paul told her.

"I know. We've given him aspirin."

"Not good enough. Hasn't he seen a doctor?"

"Our usual doctor's away till next week. We couldn't risk taking him to a stranger. He's a bit out of his head and talking too much."

"I understand. But you don't want him to die here."

"Well, have you got any better suggestion?" the tall one asked sharply.

"As a matter of fact, I have. I'm staying at a rooming house. I can take him back with me and nurse him."

The other appeared to be considering the offer.

"You don't want him to die here," Paul repeated.

"God, no! That's all we need. Okay, then, take care of him. But how are you going to take him in this rain?"

"I'll get a taxi. I've been flush for the past few days." Paul grinned. His meaning was clear: Tim—or someone—had supplied him with money.

"Well, okay. Go ahead."

After the fact Paul was to wonder at his own accomplishment, first in getting Steve dressed; then helping him wobble down the stairs into the taxi and finally into the hotel.

Once there, he put him into the twin bed nearest to the windows that overlooked the Bay. Next he shaved, changed into his usual clothes, and summoned the hotel doctor.

"No, he won't need the hospital," the doctor said, "unless, of course, he should develop pneumonia. Just keep up the penicillin and watch the fluids."

"I'll do that."

"Is he a relative of yours?"

"Son of a friend."

"Well. A friend in need. You came just about in time. Another day with fever like this . . ." The doctor shook his head. "He's lucky he came across you."

"Thank you." Paul smiled and closed the door.

From a booth in the lobby he made a telephone call to Theo Stern. He felt, as he told his astounding tale, a confusion of triumph and exhilaration along with pity for the boy who lay upstairs in his room. And over the wire, from the far end of the continent, it seemed that he could actually feel Stern's shock.

"But is he all right, Paul? The truth, please! Don't shield me."

"Yes, yes, he will be. The doctor's started him on antibiotics, and he's a strong guy."

"I'm coming right out. I'll get the first flight I can."

"Iris too?"

"I'm going to try to keep her from coming. It might be too overwhelming. She's been frantic over him. And, Paul?"

"Yes?"

"Before you hang up I just want to say that I never knew there were people like you in the world. No, don't answer."

"What am I doing here?" asked Steve when, late that night, he awoke.

"Don't you remember that I brought you here in a taxi?"

"Vaguely."

Steve sat up and looked around at the room, which was quiet and restful in lamplight. The chairs and curtains were flowered in lemon yellow and leaf green. Engravings of old California hung on the walls. A handsome French armoire concealed a television between the windows. Supper had been wheeled in and set up on a table between the windows. Paul, seated at the table, was peeling some fruit.

Steve stared. His eyes, though puzzled, were clear, and it was evident that the fever had broken.

"Who are you?" he asked.

"I'm a friend of Tim's."

"Tim? I hate him. Tell him I hate him. I wish *he* was dead."

Paul's response, despite his astonishment at this, was mild. "Do you? Why?"

"Damn him. And damn me for listening to him."

Paul, aware that he must tread very carefully on unknown ground that might be laden with mines, said softly, "He only wanted to know what had happened to you, whether you—"

"Whether I was alive?" the boy asked brutally. "Oh, you can tell him I'm alive, all right. But *she's* dead. She—where's my jacket? There's stuff in the pocket. Here, read. Her picture's in the paper, page nine."

As if he had received a command, Paul read the rumpled clipping. There, indeed, was a photo of a young girl with braids hung on either side of a childish face. "Wealthy mother baffled . . . why girl left home. . . . 'We never had any disagreements,' the mother said tearfully. 'She had everything a child could ask for. . . .'" Paul read on. "House used as bomb factory . . . fragment of man's torso found under bloody rubble last night . . . the police are searching . . . no trail to follow. . . ."

"I would have been there if I hadn't gotten sick." Steve's eyes filled and he turned away. "I should have been there. She's dead! Susan's dead, and it's my fault. My fault."

As the boy wept, Paul's own eyes filled. So the story unravels, a pitiable love story, this boy's first love, perhaps, caught in that mess, born and died in that mess.

"It was his fault, the bastard. The things he taught us. But I shouldn't have let her either. I promised that nothing would happen." Steve's face was contorted with despair. "She didn't really understand, she did it to please me. She tried to believe in it all, because she was lonesome and she loved me. A kid. . . . She was only a little kid. She didn't want to do it. She really didn't want to do it. He taught us. . . . And now she's dead. . . . So you see, you can go back and tell Tim from me to go to hell."

Paul got up to stand at the foot of the bed.

"I haven't got the foggiest idea where Tim is," he said, "and I don't give a damn either. I'll level with you: I wasn't sent here by him. I've come from your father."

"From my father? I didn't think he cared."

"Well, you thought wrong."

"Then why didn't he come himself, if he cares so much?"

"He's coming," Paul answered steadily. "He'll be here sometime tomorrow."

"But I don't understand who you are, why you're here."

"I'm here because it was I who happened to think of a lead that, miraculously, happened to work."

"But why? I can't figure out why you're taking all this trouble for me. This expensive room—"

"What's there to figure out? Sometimes a person wants to do something for a friend. Or for a stranger too. Either way."

Steve said nothing. It seemed to Paul, as he watched the changing expressions on the other's face, that one of them might be embarrassment, another wonderment, and one disbelief. Then something flared in Paul, sorrow, anger, and exasperation catching fire together.

"Did you think that only you and your kind knew how to give or to feel compassion?" he cried harshly. "You want to hear something? Your friends would have let you die rather than risk their cause. They're a cold, cruel lot. And your girl, that Susan, is dead—for what? Answer me, if you can."

"It was—it was to stop the war," Steve answered very low. "We thought if we kept bombing the barracks, they would stop the draft."

"It was more than that. It was to make a revolution here. The place was full of printed stuff. Don't deny it. Your Susan died for that."

There was a silence. A horn blew in the street below, voices passed in the corridor, and the silence continued.

"Revolution," Paul said. "What? Cuban style? Russian style? Goodies for all, including secret police? Come on, man, you're too intelligent for that. No, you've been used by shrewd heads, drafted into what should be, into what is, a decent cause, to halt this war. But this isn't the way to do it. Bombs aren't the answer to anything, as you've found out."

Steve closed his eyes. When he opened them, they were full of sadness.

"I know I cursed Tim and I do blame him, I do," he said. "Yet I ask myself: Can he be *all* wrong, really? The world is full of injustice, as he says. If you could hear him speak—"

Paul was about to say grimly "I've heard him," but, catching himself in time, said instead, "Many a tyrant has expressed some noble thoughts. One should examine his methods instead."

Again Steve sighed. And Paul, relentless now, pursued.

"Was there anything noble about Susan's death?"

"How will I live with myself?" Steve cried. "I can't ever undo it."

"We all have to live with things we can't undo." And Paul asked then, "Do you realize how brave your father was in his time of trouble?"

"Yes, I do," Steve said quietly. "But I—I ran away from trouble, I guess."

"You were really running away from this revolution business, do you understand that?"

"I know. The commune was a cop-out."

"In a way, one might say it was. Oh, why must we have one extreme or the other? The sane way is always the middle one. Not too much of anything. Except health," Paul reflected, as a small pain stung and slid down his left arm. Then, as it receded, he finished, "Yes, the middle way, as in peaceful protest against the war. Peaceful, and as firm as you can make it."

Steve smiled. "People who look like you don't always talk like you these days."

"Because I'm wearing this suit, you mean? Listen, a person doesn't have to go around wearing beat-up clothes to express himself every time he happens to be in disagreement with a government policy." Paul laughed. "I actually like these things I'm wearing, believe it or not." He picked up Steve's jeans. "These are a disgrace. They stink. I'm going to measure them and go out to get you some clothes while you finish resting."

"You know, you've got a handsome mug. Now that you've gotten rid of that scruffy beard, people can really see it," Paul said.

They were halfway through lunch in the hotel's sumptuous dining room.

Steve finished chewing a piece of his enormous steak before replying, "I wouldn't have shaved it off except that I figure I owe you."

"You owe me your life, that's all," Paul answered cheerfully. "I've been considering something," he continued. "I could get you a job."

"What kind?"

"In a think tank. You're good at thinking, aren't you?" Humor might be a help to this fellow right now, after what he'd been through. "Involve yourself with world peace, world problems. I know a few people. I'd recommend you if you were interested."

"What do you mean by 'involving'?"

"Research. Preparing papers. Influencing legislation. Long-range planning. Peace. Environment. Poverty. Got the idea?"

"I might like that," Steve said slowly.

"I should think you would. You'd be in Washington, where the action is." Paul looked at his watch. "It's one o'clock. Your father's due in soon. Shall I call my man now before he arrives?"

"Please. Go ahead."

Paul hung the receiver up, thinking, Well, so I've accomplished something on this trip. Then, scolding a little, he said to himself, "Don't give yourself so much credit. It's really that poor girl's death that brought him around, and you know it."

From the dining room's door he had a view of Steve, who was still at lunch. He looked good in the new suit, although he had protested that a collar and tie was a uniform, an absurdity. Paul had told him, "That may be, but you need to wear it if you want a job—and if you want to eat, you need a job. It comes down to that."

A determined young man, he was; whose genes did he carry? If only all that idealism, all those convictions, could be channeled, as Ilse's were—but then, you are comparing apples with oranges, Paul; this boy is no Ilse. However, he's surely worth every chance, because he's going to make his mark, and it will be a good mark.

Back at the table he said, smiling, "There'll be a job for you in Washington as soon as you're ready—next week, if you like. I'll give you the details later."

"I still don't understand why you're being so good to me. And I don't know how I can repay you."

"Be good to your parents. That'll repay me. Oh, I don't mean that you should act like the prodigal son, for God's sake! I don't suppose you'll ever fit with them hand in glove. I suspect you're just too different. But you might give them a chance."

"All right. Okay. I will."

"Here's a check. It's not much, but you can open a bank account, and it'll tide you over till you get your first pay."

"I don't require much," Steve said. "I don't believe in having too much."

"Fine. Then you'll do all right. And if you want to thank me, just keep remembering that I've stuck my neck out for you. Give me your hand and shake on it. Good luck."

The hotel was small and quiet. In an alcove off the lobby where drinks or just afternoon tea were served, the father and son sat talking.

"It's been two years," Theo said softly. "A long time. We've missed you."

"I'm sorry."

His father looked older than he remembered. And his hand was dreadful, with those twisted stumps of fingers. He had to look away.

"I don't mind your seeing my hand, Steve."

"But I mind." He felt a choking in his throat. "I guess I haven't realized how hard everything's been for you and Mom. The hand, and expenses, and me. . . ."

Theo gave him a tissue and Steve wiped his eyes. Then, feeling the heat of embarrassment, he tried to explain. "I'm not myself, I'm not usually like this, I—"

"Well, I know that!" Theo smiled. "Don't be ashamed. You've been through a lot yourself. Paul told me about your girl. I won't say any more and make it harder for you, except to say that I feel your pain."

"Who is Paul, anyway? He's an amazing guy."

"Yes. Yes, he is."

"Have you known him long? I don't remember seeing him at home."

"Well. I've known him more—more professionally. We go back a long time. Well. Can't ever thank him enough for this, though. Your mother's taken on new life."

Suddenly Steve wanted to do something for his father, and there being nothing else at the moment to do, he poured another cup of tea for him and passed the plate of cakes. And then, as suddenly, he said, "I'm going to be all right now, Dad."

"You're really through with those people?"

"Yes. They didn't want peace, truly. They wanted war, their kind of war. It's taken something awful to show me."

"You're not the only one, son."

Theo laid a hand on Steve's, and the two sat for a few minutes like that, while a kind of peace, something they had never before felt with one another, settled upon each.

Presently it became time to go.

"If we're going to catch the red-eye back," Steve said. And he did something he had not done in years: He kissed his father's cheek.

22

"I remember being told," Paul said, "that both Timothy and Steve were the brightest in their families. What went wrong with their intelligence?"

Ilse sighed. "Personal grudges. Insecurities. That's as neat an answer as any. And now I'd like to put this behind us and just enjoy your being home."

"I'm enjoying it." Paul stretched his legs out on the ottoman. "But I can't help wondering sometimes whether Tim can possibly be only a dupe, used by the top guys to destabilize governments. If that's the case, then Martillini's death must have knocked him off his feet. Or is he a top guy himself?"

Ilse didn't answer. The television screen flickered. Water

buffalo, rice paddies, running people, helicopters, stretchers, and fires flickered in and out.

"Sometimes I think those people in Cambodia will suffer terribly if we don't win," Paul said. "And on the other hand, I think we ought to get out now and never should have been there in the first place, as Eisenhower warned. I just don't know."

Ilse turned the television off. "Enough. There's a concert in the park tomorrow night, and we're having supper on the grass."

"Do you think Tim's an international top guy?"

Ilse sighed. "My guess is yes. What would you like for the picnic?"

"Anything you provide. It's always good. What do you think can have happened to Tim now?"

"Don't worry about him. If he's not hiding in this country, then he's very comfortable in Libya. Or Cuba, or maybe in Lebanon, in some white villa with a view of the Mediterranean."

"You're saying that the world hasn't seen the last of him and his kind."

"It's a lovely evening. Come on, let's take Lou for a walk. Then you can buy me some ice cream."

"All right. I'll drop the subject." He laughed. "You've made your point. Get the leash." He hesitated, then. "One thing, and then I promise to say no more. I've been thinking—I want to ask Theo to invite me to the house. I'll wait awhile and ask him in a month or so. I want to."

Ilse reached up and stroked his cheek.

"I'm surprised you're not fussing the way you always did and telling me that's crazy," Paul said.

"No," she answered gently. "What was true once isn't necessarily true forever."

·   ·   ·

It's going really well, Iris thought as she surveyed the table. There were nine at dinner, which was about as many as the room could comfortably hold: Theo, Philip, and herself, besides Jimmy and Laura with their spouses and, of course, Mr. and Mrs. Werner, in whose honor the family had assembled. Only Steve was missing. And at once she corrected herself: not missing anymore, merely absent.

The table was really beautiful, adorned with Anna's old French china and one of her best embroidered cloths, a little crowded, to be sure, but then crowding could also create an intimate atmosphere. The Werners had sent flowers that morning, five green orchids resting lightly in a Lalique bowl, the whole most unusual and most exquisite, chosen as though they could have known beforehand that the small table in the small room would be overpowered by a massive centerpiece.

Two or three enthusiastic conversations were going at the same time, flinging bits and pieces of themselves to where Iris sat.

"Nobody knows what the future may bring." That was Philip. "My science teacher told us that in 1937 people at the American Academy of Sciences were asked to predict what inventions might be made within the next ten years, and not one of them predicted radar or the jet engine or atomic energy."

". . . the same butterflies we used to see at Cape Cod, the monarch." That was Laura. "Can you imagine those frail things flying all the way to Mexico to winter and breed?"

Bright young people, they were. Handsome and good: Jimmy with feet on the ground, so sensibly, so happily, making his way; Laura, the sometimes willful and always charming romantic; Philip, turning now from boy into man and blessed with the gift of contentment, of easy acceptance. A mother might be forgiven for having a little pride in them. At once she corrected herself: no, not pride, but gratitude. Much gratitude.

Mr. Werner, on her right, looked as though he wanted her attention.

"The flowers," she said. "I must thank you again. They're so beautiful."

"And I must thank you for a most beautiful letter. I was much moved by it."

"Oh, I'm glad. It was a very hard letter for me to write. I really labored over it."

He was surprised. "Labored?"

"Oh, yes! How was I to begin telling you how grateful, how thankful, we are for what you did? It was a miracle. A miracle! If we were to live a thousand years, Theo and I, there wouldn't be time enough to tell you of our relief, our joy—"

He stopped her. "The joy was mine too. I've always liked to do things for young people. Boys' clubs, summer camps, settlement houses, that sort of thing. And this was a challenge. A bit different." He smiled; the smile was very kind.

At first, when he had come to the door this evening, she had been startled to find that she recognized him in spite of having seen him so few times, and each time only briefly, almost in passing. Then it came to her that there were indeed some things about the man that one would remember, chiefly his height and his elegance. There weren't too many men who possessed that combination or that particular formal, yet simple, courtesy. Theo was one of them, she thought now, and thinking so, it was her turn to smile.

". . . radiology," Janet was saying. "Then I can pretty much set my own hours. Emergency medicine and child rearing don't mix very well."

"How right you are," said Ilse Werner. "I remember it myself."

Robbie, addressing Jimmy, inquired, "And you'll do surgery?"

"I think so."

"He can take up where I left off," said Theo.

"Your husband has adjusted very well to the change in his career," Mr. Werner remarked.

"He's a courageous man, Mr. Werner."

"I'd be pleased if you'd call me Paul."

The friendly request gave her a queer feeling of guilt. If it had not been for what he had done for Steve, she would no doubt still be remembering him, if at all, with dislike. And she recalled the words she had used about him: *hovering, popping up, sneaking*—as on that day she had seen him driving away from her mother's house. And she had chastised poor Mama for merely talking to a man who was apparently, after all, only an acquaintance from years past! For this she might well feel some twinges of guilt and shame.

She spoke now with redoubled effort at warmth. "I'm sure Theo's told you we've been hearing regularly from Steve, hasn't he, Mr.— Paul?"

"Yes, and I'm glad."

"He seems to be liking his new work. That was a wonderful suggestion on your part."

"It's good that you don't expect too much too fast. He has to rebuild himself patiently, and that takes time."

"At least he's building instead of dynamiting."

Theo spoke. "He never did actually dynamite anything, Iris. He swore that to me."

"Thank God." And she raised her eyes to the opposite wall, where now hung the portrait of her mother that, for as long as she could remember, had hung above the mantel in her parents' living room. Theo had wanted it to be put in this prominent position between the dining room's two windows, and now at every meal, Anna, in the pink evening gown that her proud husband had had made for her in Paris, gazed down at her descendants.

"My mother would be so relieved if she could know," Iris said. "She worried so about us all."

"A good mother."

"Yes, I had good parents. I often think how different their lives were from mine. How far they came! Papa grew up in back of a grocery store on the Lower East Side. His mother supported them when his father went blind. And then when Papa was successful—I guess that's why he couldn't give my mother enough. He wanted to make up for everything that neither of them had had when they were young. He would have given her the world."

Suddenly, she became conscious of Werner's intense expression. He had turned his head to look at her, and it crossed her mind that perhaps she was boring him with these personal remarks, so she sought hastily for something else to say.

"Did you grow up in New York too, Mr.— Paul?" she asked.

"What are you talking about so seriously?" asked Ilse Werner, from across the table.

"Not seriously," Iris answered her. "I just asked Paul whether he grew up in New York."

"He did, and he can tell amazing things about the city that used to be, things you wouldn't even recognize," Ilse said with affectionate pride.

Robbie spoke then. "Tell us. I'm a midwesterner, and New York still dazes me."

"I hardly know where to begin," said Paul. "There are so many pictures in my head. Electric automobiles and organ-grinders with their monkeys. And, oh, yes, the Dakota apartment house on Central Park West. I could always get my bearings from it when I was a child because it stuck so far up into the sky. My grandmother called it a sore thumb, but my father said it was very fine and someday the whole West Side would be built up like that, all the way to the Hudson River where the farms were."

"Farms!" cried Laura.

"Yes," Paul continued, with evident enjoyment, "they were vegetable farms mostly, with goats climbing on the rocks behind the houses. I used to think it would be nice to live in one, I remember. Looking back, I suppose they were nothing more than shanties," he mused.

"New York is fabulous," Janet said. "I can't wait until we live here."

Laura shuddered. "Robbie and I wouldn't take it as a gift. Can't be too far out in the country for us."

"And we're in between, your mother and I," Theo remarked. "We've gotten to like this house and our little garden. But maybe it would be nice to move a little farther out and have a bit more garden space."

"And room for a pool," Iris told him, "since your favorite exercise is swimming."

"Expensive," Theo said.

"You deserve it," she responded firmly. "It's something you always loved, and you should have it."

He worked hard, he earned enough now, and it was time again for some luxuries. To her slight surprise Paul Werner gave agreement.

"I think he does. And you deserve something too, as a reward for labor, don't you?"

"What labor?" she countered.

"Why, earning your doctorate. Theo tells me you're almost finished with your thesis."

"I've enjoyed it too much to call it 'labor,' " she said, but was pleased, nevertheless.

Presently the dessert appeared, a lemon mousse with a fresh raspberry sauce.

"Laura made it," Iris proclaimed. "You all know perfectly well that I didn't. She's a much better cook than I am."

Everyone laughed, and Laura said, "It's from Nana's recipe, naturally. My grandmother was one of the world's best cooks," she explained to Paul.

When dinner was over, they all went to the living room. Theo served brandy, Philip consented to play some jazz, and Jimmy, one of those people who remember jokes, brought out a string of them.

The little house glowed, and Iris, watching and listening, felt the glow. She was really sorry they hadn't invited Paul Werner before now. They had been remiss; she had said so to Theo earlier today when they were dressing.

"You weren't thinking, were you, that I could possibly have any feeling toward him, after what he's done for us, but the most grateful?" she had asked.

And Theo had answered, "Of course not. I just never thought he'd want to come."

"But why on earth wouldn't he want to? We're nice people, aren't we?"

To that Theo had given her no answer. Well, she decided now, it's of no moment. We shall certainly invite them again.

The evening came to an end when Paul Werner said, "Now that we've had a good time and solved the world's problems, it's time to go home. At least it is for me."

He thanked them, shaking everyone's hand in turn, complimenting the hostess on the dinner, and all of them for their hospitality. They watched the Werners go down the walk with Theo, who escorted them to their car.

"Such a pleasant man," Iris said. "He gave me the feeling that we had known each other forever. And I liked his wife too. You can tell how much she loves him."

"A nice time, wasn't it?" Theo remarked later in their room upstairs.

"Very. But you were so quiet! I'm used to seeing you take the lead, and tonight you were sort of lying back and observing. Was there any reason?"

"Not at all. I wasn't even aware of it. I guess I was just listening to Paul."

"Oh, he's quite charming, so full of life! And to think how I used to dislike him!"

At this same time, while Theo and Iris were talking to each other, Paul and Ilse were on the parkway traveling toward New York. To Paul it was as if the evening had been a dream, as if the fulfillment of so many years' longing were too much to have been granted to him.

"How lovely she is! How lovely!" he said. "All of them. . . . The two young couples in love. . . . Jimmy's strong, the kind of young man I like. . . . Must be a consolation, in a way, for all their trials with that other. . . . But I have a feeling that that one will come out all right too, in the end; he won't eat crow before his parents, that's for sure, not with his fierce opinions. But at least he's working well at the job, and that's progress. He reminds me a little of my socialist aunt. This family breeds types. I guess all families do. . . . The boy at the piano has a fine head. . . . And Laura . . ." He stopped, thinking, Laura is Anna . . . almost. . . . You were right, Anna . . . you kept them together instead of coming to me all those times when I begged you to leave your husband. . . . You were right. . . . You gave them something to stand by."

In the darkness in the little car Paul felt himself smile.

I helped too, he said to himself. The day I walked into Theo's office and found everything in chaos, I helped too. And I thank God I could, because tonight is the result, and they're all right together, the two of them. Even a blind man could see that. Theo . . . Iris. . . .

"I can feel you smiling," Ilse said.

"Yes, I was happy. I was so happy tonight."

"Yes, dear, I know. I'm glad."

"I hope they'll ask us to come again sometime."

"I'm sure they will, dear Paul." Passing lights fell full upon Ilse's face, revealing a sweet expression of purest love.

"I wish life could go on awhile just like this," he said.

Then, not very many days later, the pain came again, and he was taken away.

He lay in the intensive care room. Something seemed to have happened in his head, because it was difficult, although not impossible, to frame words. Could it be both heart and stroke, he wondered, a double blow? Tentatively, he tried to move his arms and legs; they moved, so he was not paralyzed. He gave a sigh of deep thankfulness.

People were coming and going. He was aware of low, considerate voices. He knew, without opening his eyes, when people were standing by his bed. He knew Ilse was there always. He was aware of Theo. When Leah came he recognized the jingle of her bracelets and was amused. He knew Meg's voice. He wished that Iris and her children would come, but of course they would not; why should they? They were acquaintances, people he hardly knew.

One day he awoke and looked into the brown, weepy eyes of the Hindu intern.

"He's awake," said Ilse.

"Do something for me," he murmured, and she bent low.

"The dog. Give him to Meg, unless you want to take him back to Israel."

"My dearest, who says I'm going back to Israel?"

"You will. You should. You came to stay with me because you knew I was going to die."

He drifted. Inside his head there was a flickering of pictures that flared, faded, and overlapped. In myriad colors they came: his parents and his grandmother Angelique in black and gray; Meg in a blue haze carrying babies, so many babies; Ilse, young, with black satin hair, in her white doctor's coat; Anna, always she returning again and again, all gold and scarlet; and Iris's face . . . her face.

A nurse spoke far above his head. "He's smiling."

And someone answered, "It's only a reflex. He can't be, in his condition."

They always said, he remembered, that no one really knew whether a person in a coma could hear or understand. He could have told them, he wanted to tell them, that, yes, he did hear and did understand. But he hadn't the energy, and anyway, it didn't matter. I am old, he thought again. It's wonderful to have lived, but now it's time.

They buried him in Westchester on a gilded autumn morning, a burnished day. In the windless air the last yellow maple leaves dropped, slowly turning, and fell on the roof of the granite mausoleum in which two generations of the Werner family already lay.

It was surprising, Theo reflected, how many had come to the graveside. Almost a hundred people had followed the hearse. There were young men in Wall Street suits, prosperous middle-aged couples, a group of well-dressed blacks representing, he supposed, some organization Paul had benefited; there were even a few young people wearing jeans. And yet, among all these, there was not one descendant except Iris.

The rabbi asked family members to take the front row of seats. First, of course, came Ilse, slender in a black suit, with deep grief on her fine strong face. There was a younger woman in some sort of western outfit, with a single braid of gray hair falling down her back. There were two couples, both in late middle age, one of them expensive and urbane, the other appearing to be country people; the woman was fair with a gentle, pink, English face, an elderly tweed suit and sturdy brogues.

"Come, Leah," he heard the fair one say. "Sit here."

"That's Léa from the dress shop," whispered Iris. She felt nothing but curiosity. All other feelings and memories connected with that place and time had been overcome and cast away.

The rabbi began the Kaddish. A murmur of accompanying voices filled the quiet space beneath the trees.

"Astonishing prayer," Iris said to herself, "thanking God even in death for life, and asking for no bountiful reward in heaven. Only thanks. Astonishing, when you think about it." And her eyes filled with tears.

Theo was sure that she was thinking of her parents. But then, she cried even when she saw a strange bride and groom driving away together after their wedding. Tender soul! And he took her hand, remarking silently how odd it was that of all the people here, he was the only one who knew the truth about her.

Most of the young these days, not all of them and not everywhere, yet certainly here in this sophisticated city, wouldn't be shocked at all by that truth. But he had made his pledge, and to break it would be not only to savage Iris, but to haunt his conscience forever with the reproaches of Anna—and he could see her wide, gold-lashed eyes as clearly as if she were standing here next to him—and of the man whose body was now being laid within the little gray stone house.

No. Never. This truth would go with him to his own grave.

The ceremony was over, and people were dispersing, walking slowly over the grass toward their cars.

In back of Theo a woman was saying, "He did for everyone in the family. We all leaned on him. He was so strong, and with it, so unassuming."

Another voice asked, "And so you'll be going back to Israel, Ilse?"

"Yes. He wanted me to, anyway," Ilse replied.

At the open neck of her blouse, as she passed Theo, he remarked a pendant, a miniature set elaborately in gold and diamonds, striking against the background of black. Vaguely it crossed his mind that once in another world, another life, his mother had worn one like it.

He started the car, and they drove away. This was an area in which some large estates remained, with woodland patches and open fields still brilliantly green. In one of them a flock of Canada geese, heading southward, came coasting to earth with a great bustle and honk.

"Oh, just look at them!" cried Iris. "Let's stop a minute and get out. Oh, how beautiful!"

And as they walked down the slope toward the field, she said,

"Do you remember how my mother loved birds? Anything from a parakeet to an eagle."

The geese fluttered and stalked. The sun was not hot, merely warm, like a soothing bath. Theo's arm, loosely held around Iris's shoulders, slid to her waist, tightening as he pulled her to himself.

"Darling Theo," she said.

He raised her face and held her for a long time with his lips on hers. So they stood in the warmth, in the silence broken only by the whir of a car passing on the road above the slope and by the rustling and flapping of the geese.

"I feel so happy," Iris said when they broke apart. "That's awful, isn't it, having come directly from a funeral?"

"No, it's nature. People have always had funeral feasts, haven't they? It's because they're glad they're still alive, with time still left. That's all it is."

"But to feel like making love," she asked, almost shyly, "after they've just buried that good man?"

Theo spoke gravely. "He would have understood that too. He knew about loving." And he thought, There was a whole lot more in that man's life than I'll ever know. Paul's eyes had had a kind of twinkle, as of hidden amusement at the world.

"I keep thinking how I used to say nasty things whenever his name came up, even when you first told me he had offered to look for Steve. How terribly wrong I was!"

"We're all wrong sometimes. It's nothing to worry about."

"I really intended to invite him soon again. He seemed to have such a good time at our house. And, you know, he seemed to pay a special attention to *me*! I mean, he had a curious expression whenever he looked at me, and he kept looking often, which ordinarily would have made me uncomfortable, but didn't at all then. It was, well, it was rather odd, but also very *kind*. Do you know what I mean? I didn't mention it to you that night because it seemed too silly."

"I don't think it is."

"And when he left, when he thanked me for the evening, he said, 'God bless you.' It was lovely, but not what people usually say. It was so—so intense. Don't you think it was strange of him?"

"Oh," Theo said, "maybe you reminded him of someone, that's all. It can happen. Who knows? Come, darling, let's go home."